A GUIDE FOR PROGRAMMERS

MARILYN BOHL

IBM Corporation

PRENTICE-HALL, INC. *Englewood Cliffs, New Jersey* 07632

Library of Congress Cataloging in Publication Data

Bohl, Marilyn.
  A guide for programmers.

  Includes bibliographies and index.
  1. Electronic digital computers—Programming.
I. Title.
QA76.6.B62   001.6'42   77-14982
ISBN 0-13-370551-X
ISBN 0-13-370544-7

10 9 8 7 6 5 4 3 2 1

Printed in the United States of America

PRENTICE-HALL INTERNATIONAL, INC., *London*
PRENTICE-HALL OF AUSTRALIA PTY. LIMITED, *Sydney*
PRENTICE-HALL OF CANADA, LTD., *Toronto*
PRENTICE-HALL OF INDIA PRIVATE LIMITED, *New Delhi*
PRENTICE-HALL OF JAPAN, INC., *Tokyo*
PRENTICE-HALL OF SOUTHEAST ASIA PTE. LTD., *Singapore*
WHITEHALL BOOKS LIMITED, *Wellington, New Zealand*

CONTENTS

PREFACE

This book is for programmers, for persons who are learning to program, and for all others who want to know how to make computers do useful work. Its contents are suitable for persons with experience using one or more programming languages, and for persons with no prior programming experience. This book is designed to provide supplemental material on programming and program development for use in a wide variety of situations — specific programming-language courses, general programming courses, career-oriented curricula, courses in subject areas such as accounting or business problems where students are expected to pick up programming on their own to a degree sufficient to solve programming problems in those areas, and so on. Because of its coverage of current programming techniques and technologies, this book is well suited for self-study and on-the-job reference as well.

My objectives in developing this book are to help the reader/programmer to understand more fully the programmer's job, to become familiar with many of the tools at his (her) disposal, and to know more about the environment in which programs operate — in short, to develop skill as a programmer.

The most important tool available to the programmer is, of course, the computer system itself. So, after a brief look at the ever-increasing use of computers in Chapter 1, Chapter 2 provides an overview of computer-system components. The hardware of the system comprises the central processing unit (CPU), storage devices, and input and output devices. This hardware operates as directed by stored-program instructions, or software, created initially by the programmer or made available for his use. Most modern computer systems also contain firmware, or microcode instructions, developed to tailor further the systems to users' data-processing requirements.

In Chapter 3 we take our first close look at the program-development process, noting especially how the programmer approaches a problem. The responsibilities of the programmer in a team environment are described. Chapter 4 explains what an algorithm is, stresses the top-down approach to program development, and introduces structure charts, HIPO diagrams, and other design languages. Two additional tools of program planning, program flowcharts and decision tables, are explained in Chapters 5 and 6 respectively.

Chapter 7 deals with program coding. Here we consider the large number and variety of programming languages available. We then discuss how to choose a programming language that is well suited to the problem to be solved. We show how to move from the design representation of a solution algorithm (say, a program flowchart) to its computer-program form, in both batch and interactive programming environments. Additional factors that must be considered when writing code to be run in a virtual environment are pointed out. Actual coding examples are used in this and other chapters to demonstrate good coding practices that should be followed consistently when programming.

Chapter 8 covers structured programming. After a brief look at the motivation for its development, we study the basic control structures and show how pseudo code can be used to express them. Then we show how the COBOL, PL/I, and FORTRAN languages as commonly available can be used to write structured programs.

In Chapters 9 and 10, we talk about preventing and eliminating errors by using techniques that begin at the problem-definition stage and continue throughout the program-development cycle. Numerous testing and debugging techniques are described.

The key role that documentation can and must play throughout program development is emphasized repetitively in this book. The form and content of that documentation is fully explained where appropriate. A unique feature of the index is the use of italics for all terms pertaining to documentation; thus, a ready guide to the whats, whys, whens, and hows of program documentation is provided.

Each chapter is followed by an annotated bibliography. Questions and exercises that require a greater knowledge or understanding are provided. Those that assume an ability to write programs are marked by asterisks, so they can be skipped or referred to easily at appropriate times. Answers to selected questions are given in the appendix.

Both masculine and feminine pronouns appear early in the book, to emphasize the fact that both men and women are choosing to become programmers. (I worked as a programmer for a number of years and am currently managing a group of male and female programmers.) Use of only masculine references later is solely for convenience purposes.

MARILYN BOHL

1

USING
THE COMPUTER

Since very early times, people have looked for ways to make their work easier, to solve their problems more efficiently. Many of these problems involve quantities and numbers, so people have looked for easier ways to count, and to add, subtract, multiply, and divide. As society has grown in both size and complexity, so has the data that is generated within it. But data in the form of quantities and numbers by themselves is of little value. Like coffee beans, iron ore, and other raw materials, data is of little use until it is processed. Only when it is collected, used in computation, and analyzed does it have real value.

Because of the rapid growth of society, our need for processed data, or information, has increased greatly. Clerical tasks have multiplied. Most if not all organizations, whether government, business, or social, tend to be overwhelmed by paperwork. For example, consider the paperwork required in a company that manufactures fabrics for the wholesale market. The research scientists in this company work daily to improve the quality of current materials; to develop new fabrics with greater resistance to wear, heat, and chemicals; and so on. These scientists record data from their experiments, use the data in calculations, and summarize their findings in recommendations and reports.

In the same company, the manufacturing division requires summarized data to control production. What items are needed? What raw materials are available to produce the items? What materials must be purchased? What human and machine resources are needed to meet current production goals?

Financial departments within the company process data to produce accurate records of the company's financial transactions. Costs of materials, operating expenditures, personnel time, and other charges are posted in the appropriate ledgers. These records reflect the total worth and profitability of the company. Executives analyze such information when developing both short-term and long-term objectives, which serve as directional guidelines for operations throughout the organization.

DATA-PROCESSING SYSTEMS

Data processing, the modern name for paperwork, is the collecting, processing, and distributing of facts and figures to achieve a desired result. The equipment (devices) and procedures by which the result is achieved form a *data-processing system.* (See Figure 1-1.) The devices vary. In some data-processing operations, all work is done using manual procedures. These sys-

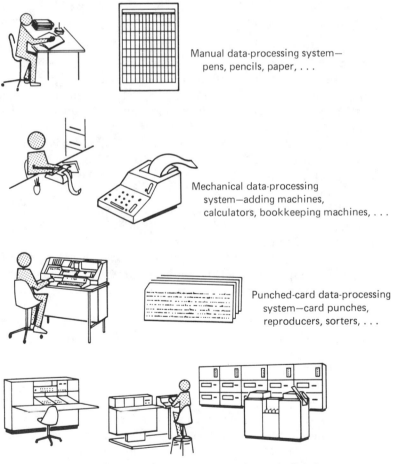

Manual data-processing system—
pens, pencils, paper, . . .

Mechanical data-processing
system—adding machines,
calculators, bookkeeping machines, . . .

Punched-card data-processing
system—card punches,
reproducers, sorters, . . .

Electronic data-processing system—electronic digital computers, . . .

Figure 1-1   Data-processing systems

tems employ tools and materials such as pencils, pens, multiple-copy forms, carbon paper, accounting pegboards, and filing cabinets. Mechanical data-processing systems use a combination of manual procedures and mechanical equipment such as typewriters, calculators, bookkeeping machines, and duplicating machines. Punched-card data-processing operations are performed by a wide variety of card-handling equipment—card punch, verifier, repro-ducer, interpreter, sorter, collator, and so on. As indicated in Figure 1–1, an electronic data-processing system has, as one of its components, an electronic digital computer.

Regardless of the kind of data processed or the kind of equipment used, all data-processing systems involve at least three basic elements:

- the source data, or *input*, entering the system
- the orderly, planned *processing* within the system
- the end result, or *output*, from the system

To examine further what these terms mean, let's consider a familiar situation. We assume that a utility company is preparing bills for customers to whom it furnishes electricity. First, an employee of the company reads a customer's meter, on which all electric usage has been recorded. The previ-ous meter reading (recorded at the end of the last billing period) is sub-tracted from the current reading to determine the amount of electricity used by this customer during this billing period. The resulting amount is then multiplied by a rate factor to determine how much money the customer owes. The amount owed is recorded in the company's accounts receivable files, and the customer's bill is prepared and mailed to him.

In this example, the *input* is the previous and current readings on the meter. The *processing* is the subtraction of one of these numbers from the other and the multiplication of the result by the appropriate rate. The *out-put* is the customer's bill and the company's record of the amount owed. All together, these functions constitute a data-processing system.

We can treat the terms *data* and *information* as synonymous, or we can distinguish between them by saying that data is raw material gathered from one or more sources, and that information is processed or "finished" data. Generally, *information* implies data that is organized and meaningful to the person receiving it. Since knowledge and decision-making activities are im-portant in many different areas, and at many different levels, one person's information may be another person's data.

INFORMATION SYSTEMS

A *system* can be defined as a group of interrelated components that seeks the attainment of a common goal, accepting inputs and producing outputs by means of organized processing. Thus the basic operational system of a

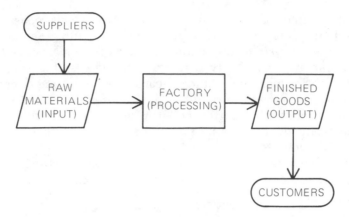

Figure 1-2   The basic operational system of a manufacturing company

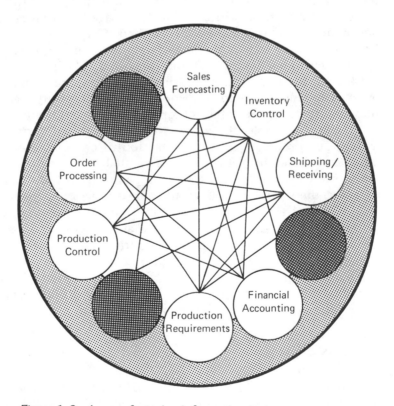

Figure 1-3   A manufacturing information system

manufacturing company, such as the fabrics producer above, accepts raw materials as inputs and produces finished goods as outputs. (See Figure 1-2.)

The successful functioning of this operational system is dependent upon several data-processing systems. For purposes of clarity, let us refer to these specifically identifiable units within the organization as *subsystems*. Some of them are shown in Figure 1-3.

To emphasize the input-processing-output characteristics of these subsystems, we summarize four of them briefly.

- Order-Processing Subsystem: Processes sales orders received from customers as inputs and produces invoices for customers and data needed for sales forecasting, inventory control, and financial accounting as outputs.

- Sales-Forecasting Subsystem: Receives data concerning customer orders and about the current and anticipated business environment in which the company operates. Produces sales forecasts for inventory control and operations (production) management.

- Inventory-Control Subsystem: Receives data concerning customer orders, sales forecasts, production control, and receipts and disbursements of inventory from company stock locations. Produces shipping documents, issues reports on products moving through the various stages of production, monitors current stock levels, and provides data needed for production requirements generation and the filling of customer orders.

- Production-Requirements Subsystem: Receives data concerning finished goods needed from the inventory-control subsystem. Determines manufacturing process, material, machine, and labor requirements, produces purchase requisitions for required materials, and develops a production schedule for the factory.

These and other interrelated subsystems are the basis of a comprehensive *information system*, collecting and processing data and disseminating information throughout the entire organization. As we see here, an information system may utilize several data-processing systems as subsystems. Some computer scientists treat the terms *data-processing system* and *information system* as synonymous, but it is often convenient to distinguish between them. A data-processing system is a device-oriented concept (a manual data-processing system, a mechanical data-processing system, a punched-card data-processing system, and so on). An information system is organization and application oriented (a business information system, a management information system, a marketing information system, and the like).

COMPUTERS IN SOCIETY

Probably the most-discussed and, to some, the most awesome tool that men and women, working together, have developed to simplify data-processing tasks is the electronic digital computer. It is *electronic* in that it depends, not on the functioning of mechanical parts, but on the swift motions of electrons. It is *digital* in that it operates on discrete quantities, which we commonly measure or represent in terms of numbers. Modern computers are the result of a long series of events that began as early as the 1600s. Most of the organized effort to develop computers and related equipment has occurred in the relatively brief period since 1945, however; they have emerged rapidly as fantastically complex, fast machines.

Because computer usage has spread widely, people are becoming increasingly aware of computers. Much has been written about them and their effects on society. Today the computer is doing many jobs, from figuring taxes and checking tax returns, to keeping track of airline flight schedules and available seat locations, to predicting and then tallying election results. In our nation's classrooms, computer-assisted instruction (CAI) techniques permit students to learn at their own pace, and to interact independently with computers via television-like screens and associated pencil-like devices (known as light pens or selector pens) or data-entry keyboards. Physicians now diagnose, test, and evaluate human ailments with computer help. Federal, state, and local governments depend heavily on computer capabilities (witness the Federal Bureau of Investigation, Departments of Motor Vehicles, Department of Agriculture, and so on).

To appreciate just how much computers are involved in our daily lives, let's consider a typical example:

Mrs. Adams, a busy housewife, plans to shop for groceries and other daily household items at a nearby shopping center. She phones a department store at the center to find out whether it is open at this time, because she wants to look for a new lamp during the same trip. A computer assigned the local telephone numbers and prepared the directory that she refers to before making her call. A computer times her call. Upon receiving an affirmative answer, she turns out the lights in her home, shutting off electricity that comes from a power plant designed with the aid of a computer and controlled by another computer.

Mrs. Adams gets into her car, designed and built with computer direction, and drives along a highway laid out by a computer. The computer also helped to figure construction costs for the road. On the way, she stops at traffic signals controlled by a computer. Her destination, the shopping center, was planned with computer help. Mrs. Adams enters the supermarket. The lighting, the height of the shelves, and the location of each department she visits were planned with computer help. The brand of soap she purchases was named with the help of a computer. To pay for her purchases, she cashes a paycheck that was figured automatically by a computer. In fact, the check was printed with computer assistance. The register at the checkstand is a computer terminal, connected to the computer to send data to it and obtain information from it.

So great is the involvement of computers in our daily lives that we can no longer ask whether or not we want to use computers. Each of us uses them frequently, perhaps without even being aware of doing so. Some people fear that computers will take away their jobs; others fear that computers will invade their privacy; still others point to depersonalization, expressing concern that computers are a threat to our individuality. Some members of society actually fear that computers will take over the world.

Maybe so, you say? No? Yes? I doubt it? As your direct experience with computers increases, you will realize that the computer has no magical power. Like its predecessors — the calculator, the slide rule, pencil and paper — the computer is only a tool. It was developed as a refinement of its predecessors because the problems to be solved in our modern world have become more refined and more complex. Given the rapid pace at which we are working and living, there are indeed more data generated and an ever-increasing number of potential computer applications. Calculating the position of a spaceship traveling about our earth or generating tons of reports about the checking account activities of millions of bank customers exceeds the capabilities of a labor force using yesterday's tools. But everything a computer does is dependent on the people who use it and the instructions they supply. True, a computer operates swiftly and accurately; but just as a hammer cannot drive itself, a computer cannot work without direction. The purpose of this book is to help you learn how to direct computers effectively.

QUESTIONS

Q1. What is data processing?

Q2. (a) Name four types of data-processing systems. (b) Give an example of each.

Q3. (a) What three basic elements are involved in any data-processing operation? (b) Identify each of the elements in the example systems you named in Q2b above.

Q4. Distinguish between data and information.

Q5. What does it mean to say that "one person's information may be another person's data"?

Q6. What is a system?

Q7. (a) Distinguish between the terms *data-processing system* and *information system.* (b) Give an example (other than the one given in this chapter) where several of the former are included in one of the latter.

Q8. Give some examples in current society where the computer's capabilities are used advantageously.

Q9. What are some of the fears people have of computers?

Q10. (a) What is a tool? (b) Assuming your definition, is it correct to call the computer a tool? (c) Why, or why not?

EXERCISES

E1. Select one modern business organization (such as a travel agency, a telephone company, an employee placement service, or a large grocery chain). Show how that organization might take advantage of electronic data processing.

E2. List five uses of computers that directly affect you.

E3. List five activities in your immediate environment where computers may be used advantageously in the future.

E4. Suppose a colleague expresses grave concern over the computer's threat to society. What might you say in response?

E5. Investigate and report on one of the following computer applications: weather forecasting, identification and tracking of suspected wrongdoers, ground or air traffic control, translation of manuscripts from one language to another, computerized match-making, the diagnosis, monitoring, and treatment of human ailments, or the playing of chess games.

REFERENCES

ACM Committee on Computers and Public Policy. Daniel D. McCracken, Chairman. "A Problem List of Issues Concerning Computers and Public Policy," *Communications of the ACM* 17, 9 (Sept 1974): 495-503.

Bemer, Robert W. "The Frictional Interface Between Computers and Society," *Computers and People* (formerly *Computers and Automation*) 24, 1 (Jan 1975): 14-19.

Gilder, Jules H. "'Smart' Cars Coming down the Road in 1977," *Computer Decisions* 8, 9 (Sept 1976): 14.

Kindred, Alton R. *Introduction to Computers*. Englewood Cliffs, N.J.: Prentice-Hall, 1976 (an introduction to computers and programming, with much about computers in society and societal issues).

Myers, Edith D. "Working at Home and Liking It," *Datamation* 21, 1 (Jan 1975): 103-06.

Rothman, Stanley, and Charles Mosmann. *Computers and Society*. 2d ed. Chicago: Science Research Associates, 1976 (a readable text emphasizing social implications).

Yasaki, Edward K. "Toward the Automated Office," *Datamation* 21, 2 (Feb 1975): 59-62.

2

AN ELECTRONIC
DATA-PROCESSING SYSTEM

As noted in Chapter 1, there are many types of data-processing systems. Each type of system performs one or more required operations on data by means of various devices. When a machine performs most of the required operations, the system is called an *automatic data-processing system*. More particularly, when that machine is an electronic digital computer, the system is described as an *electronic data-processing (EDP) system* (or, sometimes, simply as a *computer system*).

In the broadest terms, an electronic data-processing system consists of (1) the *hardware*, or machinery, that performs the mechanics of operations; and (2) the *software*, or prewritten sequences of instructions, that directs those operations. Most modern EDP systems also contain *firmware*, or microcode instructions, developed by the computer manufacturer to permit tailoring of the system to meet particular data-processing requirements.

HARDWARE

Describing the hardware of a computer system is somewhat like trying to describe the features and characteristics of the broad category of vehicles commonly referred to as automobiles. Obviously, the special features of a Volkswagen and of a Cadillac cannot be encompassed in a single description. Even within a family of automobiles, such as the various Chevrolet models, there are significant differences in features, price, and performance. So, too, with computer systems. There are microcomputers; compact, low-cost mini-computers; and small-sized, medium-sized, and large-scale computers. Some can be purchased for $5000, whereas the minimum monthly rental charge for others is from 5 to 25 times that much—from $25,000 to $125,000. One computer may perform in 1 millionth of a second (1 microsecond) a calculation that another computer takes 1 billionth of a second (1 nanosecond) to perform. One may allow us to store millions of data items, but another may limit us to a few thousand items. One computer system may include a device for reading data from punched cards and providing output on punched cards; another may accept input from a television-like screen or a keyboard, and provide output as printed reports. Nevertheless, an EDP system typically consists of four types of functional units: the central processing unit, secondary-storage devices, input devices, and output devices. The interrelationships of these units are shown schematically in Figure 2–1 and explained in the paragraphs that follow.

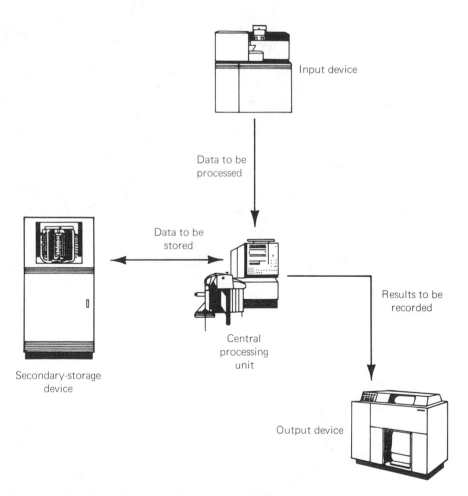

Figure 2–1   Functional organization of an EDP system

Central Processing Unit

The central processing unit (CPU) is the "computer" part of an EDP system. Its relation to the rest of the system is analogous to the relation of the human brain to the rest of the body: It is the control center of the entire system. As such, it contains a *control section*, an *arithmetic/logic unit*, and an *internal storage unit* (also called *primary storage* or *main storage*).

The control section of the CPU directs and coordinates the operations of the EDP system according to a prewritten sequence of instructions stored within it. This sequence of instructions is known as a *stored program*. (It is a part of the software of the system, soon to be discussed.) The control section selects instructions from the stored program, interprets them, and generates signals and commands that cause other system units to perform required operations at appropriate times. It controls the input and output devices, the arithmetic/logic operations of the CPU, and the transfer of data to and from storage. In fulfilling its role as controller, it performs no actual processing operations on data; such processing must be carried out by other system units.

The arithmetic/logic unit contains the circuitry necessary to perform arithmetic and logical operations. The arithmetic circuitry calculates, shifts numbers to the right or left, sets the algebraic sign of a result, rounds, compares algebraically (taking the sign of the number, plus or minus, into account), and so on.

Sometimes, arithmetic operations are performed on numbers represented in *binary form*. Under this approach, each decimal numeral (the form that is familiar to us) is converted to an equivalent binary numeral, a combination of the binary digits 0 and 1, before being stored in the computer. For example, the decimal numeral 9 is converted to 1001 ($1 \times 2^3 + 0 \times 2^2 + 0 \times 2^1 + 1 \times 2^0$). The decimal numeral 67 is converted to 1000011 ($1 \times 2^6 + 0 \times 2^5 + 0 \times 2^4 + 0 \times 2^3 + 0 \times 2^2 + 1 \times 2^1 + 1 \times 2^0$).

Under another approach, arithmetic operations are carried out on numbers represented in *binary coded decimal*, with each decimal digit of a numeral represented separately by four binary digits. For example, the decimal numeral 498 is represented in binary coded decimal as 0100 1001 1000. (We have shown spaces between the groups of four digits, for readability.) Similarly, the decimal numeral 67 is represented in binary coded decimal as 0110 0111.

The choice of data representation in the computer depends not only on the hardware design of the computer but also on the type of instructions causing the operations to be performed on data. The usual practice is to classify all arithmetic/logic operations other than addition, subtraction, multiplication, division, and shifts as logical operations. The most basic and widely used are logical comparisons and tests. Logical comparisons are performed *bi*nary-digi*t-by-bi*nary-digi*t* (bit-by-bit) or character-by-character, without recognizing the sign of either value. Tests may be applied to determine whether a value is positive, negative, or zero. Most computers can also test the states of indicators and switches; for example, to determine whether or not an error has occurred during the reading of data. In general, the logic circuitry of the CPU performs a decision-making function. It checks to see whether a certain condition or combination of conditions is present in the system and determines the next instruction to be executed accordingly.

The internal storage unit, or primary storage, of the EDP system is somewhat like an electronic filing cabinet or a group of numbered mail boxes at a post office. Each "box," or *location*, is capable of holding data or instructions. Just as each post office box is identified by a number, so each storage location has an assigned *address*. Using the addresses, the control section of the CPU can locate data and instructions as needed. The size, or *capacity*, of primary storage determines the amount of data and instructions that can be held within it at any one time. In some computers, storage capacity is measured in millions of digits or characters (for example, 1024K or 2048K, where each K represents 1024 8-bit *bytes*, and each byte provides space for one 8-bit character representation or two 4-bit character representations). The typical storage capacity of a minicomputer is, in contrast, 8K or 16K where each K represents 1024 12-bit or 16-bit computer *words*. As we might expect, the design and capacity of the storage unit affects the method by which data is handled in an EDP system and the applications for which it can be used.

Secondary-Storage Devices

Frequently, the data-processing operations required to satisfy a user's information needs require access to more data than can be held in primary storage. In such cases, the data is retained on *secondary*, or *auxiliary*, *storage devices*, from where it can be retrieved as needed during processing (albeit, somewhat

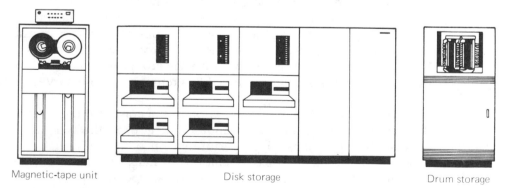

Magnetic-tape unit   Disk storage   Drum storage

Figure 2–2 Secondary-storage devices

slower than if it were already in primary storage). Programs and/or portions of programs not currently in use can also be kept on secondary storage. Various types of devices have been developed to provide these capabilities. The most common are magnetic-tape units, disk storage units, and drum storage devices. (See Figure 2–2.) Some manufacturers are currently offering even larger-capacity bulk-storage units, but the data-recording techniques and media used are generally the same as those of these common devices.

Processing restrictions that are due to the limited amount of primary storage available in an EDP system may be somewhat alleviated by the introduction of *virtual storage*, a facility that permits instructions within a program being executed by the computer to refer to other instructions and data on auxiliary storage as well as to primary-storage locations. When data or instructions referenced during execution are on auxiliary storage but not in primary storage, they are moved to primary storage immediately. Processing continues as though no such movement had occurred. (In Chapter 7 we look at how the fact that a program may be executed in a virtual-storage environment affects the writing of the program.)

Input and Output Devices

Before data can be entered into the computer, it must be converted from a form that is intelligible to us to a form that is intelligible to the computer. An *input device* performs this function. The input data is recorded on cards and paper tape as punched holes, on magnetic tape as magnetized fields along the length of the tape, on paper documents as printed characters, and so forth.

An *output device* accepts data that has been processed. The results may be in a form that we can understand or in a machine-readable form that is to serve as input to another machine. For example, an output device like the printer can display data in a form that is meaningful to us. However, a magnetic-tape unit used as an output device carries data in a form that is useful only as input for further processing. Other output devices record information from the computer on cards or paper tape; generate signals for transmission over communication lines; produce graphic displays and microfilm images; and even provide output as spoken words.

The number and types of input/output (I/O) devices included in an EDP system depend on the design of the system and the kind of processing for which it is used. Some devices are used only for input, some only for output, and some for either. They may be linked directly to the CPU by means of cables or attached via communication lines. In practice, the variety of I/O devices available seems almost unlimited. Some of the most common ones are shown in Figure 2–3. Note that a magnetic-tape unit appears here and in Figure 2–2. It may be regarded as both a secondary-storage device and an input or output device.

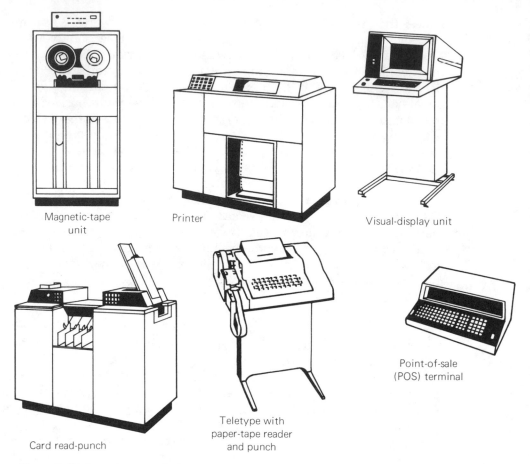

Magnetic-tape unit

Printer

Visual-display unit

Card read-punch

Teletype with paper-tape reader and punch

Point-of-sale (POS) terminal

Figure 2–3   Input/output devices

SOFTWARE

A central processing unit can accept input data from a card reader, make rapid calculations, process other data stored previously on magnetic tape, send results via communication lines to distantly located printers, and so on. But organizing these functional units into a coherent system capable of solving problems depends on computer programs. Each program is a sequence of instructions that has been written and then stored within the computer to direct its operation (recall the requirement for a stored program, mentioned above). The individual who writes the program is known as a *programmer* or *problem solver.*

Collectively, computer programs have been given the somewhat facetious name *software* to indicate that they are distinct from, but parallel to, hardware as we have just discussed it. Just as the term *hardware* can be expanded to include all tangible EDP materials, especially data-recording media such as punched cards, paper tape, magnetic tape, and so on, the term *software* can be expanded to include (1) training of the people who will use the EDP system, operate or service the equipment, and maintain the programs or develop new programs; (2) all nontangible EDP-system considerations such as the policies and procedures required to manage and control the user installation; and (3) the documentation of the policies and procedures as well as specific operating instructions, detailed information about the programs to be run, and comprehensive system information.

Since programs are required to direct all jobs that a computer does, and we know that a computer can do many different things, we might expect that many different programs must be prepared to direct it effectively. Generally, this is true. A large number of programs are designed, written, and tested, then stored in one or more *system libraries* on secondary storage, from where they can be retrieved as needed during processing. Programs developed to solve problems in direct response to user needs are called *applications software*. Other programs, called *systems software*, are developed to facilitate use of the EDP system itself.

Systems Software

Systems software comprises programs to help individual programmers, or problem solvers, use the computer as a problem-solving tool and programs to help insure that the system as a whole operates efficiently. Included in this category are:

- language-processor programs, also known as language translators
- program generators
- operating systems
- data management systems
- utility routines
- library routines

Language-Processor Programs

Initially, computer programs had to be written in *machine language.* Each instruction consisted of a difficult-to-remember string of binary digits, or bits. Imagine, for example, trying to write correctly a program consisting of instructions such as:

```
01011011 00100000 00000100 00101000
01010000 00100000 00000100 00101010
```
.
.
.

Each bit in a machine-language instruction corresponded directly to a bit position in primary storage, and the instruction itself was loaded into storage, interpreted, and acted upon by the computer.

Obviously, machine-language programming was time-consuming, tedious, and error-prone. The programmer had to know exactly what operations the computer at his disposal could perform, and he had to know the bit combination, or operation code, for each operation. Furthermore, he had to determine the exact locations that each instruction in the program and each data item referenced by it would occupy when loaded into primary storage. Having done so, he had to specify the addresses of those locations (using binary digits) whenever he referred in one instruction to other instructions or data items. Because the program was tied very closely to the machine operations of a particular type of computer, it could be run only on that type of computer.

Assembler languages are the next level of programming languages. They were developed to eliminate many of the difficulties of machine-language programming. These languages are commonly referred to as symbolic languages, because convenient alphabetic abbreviations called *mnemonics* (memory aids) are used when writing programs. For example, the symbol S or SUB (depending on the particular assembler language) can be used instead of 00000111 as the operation code for subtraction. In the same way, A can stand for addition, L for load, ST for store, and so on. Each assembler language has its own mnemonic operation codes, but, once learned, they can be remembered easily.

Futhermore, a programmer who uses an assembler language need not know the exact storage locations of data and instructions. He can select a symbolic name, or label, for an instruction or a data item, and use that label when he refers to the instruction or item. These labels can be any terms meaningful to the programmer, subject only to minor restrictions of the particular assembler language. (One restriction might be, for example, that each label must begin with a letter; another might be that no label can exceed eight characters in length.)

A representative sequence of assembler-language instructions is shown as an example in Figure 2–4. These instructions cause the contents of the primary-storage locations represented by the symbolic name GROSS to be loaded into CPU register 5; the contents of TOTPAY to be added to that value; and the sum (placed automatically in register 5 as part of the preceding operation) to be saved in GROSS for subsequent use.

```
L      5,GROSS       LOAD GROSS INTO REG 5
A      5,TOTPAY      ADD TOTPAY TO GROSS
ST     5,GROSS       SAVE THE RESULT
```

Figure 2–4   Example of assembler-language programming

Assembler-language programming has, as a prerequisite, the development of a *language-processor program*, or *language translator*, to operate on the programmer's assembler-language instructions as data. In effect, the translator accepts the assembler-language program as input and produces as output a corresponding machine-language program. Most computer manufacturers develop an assembler language and an associated language translator (specifically, an *assembler program*) as part of the systems software for use with their computers.

Though assembler-language programming offers certain advantages over machine-language programming, it is still machine-oriented; assembler-language instructions correspond closely to their machine-language equivalents. The programmer must write long series of detailed instructions to accomplish even simple data-processing tasks. Some improvement was experienced with the development of *macro-instruction* capabilities, which permit several machine-language instructions to be generated from a special type of assembler-language instruction known as a macro instruction. In general, however, a one-for-one correspondence between assembler-language instructions and machine-language instructions is typical.

GROSS = GROSS + TOTPAY

Figure 2-5 Example of high-level-language programming

Machine languages and assembler languages are often referred to as *low-level programming languages*. In contrast, *high-level programming languages* — the next advancement in programming-language technology — remove the programmer a considerable distance from any particular machine. The programmer who uses a high-level programming language writes statements that closely resemble familiar English or standard notation of mathematics. He directs his attention to the steps necessary to solve the problem at hand rather than to the exact operations that the computer itself will carry out. If multiplication is to be performed, for example, the programmer need only be concerned with what value is multiplied by what value and what the result is. He does not have to be concerned with placing either value in a certain CPU register beforehand, or with setting up a special area for temporary storage of intermediate results. Similarly, the addition operation set up by the three assembler-language instructions in Figure 2-4 can be described by a single high-level-language (in this case, *FORTRAN*) statement, as shown in Figure 2-5.

High-level-language programming is possible because of the development of language translators known as *compiler programs*. The single high-level-language statement in Figure 2-5, for example, may be translated by a FORTRAN compiler program into a dozen or more machine-language instructions. This capability reduces the time and effort needed for programming because fewer instructions are required to direct a sequence of processing steps than would be necessary if an assembler language or a machine language were used. It cuts down the likelihood of errors, because the sequences of instructions inserted to replace high-level-language statements are pretested, correct *routines* (also called *subroutines*) built into the language itself.

Representatives of computer manufacturers and user groups have cooperated in attempts to standardize various high-level programming languages, to help insure that a program written in one of them is to a large extent machine-independent. Thus, for example, a program written in the *COBOL* programming language can be executed on any of several computers, provided that a COBOL compiler program is available for the one selected, to translate the programmer's COBOL statements into machine-language equivalents.

Program Generators

The programmer who takes advantage of program-generator routines does not write statements that represent sequential processing steps to be carried out by the computer. Instead, he completes short descriptions, known as *specifications*. They indicate the form of the input data, the I/O devices and data files to be used, the calculations needed to solve the problem, and the type and format of desired output. Given these specifications, the program generator builds a machine-language program to direct the computer in performing the required operations and producing the output.

The earliest program-generator routines were report program generators introduced in the late 1950s to simplify the preparation of business-oriented printed reports. Several versions of the *Report Program Generator (RPG)* language and associated program generators have been developed. RPG is especially valuable for minicomputer and small computer users because, unlike COBOL, for example, it does not impose large storage requirements. *MARK IV* is a highly successful systems software product (rather than a generally available programming language) that is especially useful for report generation and file maintenance. Significant savings in both cost and time required to prepare programs for many types of straightforward business applications can be achieved through use of this product; satisfied users point to substantial increases in programmer productivity.

Operating Systems

An *operating system* is an integrated set of computer programs designed to maximize the amount of work that an EDP system can do. It does this by allocating the resources of the system (CPU processing time, primary storage, secondary-storage space, I/O devices, programs, and so on) to specific, independent *jobs* (programs, or series of related programs) in an optimal manner. It minimizes the amount of human intervention required during processing by performing many functions that were formerly the responsibility of the computer operator. For example, an operating-system job scheduler reads *job-control statements* indicating what programs are to be run, takes into account priorities and the availability of required EDP-system resources, and causes other operating-system programs and systems software, and applications programs, to be loaded into primary storage and executed at appropriate times.

The operating-system monitor, or executive, supervises the execution of the various programs, their use of I/O devices, and the overall flow of work through the EDP system. Because the monitor is the major component of the operating system, at least some parts of it are resident in primary storage whenever the EDP system is in use.

Operating-system service programs perform common routine and repetitive functions needed by most, if not all, EDP-system users. For example, the librarian catalogs, manages, and maintains a directory of the programs, routines, and subroutines stored in the various libraries of the system. The linkage editor determines the specific locations that instructions and data will occupy when loaded into primary storage, assigns addresses accordingly, and links program units together to form an executable program. In some operating systems, a combined linker-loader performs not only linkage editing but also loading of programs.

Because an operating system is very complex and, of necessity, closely tied to the internal operations of the EDP system for which it is developed, it is usually supplied by the computer manufacturer or a software development firm that specializes in systems work. The EDP-system user (i.e., programmer or problem solver) must become familiar with the operating-system components at his installation and prepare the job-control statements for his programs accordingly.

Data Management Systems

A *data management system* is a generalized set of computer programs to control the creation, maintenance, and utilization of computer-based files. The earliest programming aids in this area were macro instructions that could be used to specify I/O operations. By writing a simple GET or PUT macro instruction, for example, the programmer invoked pretested I/O subroutines of an *input/output control system (IOCS)* to perform not only reading or writing but also checking of device addresses and conditions, checking for errors during the read or write, blocking or deblocking of records, and so on.

In the 1960s, when applications were first implemented as integrated systems rather than as independent or loosely related programs, *file systems* offering various file organization and file accessing capabilities were provided.

File organization is concerned with the techniques used to arrange blocks of records within a file on the physical storage medium. In a file that is organized sequentially, the blocks occupy contiguous storage positions on the storage medium. In a file that uses linked organization, the blocks occupy random portions of the storage medium, with a pointer field in each block giving the address of a succeeding block.

File access is concerned with the manner in which the blocks within a file are read or written. In *sequential* access, the blocks are read in the order that they are positioned on the storage medium. When using *direct* access, there is no concept of a "next" record; each record contains a *key field* (say, item-number or user-id) which is used to determine the (random) position of that particular record on the storage medium.

The term *data management* came into common usage in the late 1960s as users insisted that the costs of file storage and maintenance be reduced and that duplication of data within systems be eliminated. They wanted to store data in a way such that it could be readily accessed, retrieved, and manipulated in a variety of ways, by any of several programs, to meet constantly changing and ever-expanding information needs.

A significant next step was the establishment of integrated collections of related data, or *data bases*. Under this approach, systems designers no longer direct their attention to collecting data in individual files for use by a particular program or as dictated by hardware. Instead, their objective is to provide for collecting, organizing, and accessing data in ways that model the natural relationships of that data in the user's environment. Common examples are a student data base containing enrollment data for all persons currently attending classes, and a parts data base established for inventory-control purposes.

Dozens of vendors now offer data management software that interfaces with both operating-system programs and user-written applications programs in the creation, maintenance, and utilization of data bases. These offerings range in sophistication from report program generators, such as the MARK IV software product mentioned earlier in this chapter, to highly complex data base management systems. Users look to these systems for protection mechanisms to prevent misuse or corruption of stored data, privacy controls that can be employed to prevent unauthorized access to data or unauthorized types of usage, and reconstruction facilities sufficient to permit complete restoration of all data bases if need be, as well as for convenient, extensive manipulation and retrieval capabilities.

Utility Routines

Utility routines, or utilities, are general-purpose programs that perform common functions auxiliary to the running of other programs. Examples are:

- Sort and merge programs — arrange records in one file, or combine two or more similarly sequenced files into one file; often the most-used utilities at an installation; separate programs are required for tape files and disk files.

- File-conversion programs — copy data from one storage medium to another, without changing the information content of that data; examples are tape-to-tape, tape-to-disk, card-to-tape, and tape-to-printer; more complex file-conversion programs reformat files acceptable to one EDP system so that they can be processed by another.

- File-preparation programs — preformat direct-access storage media for use in subsequent processing.

- Dump programs — write out the contents of all, or selected areas, of primary storage, usually for error-detection purposes.

- Trace programs — print out a visible record of the step-by-step execution of a program, usually for error-detection purposes.

- Housekeeping routines — perform miscellaneous functions such as clearing primary storage; presetting indicators, switches, and registers; determining whether I/O devices are readied for processing; and checking labels on volumes and files.

- Language-conversion programs — translate programs initially written to run on one computer into a language suitable for another.

- Simulator programs — control the computer in such a manner that it is made to imitate the operation of another, thereby permitting programs written for one computer to be run on another computer operating under control of the simulator.

This list is not exhaustive, but it should give you an idea of the kinds of tasks that utilities are used for. The programmer who uses a utility supplies specific values for one or more parameters, to tailor the general-purpose program to meet particular data-processing requirements. For example, to use a dump program, the programmer usually supplies the boundaries (lower and upper addresses) of the primary-storage area to be copied. These values are punched into specific columns of a control card or typed as direct input from a typewriter-like device. The dump program is loaded into storage, the parameter values are read, program execution is initiated, and the printout occurs.

Library Routines

Library routines are typically prepared by computer manufacturers, software development firms, or computer-user groups, then distributed for widespread use. Each routine is a program segment that performs a specific function, written in such a way that it can be used in a wide variety of programs. Generally, it uses, as input, data in primary storage and provides its output in primary storage for use by the remainder of the program. If the program segment is designed for incorporation at specific points in the program and translated to machine language along with the rest of the program, it is called an *open subroutine*; if it is attached to the program, but remains a separate program unit, it is called a *closed subroutine*.

The library routines available at an installation tend to reflect the types of processing done at that installation. Thus, a civil engineering firm maintains a different repertoire of library routines than the accounting department of a large corporation does. In practice, the most-used routines are those built into high-level programming languages. Literally hundreds of routines have been developed for some. To avoid "reinventing the wheel," each programmer should become familiar with the library routines at his disposal; if necessary, he should encourage EDP-system management to see whether or not more can be obtained. The brief listing in Figure 2–6 gives some idea of the general character of routines in common use.

Binary to decimal conversion	Means	Matrix inversion
Decimal to binary conversion	Standard deviations	Eigenvalues and vectors
Random number generator	Correlations	Integration by quadrature
Next prime number	Exponential smoothing	Newton interpolation
Greatest common divisor	Curve plotting	Bessel interpolation
Least common divisor	Probability functions	Legrange interpolation
Date	Exponential functions	Modular arithmetic
Time	Trigonometric functions	Absolute values
Error diagnosis	Logarithms	Truncation
Selective dump	Square roots	Rounding

Figure 2-6   List of library routines

Applications Software

A *computer application* is the use of a computer to accomplish a specific operation or to solve a specific problem. It follows, then, that applications software directs a computer to perform data-processing activities in response to specific user needs. This software can be subdivided into two categories:

- user-written programs, prepared by programmers of a computer user

- applications packages, also known as canned programs, proprietary software, packaged applications, and so on

How to develop user-written programs is the major theme of this book. Computer users do have unique information needs, and programs can and should be prepared to satisfy them. A large company often develops business applications programs to handle its payroll, order-writing, customer billing, and so on. Scientific applications programs are created to perform complex statistical analysis, curve fitting, modeling, and the like. Still other applications programs are developed by users in areas such as medicine, law, education, and the social sciences.

In contrast, there are indeed specific problems that are common to a large number of user groups, businesses, or organizations. Hence, there are occasions when ready-to-use, canned applications can be used to advantage. In a canned application, the experience gained in programming the same application for a large number of users is consolidated into a generalized program that can be used by many. Specialists in software development, who are familiar with both the applications area and the computer in use, work to develop an efficient, high-quality software product. Much of the costly, time-consuming effort that otherwise would be required on the part of each user is eliminated. The number of programmers that must be employed at the user installation is minimized.

Thousands of applications packages have been developed, and new ones are appearing daily. A growing trend initiated by various software development firms is to develop complete systems packages, encompassing the typical data-processing requirements of a whole industry, such as insurance, retailing, or construction. Figure 2-7 serves as a small but representative sampling of the applications packages available.

Accounting: Hospital accounting; demand deposit accounting; bill of material explosion; mortgage loan accounting; labor cost accounting; insurance accounting.

Banking: Bond swap and investment analysis; risk analysis; bond pricing; bond yeild; cash flow analysis; interest computation; credit ranking; installment-loan monitoring.

Management: Program Evaluation and Review Technique (PERT); Critical Path Method (CPM); generalized information systems; management information systems; sales forecasting; market evaluation; production scheduling.

Engineering: Optical systems design; mechanism design; industrial engineering; linear programming; facilities location; plant engineering and maintenance; stress analysis.

Science: Chemical simulation; chemical analysis; weather forecasting; simulation of physical phenomena; patient monitoring; dietetic planning; test data reduction.

Figure 2-7 List of applications packages

FIRMWARE

In recent years, computer manufacturers have recognized that the distinction between the hardware and the software of an EDP system is not a simple, straightforward matter. Although basic operations such as multiplication and division can be built into a computer as part of its hardware in the form of permanently wired circuitry (called "hard-wired circuits"), more flexibility is possible if some of the basic operations are controlled by special stored-program instructions sometimes referred to as the *firmware*, or *microcode*, of the computer. For example, microcode instructions can be used to set up the precision with which multiplication is performed or to modify the internal operations of one computer so that it can execute machine-language instructions originally set up for another.

Sequences of microcode instructions, called *microprograms*, are provided with some computers by the computer manufacturer. The microprograms for a computer are placed in *read-only storage (ROS)*, where they can be interpreted by the computer during processing. Unlike other internal storage, the read-only storage cannot be occupied or altered by regular stored-program instructions. The user who selects such a computer acquires a machine that has certain standard features plus the optional features that he needs. Through microprogramming, the basic operations of the computer are tailored to meet that particular user's data-processing requirements.

Because microcode instructions control operations that are basic to the computer, a detailed knowledge of computer circuitry is required to use them. In practical usage, only computer systems designers need be familiar with the techniques of microprogramming and of specific microcode. Few, if any, programmers at typical user installations become involved with microprogramming. It is anticipated by some computer professionals that many functions now performed by software will soon be performed by microcode, but that is not to say that the need for systems and applications software will disappear or even diminish. The number and variety of problem-solving tasks for which applications programs are being written to provide computer solutions is increasing daily. The basics of EDP-system resource sharing and control are likely to remain operating-system functions.

QUESTIONS

Q1. Define the terms *hardware*, *software*, and *firmware*. In doing so, show how they are related to one another.

Q2. (a) List the four types of functional units of an EDP system. (b) Explain each briefly.

Q3. (a) What are the three major parts of the central processing unit? (b) Discuss the functions of each.

Q4.   Distinguish between the terms *location* and *address*.

Q5.   (a) List three types of storage that may be available in an EDP system. (b) In what ways are these types of storage alike? (c) How do they differ?

Q6.   (a) Name two types of software generally available on an EDP system. (b) Distinguish between the two, giving examples of each.

Q7.   (a) How does symbolic-language programming differ from machine-language programming? (b) As a programmer, which would you prefer and why?

Q8.   (a) Explain the terms *low-level programming language* and *high-level programming language*. (b) Give examples of each.

Q9.   Why is standardization of high-level programming languages generally viewed as desirable?

Q10.   What are the functions of an operating system?

Q11.   Who uses job-control statements and why?

Q12.   Trace the development of data management systems.

Q13.   Distinguish between the terms *file system*, *file organization*, and *file access*.

Q14.   What is a computer application?

Q15.   List three advantages of applications packages.

Q16.   (a) What is another name for microcode? (b) IIow is it used?

EXERCISES

E1.   Describe the hardware characteristics of the EDP system available to you. These should include: (a) the overall system size classification, (b) CPU processing speed, (c) primary storage capacity, (d) secondary-storage device types and capacities, (e) commonly used I/O devices and their functions, and (f) communication facilities.

E2.   Become familiar with the operating-system capabilities available to you. Which of these capabilities are especially useful to you?

E3.   Find out what language-processor programs and program generators are run on the EDP system available to you. For each, state: (a) how it was obtained, (b) who maintains it, and (c) what documentation is available for it.

E4.   Investigate one of the data management products currently being marketed. Describe its functional capabilities, hardware systems supported, terms of acquisition, documentation, education and/or support services, and any other characteristics that should be noted when selecting a product of this type.

E5.   Find out what utility routines are run on the EDP system available to you. (a) List those apt to be most useful to you. (b) Describe one of the routines that you listed in greater detail.

E6. (a) What applications packages are available on the EDP system available to you? (b) Describe one of the packages that you named in greater detail.

*E7. This project is designed to help you become familiar with the job-control language, operating procedures, and physical environment of the EDP system available to you. Your instructor will supply to you a deck of punched cards containing a program to be run, and the documentation for that program. You should: (a) study the documentation carefully, (b) find out what job-control statements are needed to run the program on the EDP system available to you, (c) submit the program to be run, (d) verify that the actual results of execution match the expected results described in the documentation, and (e) if any discrepancies are detected, determine their cause.

REFERENCES

An Introduction to Microprogramming. IBM Corporation manual (GF20-0385). White Plains, N.Y., n.d. (The n.d. (no date) indication is given in this text for IBM manuals, because the latest edition of a publication, together with any technical newsletters providing updates, contains the most current information on a subject and will be provided by IBM in response to orders for the publication.)

Awad, Elias M. *Business Data Processing.* 4th ed. Englewood Cliffs, N.J.: Prentice-Hall, 1975 (a comprehensive 700-page hard-copy tutorial of systems, hardware, software, and management of business data processing).

Bohl, Marilyn. *Information Processing.* 2d ed. Chicago: Science Research Associates, 1976 (provides up-to-date coverage of hardware, software, and systems concepts at a generalized introductory level).

Flores, I. *Peripheral Devices.* Englewood Cliffs, N.J.: Prentice-Hall, 1974 (covers unit-record devices, tape, disk, and other I/O units, and the relationship of these devices to the computer and the software system).

IBM System/360 Principles of Operation. IBM Corporation manual (GA22-6821). White Plains, N.Y., n.d.

IBM System/370 Principles of Operation. IBM Corporation manual (GA22-7000). White Plains, N.Y., n.d.

Pomeroy, J. W. "A Guide to Programming Tools and Techniques," *IBM Systems Journal* 11, 3 (Sept 1972): 234-54 (describes software aids).

Wu, Margaret S. *Introduction to Computer Data Processing.* New York: Harcourt Brace Jovanovich, 1975 (a well-illustrated basic tutorial, especially good for those interested in programming).

3

PROBLEM SOLVING

THE STEPS OF PROGRAM DEVELOPMENT

Computer programming is the task of developing a program. This task is not difficult, but it must be done carefully. It involves much more than just writing instructions. To use the computer effectively as a problem-solving tool, several program-development steps must be carried out. These steps are:

- Defining the problem — describing the problem, the input data associated with the problem, and the desired results in everyday English as clearly and completely as possible.
- Planning a solution algorithm — deciding how to proceed in solving the problem; breaking the task into specific operations that the computer can perform.
- Coding the solution — writing a program to direct the computer in performing the operations identified in the solution algorithm.
- Checking out the program — debugging and testing the solution algorithm, and its computer-program form of representation, to insure that the desired results are provided as output.
- Completing the documentation — gathering and verifying all documents associated with the program and assembling them in a *run manual* that can be referred to by anyone needing to know about the program.

The first four of these steps are generally performed in sequence: definition is basic to planning a solution algorithm, which must occur before programming, which must be followed by debugging and testing. Developing a successful program may involve some backtracking to rethink and rework earlier steps; for example, during the coding phase, the programmer may decide that further definition or planning is needed. As we shall soon see, computer professionals are emphasizing that program checkout should begin early in program development; it is both possible and desirable to detect and remove certain types of errors at the time of problem definition. Still others can be detected when formulating the solution algorithm. Documentation is a vital task, and it must be a continuing one. Concise, accurate documentation is required at each step in the program-development cycle.

ASSESSING PROGRAM QUALITY

There are many ways to write a program and many ways to judge the quality of a program. One of the most widely applied measures of program performance is quality of output — precision and accuracy of numeric values, appropriateness and level of content, readability, understandability, timeliness, and so on. A program can also be measured in terms of storage utilization, running time, reliability, understandability, and ease of maintenance. In the past, good programmers were thought to be those who could write a given routine in fewer steps than anyone else; tricky, concise program routines were marvelled at. There may have been valid reasons for such attitudes in the early days of computers, when storage space was very costly and machine operations were much slower than they are today. The result, however, was programs that were difficult, if not impossible, for someone other than the original programmer to read and to maintain. Even the original programmer often had trouble, one year, one month, or even one week later.

Another problem with programs has been a high frequency of errors, or *bugs*; the difficulty in isolating, identifying, and correcting those bugs; and the care required to avoid creating new bugs when correcting existing ones. A common misconception is that programming consists of a minimal amount of strategic thinking at the top (program design) and a large amount of detailed coding at the bottom. Statistics have shown that the number of debugged instructions coded per person-day during a programming project ranges from 5 to at most 25 in the vast majority of cases. Few if any persons knowledgeable of computers would expect the programmer time required to code such instructions to exceed more than a few minutes of an eight-hour work day. What do programmers do with their remaining time? Mostly, they debug and test programs. Programmers are also apt to spend a lot of time reworking code (and then debugging that code) due to faulty logic, incorrect program interfaces, and other misconceptions stemming from inadequate problem definition and/or faulty communication with systems designers and other programmers. In short, it is thinking errors, more than coding errors, that limit programmer productivity.

While the costs of EDP-system hardware have decreased significantly over the past years, the same cannot be said of software. Indeed, a typical data-processing installation may spend up to 85% of its annual budget on programming work. The original program-development costs for a project often appear small in relation to the aggregate maintenance costs over a few years of operation.

Recently, computer professionals and businessmen in the field of software development have done some rethinking. Whereas the primary objective of software development has been to make the most of the capabilities of available hardware, today other factors are recognized as requiring special emphasis. These factors are reliability (capability of performing over a period of time without error), maintainability (provision for isolation, identification, and correction of errors when they occur), and extensibility (facility for changes to existing functions and/or addition of new functions to accommodate changes in the task to be accomplished or the problem to be solved). To provide for these factors, we must design and implement software in a way that minimizes the number of errors and maximizes the ease with which errors that do occur can be corrected and modifications made.

TEAM OPERATIONS

An approach to software development that is currently receiving much attention is one of overall programming organization as well as of programming technology. In the early days of computer usage, most programmers worked individually. Each programmer was given an assignment; he withdrew to his office or working area, then re-appeared weeks or even months later, having "done his thing." In effect, programs were designed, coded, and implemented as independent components, without much thought of how one problem or its solution related to another.

As the number and types of applications to be computerized increased, the need to view certain programs as sets of related programs, or systems, was recognized. Programmers began to work in small groups or teams, though interrelationships remained largely unformalized and occurred on a when-recognized-needed basis. This type of organization is still practiced in some program-development environments.

In program-development environments where large software-development projects are undertaken, programmers are usually organized into teams on a more formalized basis. Each team has from three to eleven members. Probably the most disciplined approach here is the *chief programmer team* concept, first introduced in an IBM programming effort on behalf of *The New York Times.* IBM implemented a complex information retrieval system comprising over 83,000 lines of original high-level-language coding in 22 months, through the work of only a few programmers and specialists reporting to the project's chief programmer. Further, the system demonstrated an unprecedented absence of major errors. For example, in the first 13 months of operation of the online retrieval system, only one program error that resulted in system failure was detected. The chief and backup programmers (see below) produced code that had one detected error per 10,000 lines of coding, or one error per person-year.* Because of the high programmer productivity rates and extremely high-quality code achieved during this project, it has received widespread attention. Subsequent efforts both in IBM and elsewhere have been patterned after this project. It is important for us to understand what the chief programmer team concept is all about.

The nucleus of a chief programmer team consists of a chief programmer and a backup programmer (both senior-level personnel), and a programming librarian. Additional programmers, analysts, and technicians are added to the team as needed, depending on the size and type of system under development. The chief programmer is a technical manager to whom all team members report directly. He also writes at least the main line of the system under development and defines segments to be written by other team members. The code created by others is reviewed and incorporated into the system under the direct supervision of the chief programmer.

The backup programmer is a peer of the chief programmer in program design and development. He is involved in every aspect of the work and participates in all important decision-making. In addition, he may serve as a special research assistant for the chief programmer in programming strategy and tactics (for example, investigating alternative design approaches), allowing the chief programmer to concentrate on the main line of system development. He may be called upon to coordinate test planning for the system independently of the chief programmer, but normally he is an active participant in all activities, so that he can assume the chief programmer's responsibilities temporarily or permanently at any time if required.

The programming librarian maintains the records of the project in a highly visible, standardized way in a *development support library (DSL)*. These records are kept in both an internal (machine-readable) and an external (human-readable) form. Examples of internal records are the job-control statements needed to execute the system under development, the programmers' coding as it has been punched into cards, and system test data—all of which are maintained on disk storage. External records consist of filed listings: current copies of all coding and current directories, or tables of contents, for all internal data sets. When current copies and directories are updated and replaced, the replaced copies are logged in historical journals (archives). All results of test runs are also maintained in journals. The librarian not only performs clerical and secretarial functions but also submits all

---

*For additional details of this project, see F. T. Baker's "Chief Programmer Team Management of Production Programming." The chief programmer team concept is further described in "Chief Programmer Teams; Principles and Procedures" by H. Mills.

jobs to the computer for processing and retrieves results, to be filed as part of the public record of the project. (See Figure 3-1.)

Chief programmer team operations provide increased productivity by sharply reducing the debugging and reworking in a project. The initial coding

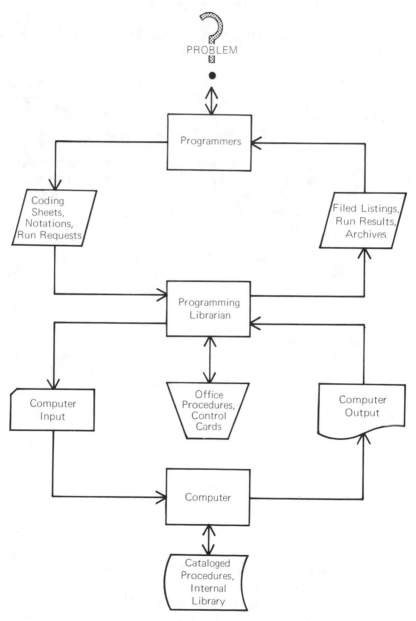

Figure 3-1   Development support library

may require the same amount of time as it otherwise would, but the design-level thinking is transmitted deeper into the coding by both technical and organizational means. The job structuring in team operations isolates functional responsibilities (data definition, program design, clerical operations, and so on) so that accountabilities are better defined. Consequently, communication among team members is sharpened and more precise. The librarian submits all jobs and picks up all computer output, good and bad, filing the results in journals. This identification of all program-related data and results of computer runs as public records, not private property, is a key principle of team operations.

The chief programmer team concept allows for professional growth and development of technical skills on the part of team members. Since clerical procedures are well established and delegated where appropriate, programmers and analysts can devote more time and energy to developing key technical skills and building the desired software. Both work habits and results are highly visible, so team members can learn from one another. Inefficient or erroneous coding habits and techniques can be identified and eliminated. Team members who work closely with the chief and backup programmers are exposed to the qualities and requirements of leadership; in many cases, they are prepared for leadership of future teams.

The chief programmer team concept is one of a set of interrelated disciplines, collectively referred to as "improved programming technologies." (See Figure 3-2.) These technologies are not all mutually inclusive; that is, a software-development group can adopt some of them without adopting others. But experience thus far has demonstrated that their combined use can result in significantly more efficient data-processing operations and substantial increases in programmer productivity. We shall discuss each of these techniques further in succeeding chapters of this book as we direct our attention, in detail, to the program-development steps listed at the beginning of this chapter.

DEFINING THE PROBLEM

A programmer begins his (or her) problem-solving task by defining the problem, making sure he knows what has to be done. To define a problem is to understand the scope of the problem. It requires determining the form and type of input data to be used, and the form and type of output required. This information, in turn, provides a basis for determining the computer operations (processing) that must be performed.

The Problem Statement

Generally, the first step leading to a computer program is someone's recognition of a need for information. A careful analysis of that need should involve both prospective users of the information and one or more trained systems

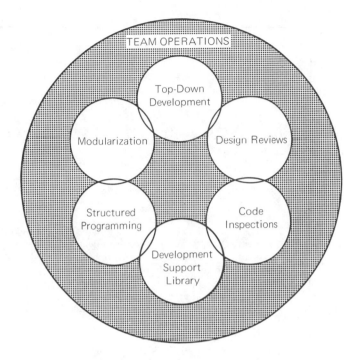

Figure 3-2   Improved programming technologies

analysts, who can perceive the full nature of the information need and how the computer can be used to respond to it. Sometimes, problem definition must occur at many levels. If a business data-processing task is to be programmed, for example, the objectives of top management in having the task computerized must be clearly identified. Then the specific information needs of each client, or user department, must be documented. Finally, individuals within each department must be consulted to determine what information each requires.

If a task is currently being done manually, steps of the manual procedure should be reviewed to determine what improvements are possible. If advisable, the procedure should be redesigned to meet the current needs of the business and to take advantage of new capabilities that the computer offers. Through experience and observation, systems analysts and programmers can determine the details of what the computer system to be used can and cannot do. The analyst is largely responsible for the efficient use of the system. The factors to be considered when defining the problem are all closely related to the success or failure of the resultant program or system of programs, as revealed in its ability to provide correct, timely output.

In a chief programmer team environment, one or more systems analysts works very closely with the chief programmer assigned to the project. An analyst identifies jobs within the system (in effect, subsets of the problem)

Job Description
    Job name
    User application
    Purpose
        Objectives

Input Information
    Identification of each input file
        Data-recording medium
        Volume and serial identification
        Name
    Identification of each record type within its file
        Name
        Identification
        Format names and arrangement of fields (data items) within record
        Expected ranges in value of relevant data items
    Organization of each record type within its file
        Individual records within file
            Sequence
            Records always present
            Records occasionally present (and why)
        Groups of records within file
            Identification of group
            Sequence within group
            Records always present
            Records occasionally present (and why)
            Sequence of groups within file

Processing Information
    Calculations to be performed
        Under all conditions
        Under specific conditions
            Determinable on the basis of input
            Arising as a result of preceding calculations
        Steps in performing calculations
        Special algorithms, formulas, and/or constants to be used

Output Information
    Identification of each output file
        Data-recording medium
        Volume and serial identification
        Name
    Identification of each record type within its file
        Name
        Identification
        Format names and arrangement of fields (data items) within record
    Organization of each record type within its file
        As for "Input Information" above
    Special output information
        Spacing charts for printed reports
        Punctuation desired for printed data items

Figure 3-3   Problem statement checklist

and assists in creating descriptions of the jobs to be passed on to the programmers selected to do them. He may also specify the formats of inputs and outputs. If he does not, the chief programmer or each assigned team programmer develops specifications for the input and output associated with a particular program. These specifications become part of the *problem statement*, a complete outline or narrative containing all information relevant to the solution of the problem (that is, to meeting the need for information).

A checklist noting the information usually required in a problem statement appears in Figure 3–3. You can use this checklist as a reminder when defining a problem to be solved.

Input and Output Descriptions

A commonly used, important form of documentation mentioned in the problem statement checklist is the *printer spacing chart* (*print chart*, for short). One of these charts is used to plan the exact layout of heading lines (report and column titles), detail lines (the columns of information created from individual output records), and summary lines (accumulated totals) on each printed report to be provided as output. A similar chart is used to plan the layout on a visual-display unit. (See Figure 3–4.) Other preprinted forms are given to the programmer, or filled out by him, to describe accurately and completely all other input and output as specified by the problem statement. A *general-purpose card punching/data recording form* is designed to help the programmer keep in mind the locations of various data items within the constraints of 80-column or 96-column punched cards. A *proportional record layout form* shows the manner in which data is written on magnetic tape or disk. (See Figure 3–5.) The completed forms are essential during programming and become part of the program documentation in the run manual.

Samples of Input and Output

Though printer spacing charts and card layouts are useful to the programmer, they may appear abstract and have little meaning to persons not familiar with computers. Typically, the persons who will provide input data to the program or receive output reports from it are in this category. To prevent surprises (cases where input or output turns out to be quite different from what these persons expect), samples of the input and output can be produced. For example, the analyst or programmer may prepare documentation such as shown in Figure 3–6. The individual or group who will be responsible for providing input data should verify that a two-place decimal is appropriate for the second type of data item (the column beginning with 8.00). Each inputter is further alerted to place zeros in positions to the right of the point when there is no fractional value. This figure may represent a dollars-and-cents amount, in which case the sample shows that no dollar sign need be specified. The second entry in the third column shows that a value of 0 is appropriate

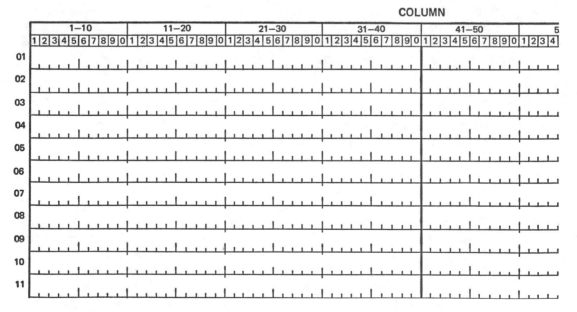

Figure 3–4 Printer spacing chart (top) and visual-display layout (bottom)

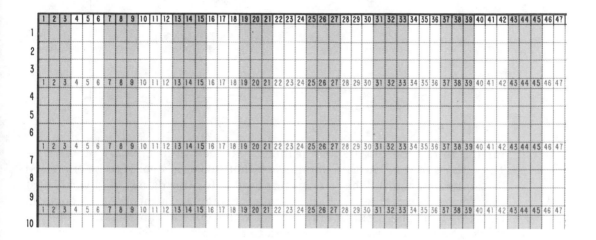

IBM GENERAL PURPOSE CARD PUNCHING/DATA RECORDING FORM

PAGE_____OF _

JOB

BY   DATE

PUNCHING INSTRUCTIONS

| GRAPHIC | | | | | | | CARD FORM NO |
| PUNCH | | | | | | | |

IBM

INTERNATIONAL BUSINESS MACHINES CORPORATION

PROPORTIONAL RECORD LAYOUT FORM

Application _____ Type of Records _____ By _____

| RECORD NAME AND REMARK | | Hex. ☐ | 01 | 05 | 06 | 0A | 08 | 0F | 10 | 14 | 15 | 19 | 1A | 1E | 1F | 23 | 24 | 28 | 29 | 2D | 2E | 32 | 33 | 37 | 38 | 3 |
| | • | Dec. ☐ | 1 | 5 | 6 | 10 | 11 | 15 | 16 | 20 | 21 | 25 | 26 | 30 | 31 | 35 | 36 | 40 | 41 | 45 | 46 | 50 | 51 | 55 | 56 | 6 |

Figure 3-5   Card-punching form (top) and proportional record layout (bottom)

37

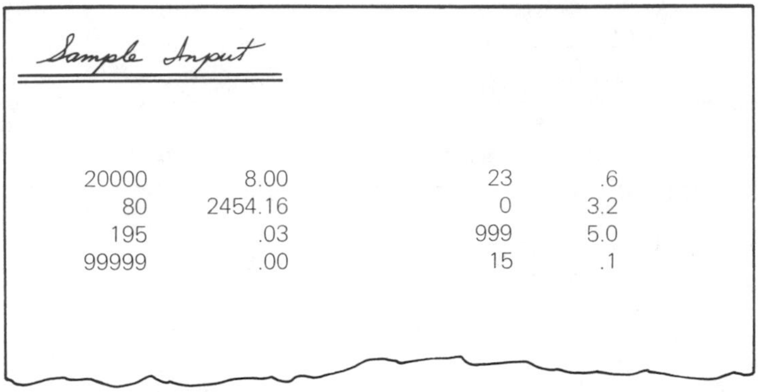

Figure 3-6   Sample input

for the third type of data item if there is no need to specify any other value. The entries in the fourth column show that this data item is to be expressed to the nearest tenth. The persons responsible for this data should verify that this format is acceptable. For example, .6 may be a measure of length in terms of feet. The inputter may recognize this but indicate that he prefers to think of values in terms of inches, and to deal only with whole numbers.

In cases where positioning of input values on the data-recording medium is a responsibility of the inputter, the sample input can serve an additional function. It can show, for example, the columns of a punched card into which values are to be punched. Looking again at Figure 3-6, we note that all values are right-aligned in column format. This alerts the inputter to the fact that input values are to be placed toward the right (right-justified) in the positions set aside for them.

In most programming situations, sample outputs can be generated easily, even when the program that will ordinarily prepare the outputs is not yet coded. A common approach is to determine manually some typical output values, then write a simple print program to display the values in their anticipated forms. (See Figure 3-7.) Report recipients can be asked whether columns are titled appropriately, whether items are arranged in satisfactory order across the page, whether sufficient space is provided for any notations that the recipients expect to make on the report, and so on. If summary lines are to be included on the report, the sample should show examples of the lines. If, as a programmer, you are not given samples of input and output, you should develop such samples *before* beginning to write the program.

DOCUMENTATION

Documentation is a term with several meanings. We can say, for example, that *documentation is the act of furnishing recorded evidence of any activity.* Since the steps of program development — defining the problem, planning a

DEPT. J49 STOCK STATUS REPORT

ITEM NUMBER	DESCRIPTION	REORDER POINT	REORDER QUANTITY	OPENING STOCK	VENDOR RECPTS	SALES/ ISSUES	STOCK ORDERS	AVAILABLE STOCK
054123	Binders, 3-ring	1,000	500	3,567	5,000	3,500	2,000	5,567
648921	Clips, Paper Jumbo	1,000	300	1,634		968	900	666
888345	Notebook, Steno	4,200	1,000	9,330	4,000	7,340	6,825	5,990
	TOTALS			14,531	9,000	11,808	9,725	12,223**
JJ1345	Ink, Stamp Pad	4,150	300	6,505	300	2,300	600	4,205
JJ3740	Ink, Drawing	600	100	1,090		1,400	2,000	######
								(310)
JJ1211	Ink, Nonrepro	1,000	100	2,060		225	500	1,835
	TOTALS (JJ)			9,655	300	3,925	3,100	5,730**
	FINAL TOTALS			24,186	9,300	15,733	12,825	17,953***

Figure 3–7 Sample output

solution algorithm, coding the solution, and checking out the program — can all be thought of as activities, recorded evidence can and should be furnished for each of these steps. That is, collecting, organizing, and storing information about a problem and its solution are an ongoing part of the programmer's job. We can also say that *documentation is the collection of records that tells what has been done, is being done, and is going to be done on a programming project.* So, we see that we are discussing both an action and the results of that action here.

Why is programming documentation necessary? First, and foremost perhaps, because the life of a program is independent of the time committed by the programmers involved to their employer. Even those who remain with the employer become involved in other projects and/or forget details of the program, over time. Complete, accurate documentation (1) puts someone else, or the programmer himself, in a position to develop related programs or modules, answer questions, diagnose program errors, and modify the program if requirements change; (2) contributes to educating incoming personnel; and (3) guides the computer operator who must monitor execution of the program. It also (4) provides a visible, understandable trail for management personnel with overall responsibility for the project and/or for the programming process as a whole, and (5) is used by external and internal auditors seeking to verify that company policies and procedures are being carried out.

Most of the documentation created during program development is collected, organized, and filed in a *run manual*. This manual is used primarily by programmers. The documents that relate to the operation of the computer console are kept in a *console run book*, intended primarily for computer operators.

When the steps of program development are carried out as they should be, documentation is not an unwelcome burden imposed upon programmers as a project nears completion. Instead, both the act of documentation and the results are an integral part of the overall program-development process. In general, the documentation standards that must be established and adhered to depend on the length and complexity of the project and the number of people involved. The availability of readily usable forms helps to minimize the time required to prepare documentation, provides guidelines leading to complete coverage of the particular aspects of the project being documented, and makes for easier reading and understanding on the part of involved personnel. A guideline well worth following is: Document onto others as you would have them document onto you.

In this chapter, we have directed most of our attention to the problem-definition stage. We discussed at length the problem statement, various I/O layouts, and sample inputs and outputs. To every extent possible, this part of the documentation should be user-oriented, expressed in terms of the problem to be solved and devoid of computer jargon. Since a misunderstanding of any facet of the problem may cause endless difficulties during later stages of program development, the communication links between all in-dividuals involved must be strong. The documents created at this point help to insure that information is communicated accurately. As requirements change, addendums or corrections to existing documents must be circulated to all concerned personnel. The importance of establishing complete, ac-curate documentation of a problem and its solution, from the outset, cannot be overemphasized because the long-range success (or failure) of the pro-gramming project depends on it.

Because documentation is an ever-present responsibility of the pro-grammer, it is dealt with repetitively throughout this book. For the reader's convenience, all terms pertaining to documentation are printed in italics in the index. This feature is intended to help the reader locate details about a particular type of documentation as needed during the program-development cycle.

QUESTIONS

Q1. List and describe briefly the five steps of program development.

Q2. What are some of the characteristics you would look for in a high-quality program?

Q3. (a) What does the term *programmer productivity* mean to you? (b) Assuming your definition, how can it be measured?

Q4. Describe the organizational changes that have occurred in many program-develop-ment environments.

Q5. (a) Explain the makeup of a chief programmer team. (b) Which team position would you prefer and why?

Q6. What are some characteristics that a chief programmer should have? (Which of the persons you know have or might be expected to develop such characteristics?)

Q7. List and explain the two types of records generally included in a development sup-port library. In doing so, give at least three examples of each.

Q8. What does it mean to say that the results of computer runs are "public records"?

Q9. (a) List as many advantages of chief programmer teams as you can, from a team programmer's point of view. (b) What disadvantages might there be, from a team programmer's point of view?

Q10. What does it mean to say that "problem definition must occur at many different levels"?

Q11. What is the purpose of a problem statement?

Q12. Explain the functions of I/O layouts.

Q13. Describe a situation where creation of sample inputs and outputs is particularly advisable.

Q14. What does the term *documentation* mean to you?

Q15. List as many reasons as you can why program documentation is necessary.

EXERCISES

E1. Complete card layout forms to depict the three types of punched cards to be processed by a Monthly Sales Report program. The cards contain the following data fields:

- Card type (A1), cols 1-2; office number, 5-10; salesperson number, 11-16; gross sales, 20-29; net sales, 30-39; commission rate, 40-43
- Card type (A2), cols 1-2; dealership, 5-10; salesperson number, 11-16; gross sales, 20-29; net sales, 30-39; commission rate, 40-43; override flag, 44; override rate, 45-48
- Card type (Z9), cols 1-2; card count, 5-10

E2. Complete a printer spacing chart for the Monthly Sales Report to be produced by the program of E1 above. Assume the cards are received in card type/office or dealership/salesperson sequence. The program computes each salesperson's gross pay on the basis of commission and override rates, and prints salesperson number, gross sales, net sales, and gross pay for the salesperson as output. A minor total line is printed when all cards for a particular office or dealership have been processed. A major total line is printed at the end of the report.

*E3. (a) Write a simple print program to create a sample Monthly Sales Report according to the format you specified in E2 above. (b) Use the program to create a sample report.

*E4. Ask someone to assume the role of user of the report you prepared in E3 above. (a) What changes, if any, would he or she like to see in the report? (b) Redo your printer spacing chart to incorporate any changes agreed upon.

REFERENCES

Aron, Joel D. *The Program Development Process: Part I: The Individual Programmer.* Reading, Mass.: Addison-Wesley, 1974 (an excellent, basic introduction to programming).

Bachman, C. W. "The Programmer as Navigator," *Communications of the ACM* 16, 11 (Nov 1973): 653-58.

Baker, F. T. "Chief Programmer Team Management of Production Programming," *IBM Systems Journal* 11, 1 (Jan 1972): 56-73.

Gildersleeve, Thomas R. "Insight and Creativity," *Datamation* 22, 7 (July 1976): 89-96.

Johnson, James R. "A Working Measure of Productivity," *Datamation* 23, 2 (Feb 1977): 106-12.

Ledgard, Henry F., and Louis J. Chimura. *COBOL With Style: Programming Proverbs.* Rochelle Park, N.J.: Hayden Book Company, 1976 (guidelines covering good program design, program structure, and program understandability for COBOL programmers).

Ledgard, Henry F. *Programming Proverbs.* Rochelle Park, N.J.: Hayden Book Company, 1975 (similar to the reference above, but more suitable for PL/I and ALGOL programmers).

_____. *Programming Proverbs for FORTRAN Programmers.* Rochelle Park, N.J.: Hayden Book Company, 1975 (as above, but for FORTRAN programmers).

McCracken, Daniel D. "Revolution in Programming: An Overview," *Datamation* 19, 12 (Dec 1973): 50–52. This issue is devoted to *structured programming* with additional articles "Chief Programmer Teams," by F. Terry Baker and Harlan D. Mills; "Structured Programming," by James R. Donaldson; "Structured Programming: Top-down Approach," by Edward F. Miller, Jr., and George F. Lindamood; and "A Linguistic Contribution to GO-TO-less Programming," by Lawrence R. Clark.

Mills, H. D. "Chief Programmer Teams: Principles and Procedures," Report No. FSC 71-5108, IBM, Federal Systems Division, Gaithersburg, Maryland, 20760, June 1971.

Weinberg, Gerald M. *The Psychology of Computer Programming.* New York: Van Nostrand Reinhold, 1971 (largely a nontechnical book aimed at sensitizing the reader to the need for scientific study of human behavior on programming tasks).

4

DEVELOPING
A SOLUTION ALGORITHM,
OR PROGRAM DESIGN

WHAT AN ALGORITHM IS

After a problem has been defined, the planning for its solution can begin. This commonly involves determining the sequence of processing steps that must take place within a program to produce the outputs from the inputs. This part of the program development cycle is known as the development of an *algorithm*, which can be defined loosely as a set of rules or instructions that specify the operations required in the solution of a problem or the accomplishment of a task. The algorithm must (1) use only operations from a given set of basic operations and (2) produce the solution, or answer, in a finite number of such operations. The concept of a "given set of basic operations" is important because the computer can perform only certain operations; its capabilities are planned very carefully by hardware designers who lay out specifications that direct subsequent construction of the machine. The concept of a "finite number of such operations" is important because each operation performed by a computer takes a certain amount of time (typically, about one-millionth of a second, or less). If an unlimited number of steps is required, it is not possible to obtain the solution in a finite amount of time.

The term *algorithm* may be new or strange to some readers of this text. It need not be awesome. Each of us follows algorithms to accomplish certain tasks in our daily lives. For example, the procedure that a person follows to get from his home to school or to work is an algorithm: he exits the house, gets into his car, starts the engine, and so on; in the last of a finite number of steps, he reaches his destination. Similarly, the steps required to barbecue a tasty steak, or to obtain tickets to the next game of our favorite ball team, constitute an algorithm. The steps to compute the total deductions to be extracted from an employee's weekly earnings, or to calculate the current handicap of each member of a bowling league, are an algorithm of a more formal nature.

In most cases, it is possible to develop an algorithm to solve a problem. If doing so becomes difficult, it may be that further definition is needed. In this case, a return to the problem-definition step is required. For example, we cannot specify how to get from where we are to Dallas, Texas, unless we know both where we are and where Dallas is. If a particular mode of transportation must be used, we need to be told that as part of the problem definition. If there is a time constraint on how long it can take to get there, we need to be told that also.

In some cases, it may be necessary and even desirable to restate a problem, but to modify it slightly. An example often cited here is that of finding the square root of two. It can be shown mathematically that no finite set of operations will produce the square root of two, which can be represented only by an unlimited number of digits (1.4142. . .). However, if we modify the problem statement to say, "Find the largest 6-digit decimal number that is less than the square root of two," we can formulate an algorithm to find this close approximation to the square root of two. It may very well meet our immediate information requirement.

A computer program can be viewed as one of many ways of expressing a solution algorithm. Commonly, in the planning, or program-design, stage, we develop the algorithm by using any of several less formal methods of representation that can be translated later into computer-program form. We shall look at many of these methods of representation.

A fundamental rule here is: *Think first, program later.* As a programmer, you must learn to examine the problem definition carefully. Consider alternative approaches to solving the problem. Look at each approach in enough detail to detect possible trouble spots or areas in which the next problem-solving step is not readily discernible. Give yourself time to polish the approach (solution algorithm) that you select before trying to program it. This will shorten the programming time, reduce the number of false starts, and permit you to focus attention on design when designing, but on programming when programming. A good design does not insure a good program, but a poor design goes a long way toward insuring a bad one.

TOP-DOWN DEVELOPMENT

The chief programmer team concept described in Chapter 3 is directly dependent on another improved programming technology: *top-down development.* As we shall see, this concept is an inclusive one; in broadest terms, it includes *top-down design*, *top-down programming*, and *top-down testing*. We shall discuss each of them in this chapter and meet them again in later chapters as well.

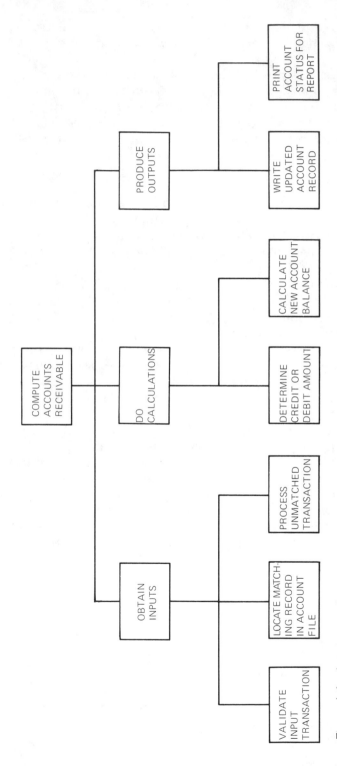

Figure 4–1   A structure chart

Top-Down Design

Top-down design is often referred to by other names — *structured design*, *composite design*, *programming by stepwise refinement*, and so on. Though the names differ, a uniform approach is generally agreed upon: we identify first the major function to be accomplished, then we identify its subfunctions, their subfunctions, and so on, proceeding from the major function to any number of lesser functions until we are satisfied that we fully understand the nature of our solution algorithm. The top-down design process consists of a series of steps to define the functions required for the solution of a problem, in terms of the problem itself.

When using the top-down approach, a specific plan of attack is developed in stages. The programmer (chief programmer, when the chief programmer team organization is used) designs a program or set of programs in *levels*. At each level of the design, only the issues relevant to that level are considered, and those issues are formulated precisely. The programmer considers alternative ways to further refine each part within the preceding level. He may take a look a level or two ahead if necessary to determine the best way to design at the present level. This design of software from the topmost level down is an interative process, continuing to successively lower levels of detail until all aspects of the solution algorithm have been defined. Determining the major function of the software, decomposing it into a next lower level of subfunctions, and so on, is not a trivial exercise. It often requires a great deal of investigation, creativity, thought, and time.

Structure Charts

As the design of a program or set of programs is formulated, it is documented in successively detailed *tree diagrams*, or *structure charts*, an example of which is shown in Figure 4–1. At this chart demonstrates, the logical structure of the design should practically jump off the structure chart pages. Each function or subfunction is described in terms of a verb (action) and an object (data affected). We can expect some if not all of the subfunctions at the third level in this structure chart to be broken down further on more detailed structure charts.

HIPO Diagrams

A key to success when using the top-down approach is not only to stress the identification of function but also to emphasize the identification of all inputs to and outputs from each function. In programming terminology, we say that the *interfaces* to the function must be defined. One of the techniques devised to help formalize this aspect of top-down design is the use of *HIPO diagrams*. HIPO is an acronym for Hierarchy plus Input-Process-Output. A typical HIPO package contains three types of diagrams:

- Visual table of contents. This diagram looks much like the structure charts we have just discussed. It contains the names and identification numbers of all the diagrams in the HIPO package and shows their relationships.
- Overview diagrams. These high-level HIPO diagrams describe the inputs, processes, and outputs of major functions in general terms. They refer to detail diagrams that provide additional information.
- Detail diagrams. These low-level HIPO diagrams describe each specific function in terms of the processes performed, the inputs it uses, and the outputs it produces. They break the functions down into the smallest details needed to understand them.

To transform the structure chart in Figure 4–1 into a visual table of contents, we add the identification numbers of HIPO diagrams in the HIPO package being documented, as shown in Figure 4–2. With this visual table of contents, the reader can locate a particular level of information or a specific diagram without thumbing through the entire HIPO package. The visual table of contents also contains a legend showing what the various symbols used in the package mean. The legend aids the reader by describing how the HIPO diagrams are to be read. If chosen appropriately, the identification numbers support the visual indication of the vertical relationships of functions along a particular path, or *branch*, of the hierarchy. For example, looking at Figure 4–2, we note (and are apt to recall later) that the leftmost branch includes *nodes* at 1.0, 1.n, and 1.n.n levels. The visual table of contents also shows horizontal relationships. For example, the 1.n level comprises nodes 1.1, 1.2, and 1.3.

Each node shown on the visual table of contents has a corresponding overview or detail diagram. The major functions at upper levels in the hierarchy contain the control logic of the program or set of programs being described. They determine when and in what order lower-level functions are to be invoked. The corresponding portion of a high-level-language program, for example, will consist primarily of CALL statements, PERFORM statements, DO loops, and IF-THEN-ELSE constructs. The lower-level functions are the workers; here simple statements to be executed sequentially will predominate.

Either an overview or a detail diagram generally consists of two parts: a *chart portion* and a *note portion.* (The chart portion is required for either; the note portion may be omitted from an overview diagram if no additional information at the particular level being diagrammed is required.) An overview diagram containing both a chart portion and a note portion is shown as an example in Figure 4–3.

The chart portion is the upper half of a HIPO diagram. It has three parts: (1) input on the left, (2) function-oriented processing steps in the center, and (3) output on the right. Inputs and outputs that are internal to the

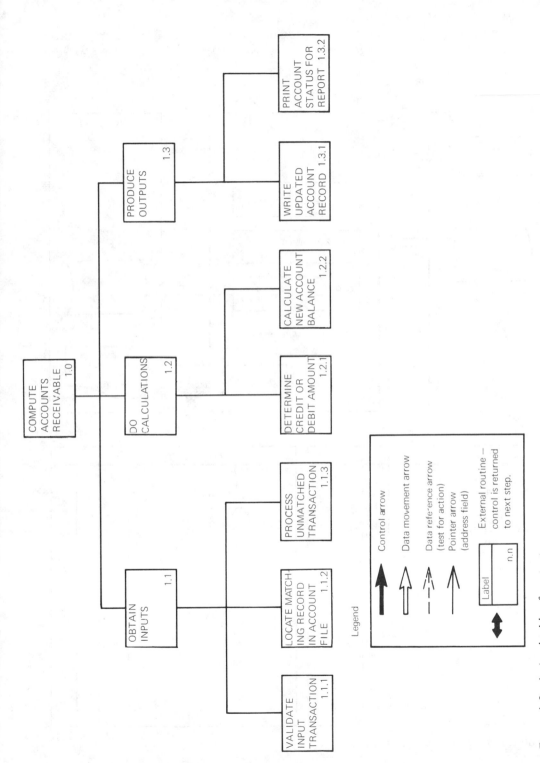

Figure 4–2 A visual table of contents

Author: B. Walton System/Program: Accounts Receivable Date: 9/25/78 Page: 1 of 1

Diagram ID: 2.2 Name: AUPDATE Description: Update Accounts Receivable Master File

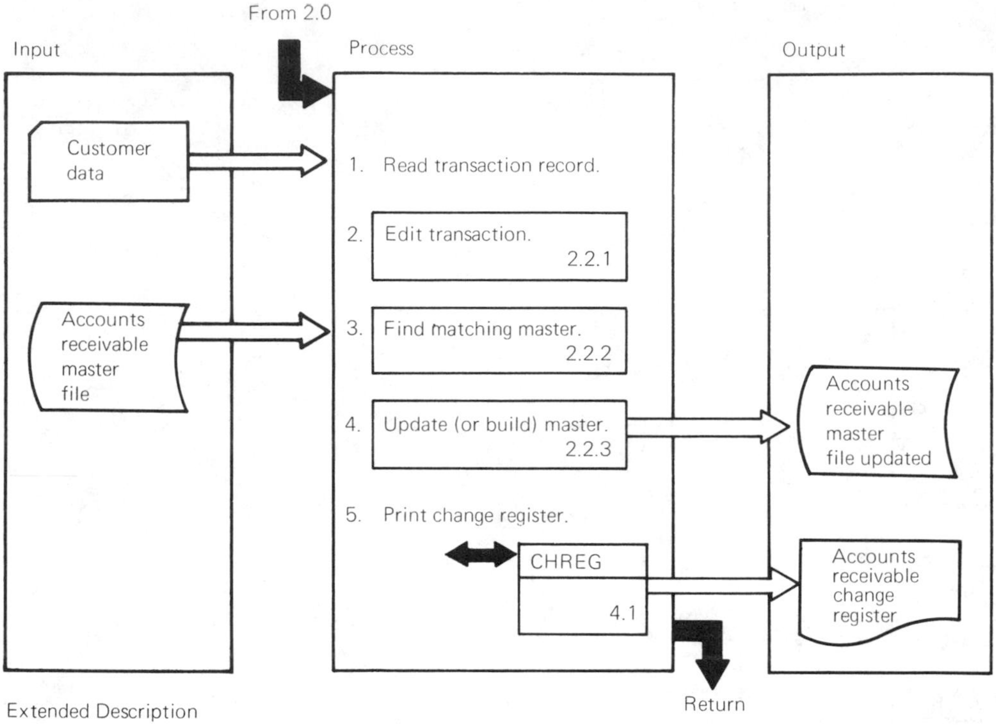

From 2.0
Input
Process
Output
Customer data
Accounts receivable master file
1. Read transaction record.
2. Edit transaction. 2.2.1
3. Find matching master. 2.2.2
4. Update (or build) master. 2.2.3
5. Print change register.
CHREG
4.1
Accounts receivable master file updated
Accounts receivable change register
Return

Extended Description

Notes	Rout	Lab	Ref
2. Customer id (CUSID) field required.		EDIN1	2.2.1
3. CUSID is search key. Create entry for new master if no match.		SRCH1	2.2.2
5. Show transaction, old master (if any), and new master, for recovery or checking purposes.	CHREG		4.1

Notes	Rout	Lab	Ref

Figure 4–3 HIPO overview diagram

overall program logic described by the HIPO package are labeled and grouped by boxes, shading, or both. If desired, inputs from and outputs to external devices can be represented by the standard flowcharting symbols for data-recording media explained in Chapter 5 of this book. If data shown in the output area is used as both input and output in the same processing step, a double-headed arrow may be used. Some processing steps on an overview diagram may be enclosed in boxes, with numbers in the lower right-hand corners of the boxes. Each number refers to a next-lower-level diagram that further describes the particular function-oriented processing step (that is, the subfunction).

The note portion, or lower half of a HIPO diagram, is often called the *extended description area.* It contains numbered notes corresponding directly to numbered paragraphs in the process part of the chart portion of the diagram. A note is included for a processing step when further explanation of that step is needed at the particular level being diagrammed. This portion of the HIPO diagram may also give cross-references to the code associated with a processing step (routine names, statement labels, and the like). It may refer to other HIPO diagrams and to non-HIPO documentation such as tape and disk layouts, program flowcharts, and decision tables (see below).

Standards for the representation of types of data, types of usage, and other program-design considerations have been proposed for HIPO users. These and other guidelines are documented, for example, in the IBM Corporation manual, *HIPO — A Design Aid and Documentation Technique.*

The number of levels of detail diagrams required to develop fully a solution algorithm depends in large part on the problem to be solved. Factors such as overall complexity, the number of functions and subfunctions to be documented, other types of documentation available, and the amount of information required by users of the HIPO package, as well as who the intended users are, must be taken into account.

When constructing HIPO diagrams, an important point to remember is that they are to show function, not detailed internal program organization and logic. This point is also a key to success in top-down design. Too often, programmers become involved in trivial details when they should be concentrating on higher-level design considerations. There is a level of design at which it is not appropriate to be concerned with whether a result should be truncated, rounded up, or rounded down.

The details of internal program organization and logic can and should be considered later. When they are, programmers often find *program flowcharts* and *decision tables* to be extremely valuable tools in helping them to see all aspects of a problem and to organize their thoughts. The reader should refer to Chapters 5 and 6, respectively, to learn more about constructing and using flowcharts and decision tables. We mention them here because they are widely used in solution planning and to clarify where and how they fit in the overall program-development cycle.

The primary goal of the top-down design process as we have described it here is to produce a design for the modular structure of a program, one in which no ambiguities exist and in which program segments, or *modules*, are relatively small and highly independent. (We say more about this later.) The overall goal of such modularization is simplicity. Our intent is to express a solution algorithm as a set of single, well-defined functions that can be programmed, tested, and maintained with ease. We hope to avoid program complexity, to make it possible for coding efforts on separate modules to proceed in parallel, and to insure that any changes to one portion of a program or set of programs need not (and will not) affect several other portions of the program as well.

Top-Down Programming

Top-down programming involves implementing a program design in the top-down manner specified for it. Indeed, the programmer might begin by preparing the job-control statements needed to run the program being implemented. These job-control statements are written in the *job-control language* (JCL) developed for the EDP system in use. They specify input-process-output for the job as a whole: (1) the input file names and the devices from which the files are to be read; (2) the name of the program that constitutes the job, or the names of several programs if the job consists of a series of programs, or job steps; and (3) the output file names and the devices on which the files are to reside. (We referred to job-control statements in Chapters 2 and 3. The programmer must become familiar with the JCL requirements at his particular installation.)

When writing the program itself, the top function, or segment, of the program is written first. This segment contains the primary control logic of the whole program. It serves as a basic skeleton, or main-line path, and contains segment names, where appropriate, referring to code that will be written later.

The simplest form of top-down programming suggests that all of the design should be completed before the code for the top segment is written. After completing the top segment, we write the code for the next lower level, then for the next lower level, and so forth. A more ambitious approach suggests that the top level of the program should be designed and then coded, before any further design is accomplished. The second level of the program is then designed and coded, then the third level, and so forth. Obviously, this means that programmers are writing code at a point in time when the overall design is not yet complete.

Most computer professionals acknowledge that there is no one correct way to do top-down programming. In practice, top-down development does not necessarily imply that all segments at a certain level must be completed before proceeding to the next level; the top-down approach is much more adaptive than that. It does imply, however, that any selected path should be implemented from top to bottom. For example, it may be desirable to write all segments related to input functions first, so that other segments that process the input data can operate on actual problem-related input, even in the test environment. As another example, it may be that one path of the hierarchy constitutes an especially critical part of the overall solution algorithm: Is the table-search routine really able to handle no-hit situations successfully? Does it execute within a reasonable amount of time? Do the various mathematical computations of slope, together with any subsequent truncations or roundings, really provide the degree of accuracy needed in the final result?

When following the top-down approach to program development, the programmer has yet another decision to make at this point: How should he arrange the code for the various functions in an overall sequence, thus determining how that code will appear in a printed listing of the program? For example, suppose a program is designed as shown in Figure 4–4a. The programmer might consider arranging the code in a horizontal manner, as shown in Figure 4–4b, or in a vertical manner, as shown in Figure 4–4c. The horizontal approach is useful for those who want an overview of the program. Having looked at the main line of the program (segment 1.0), we look next at segments 1.1, 1.2, and 1.3. If we choose to pursue further details, we look at the next lower level of segments, which follow 1.3 in the program listing.

From a program checkout or maintenance point of view, the vertical approach may be convenient. If we are tracing the flow of program logic, we look first at the main line of the program (1.0), then the code for module 1.1, then for module 1.1.1, then 1.1.1.1 and 1.1.1.2, then 1.1.2, and so on. This is the vertical order shown in Figure 4–4c.

The general question we are addressing can be summarized as follows. If we are looking at a statement in segment X, somewhere in a program, and segment X refers to segment Y, how do we know where to find segment Y? The programmer can and should provide clues for others who examine his code to follow. The use of alphanumeric identifiers patterned after the numerals in Figure 4–4 (say, S10, S11, S111, and so on) is one method. It has certain disadvantages. What happens, for example, if a segment must be inserted between S111 and S112 on the structure chart?

Some high-level programming languages (among them, FORTRAN and BASIC) permit statement numbers to be used as labels for reference purposes. The programmer can attempt to insure that the ordinal relationships between statement numbers indicate the relative positions of the segments of code they introduce. He can initially identify statements using statement numbers separated by increments of 10 or even 100 (100, 200, 300, and so on) to allow for insertions of additional statements at a later time.

The PL/I programmer can help to make statement labels visible in a program listing by placing the labels further to the left on coding lines than

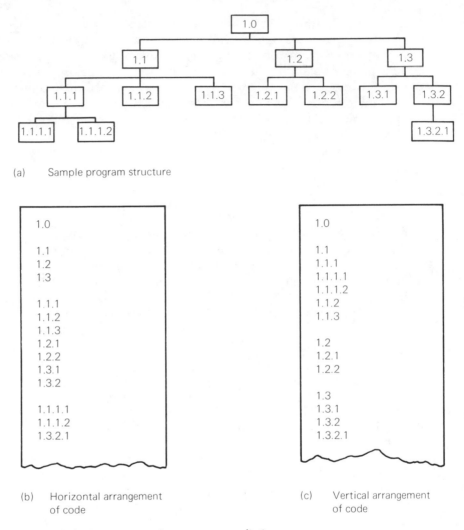

(a)   Sample program structure

(b)   Horizontal arrangement
       of code

(c)   Vertical arrangement
       of code

Figure 4-4   Arranging code on a program listing

other entries. He can also elect not to place other code on the lines that labels occupy.

Insofar as top-down development and, indeed, good programming practices in general are concerned, the main point here is that the programmer should consider this question, select one approach, and follow it consistently. When two or more members of a programming team produce code for a program, they should agree on a uniform approach before beginning to write code. Then they should follow that approach in arrangement and labeling throughout the program.

An important advantage of this phased approach is that very early in the program-development cycle and at any point thereafter, there exists a partial system that works. The systems analysts, programmers, and intended users can get a pretty good picture of what the final system will do. Another advantage is that if there are basic problems in implementing the design, they are discovered early. There are no 200 pages of design documentation that must be scrapped, because they haven't all been written yet. The painstaking work of developing them has not been expended unnecessarily.

Top-Down Testing

Top-down programming facilitates top-down testing. In effect, design, coding, and testing (or simply coding and testing, with design completed earlier, depending on the overall top-down approach adopted) proceed in parallel. The purest approach to top-down development suggests that testing of the main-line path of the program should begin as soon as it has been coded, before any lower-level segments have been designed and coded. In practice, the programmer usually finds that the main-line path and at least one or two segments at a lower level must be designed and coded before any nontrivial testing can be done. This should not be considered a violation of the top-down philosophy.

Implementation of the top-down approach to testing requires that *program stubs*, or dummy routines, be created for segments that are referred to by name in higher-level segments under test but are not yet coded. We noted, for example, that the basic skeleton, or main-line path, contains segment names referring to lower-level code. By inserting program stubs with the same names as the segments not yet coded into a program library, the programmer can execute and test this basic skeleton while design and coding of the actual segments are being carried out.

A program stub is a substitute for an actual segment. It does not perform the functions of the actual segment, but it provides sufficiently similar input/output behavior to fool the higher-level segment that references it. In most cases, a stub is a short, basic sequence of code that also provides an execution trace. For example, it may be advisable to include an output statement that causes GOT TO SEGMENT 3 to be printed as output in such a dummy routine. Another technique is to introduce a variable for use as a counter into a program stub; that variable can be set to zero initially, then increased by one and printed each time the segment is executed thereafter.

Each program stub is eventually replaced by the segment for which it serves as a placeholder. That new segment is included in the next combining of the parts of the program under development. At any point, the code already in existence provides a framework within which a newly coded segment can execute. Errors are generally easier to detect because segments are integrated into this framework one, or a very few, at a time. The requirement for test time is distributed throughout program development. This eliminates the need for very large amounts of computer test time near the end of the project. Since integration is carried out as a part of development, there is no need to undertake the horrendous task of trying to mold a large number of separately coded and tested segments into a single working system at the completion of a development effort.

MODULARIZATION

In the program-design stage, when following the top-down approach (and even when not), we consider first the general organization of the program as it relates to the major functions to be performed. Usually, we establish several main subdivisions, such as an initialization section, input, processing, and output sections, and a termination section. Most programs also contain sections dealing with exceptional conditions, such as the handling of invalid input (detected in the input section) or the action to be taken when an attempt to divide by zero occurs (in the processing section of the program).

If other than a very short, simple program is being developed, it is usually advisable to break the program into segments, or program modules. Each module should be relatively small and highly independent; it should constitute a logical unit, performing one or a small number of functions of the overall problem-solving task.

What is meant by "relatively small"? There are no absolute guidelines as to what amount of code is too large, or too small, or just right. Some computer professionals argue that a module may be any size up to that which fits in 4096 bytes, or 512 words, or 1024 words, of main storage, depending on the computer on which the program is to be run. Others suggest that a module may be defined as the amount of code that one programmer can code and test during one month; this suggests a module size of from 200 to 300 statements. Still others argue that, to present a "picture" on each page of a program listing, each module should be 60 lines of code or less in size. In some cases, several very simple functions may be included in a single module. For example, in a top-down environment, short segments at a low level may be incorporated into a segment at the next higher level (that is, a minimal redesign may prove advisable). If a function requires 100 or more lines of code, there is a good possibility that it should be divided into subordinate functions. Most programmers agree that it is much easier to work with a module contained on one page of a program listing than to flip from page to page of a multiple-page listing, or to deal with many short modules on several pages that must be ordered manually.

The most important point to grasp here is that an appropriate size (whatever that is agreed upon to be) is no guarantee of modularity. A COBOL program comprising a 300-statement main program and four or five

20-statement subroutines, or sections, referred to by PERFORM statements may or may not be modular. The size of a program module should ultimately be determined by its function.

Since size is not a definitive indication of modularity, we need to explore the concept of modularity a bit further to understand it better. We do so by pursuing a second question: What is meant by "highly independent"? Here again, there are no absolutes. In simplest terms, the concept of modularity implies that any module within a program can be changed without affecting any other part of the program. It also implies the reverse: that any other part of the program can be changed without affecting the module.

In practice, such total independence is often difficult, if not impossible, to attain. Hence, we evaluate the independence of a module in terms of how much (or how little) a change to the module will affect other parts of the program, and vice versa. Several considerations are involved:

- Module-to-module relationships. If all of the interfaces between modules have been defined, it should be possible to change any module in the program without having unexpected (and, too often, undetected) effects on any other module. It should be possible to replace any module with one that is functionally equivalent (accepts the same inputs and generates the same outputs) without having any effects at all on other modules. Some professionals claim, in somewhat oversimplification, that to the extent that we can do this, we have a modular program.

- Arguments, or parameters, to the module. We assume, by definition, that the interfaces to a module are its inputs and outputs. They may, for example, be passed to or returned from the module as the current values of arguments specified in a subroutine call. This is an area where we must expect the independence of a module to be suspect. We pursue questions such as: If the number of arguments to be specified in a call were changed, what would the effect on the module be? Or, what if the type of the second argument were changed from binary to character? Or, the length of the third argument from 4 bytes to 8? The higher the degree of module independence, the less traumatic such changes are upon the module.

- Internal variables and constants of the module. A module may depend on the values of *global variables*, which are potentially changing values known to two or more modules within a program. For example, a list of valid part numbers, or a table of possible loan amounts and corresponding rates to be applied, is apt to be defined as a set of global variables. If the structure of the list or table were changed, or even the number of entries, what would be the effect on the module?

- Structure and format of the data base. This consideration is similar to that of global variables, but it is even more likely here that changes can and will be made without knowledge or thought of their effects on any particular module. A major emphasis of the designers of current data base software (see Chapter 2) is to permit applications programs that refer to data base files to be independent of the physical structure or the definition of those files.

- Solution algorithm. To the extent that a module provides for a specific implementation of a specific algorithm, it is dependent on that algorithm. In general, the greater the number of constants specified as part of the program logic, the less flexible the modules that contain them, and the greater the likelihood that a change in the algorithm will necessitate changes in one or more of these modules.

- EDP-system environment. The programmer who writes a module makes certain recognized or unrecognized assumptions about the manner in which it will be executed. For example, if the module is concerned with accepting input, he may assume that the input always comes from a card reader. What changes would be required if the input were to be read in as blocks of records from a magnetic-tape file? Or, what changes should be made to a module if, henceforth, it were to run in a virtual environment? What changes would be required to accept input from a user at a terminal?

Obviously, module independence doesn't just happen; it may not be easily achievable, even when we design with the goal of modularity in mind. Some guidelines toward modularity are:

1. Use the top-down approach to program development. As we have seen, this approach emphasizes the identification and separation of the functions within a problem-solving task into identifiable logical units. These logical units can constitute the modules of a program.

2. Keep program segments small in size. As has been pointed out, the number of statements, or lines of code, in a program segment is not an appropriate unit of measure in determining modularity. Nevertheless, it is true that a programmer can deal more effectively with the program logic within from one to a very few pages of a program listing than with a 300-statement or larger grouping.

3. Use structured programming techniques. Edward Yourdon, in *Techniques of Program Structure and Design*, suggests that structured programming will gradually be accepted as the standard method of achieving modular programs.* Since structured programming is

---

*See Edward Yourdon's *Techniques of Program Structure and Design*, page 94.

covered in detail in Chapter 8 of this book, we shall not discuss this topic further at this time.

4. Use decision tables. A decision table is an effective tabular approach toward developing a solution algorithm. It is especially useful when a large number of possible conditions must be considered and/or a large number of possible actions or combinations of actions identified and selectively carried out. For guidelines to the construction and use of decision tables, see Chapter 6.

5. Design the program to provide flexibility. Avoid "hard coding" data values within a solution algorithm; that is, avoid entering them as constants in the program. A preferable approach is to select a meaningful symbolic name for a data item and treat it as a variable. The correct value for the data item can be read as input before the variable is referenced during program execution. This approach permits the value (that is, the solution algorithm) to be changed without necessarily having to change the program. As another example, the programmer should avoid referring to input devices or output devices by means of actual machine addresses. Most EDP systems permit physical devices to be associated with symbolic names, independent of the program in which the names are used (say, in job-control statements). To help insure module independence, this capability should be used.

6. Employ data coupling but avoid data interconnections. *Data coupling* is present when all input to and output from a module are passed as data elements, to and from that module. This is precisely the type of interface between modules that we have described. *Data interconnection* exists when a module depends on or alters variables outside its boundaries. Difficulties often occur with modules that refer to global variables or that also process input data received from an I/O device. Any externally generated changes to global variables or changes in input may cause subtle changes to the functional relationships between module inputs and outputs.

A wise design practice is to limit the sharing of data outside of call interfaces to only those data elements whose values do not change. If argument lists become cumbersome, the programmer must consider which variables are best made known to the entire program, that is, defined to be global. PL/I's EXTERNAL attribute and FORTRAN's COMMON statement provide this capability but, if used, it should be well documented by means of comments.

Another wise design practice is to concentrate I/O processing in a few, short, specially selected modules apart from the computational portion of the program. The I/O portion of the program is, by definition, the portion of the program that interfaces with the outside world; it is therefore most subject to change. The remainder of the program should neither know nor care whether input comes from a card reader or a magnetic tape, what the blocking factor is for input or output, or what operating system considerations must be adjusted to (for example, what label checking is required).

OTHER DESIGN LANGUAGES

Structure charts, HIPO diagrams, flowcharts, and decision tables are design languages. The programmer uses them to develop the solution algorithm and to communicate that algorithm to himself and others. In addition, *formal design languages* have been developed and are being used in some program-development environments. Such languages are not pictorial in nature as are those we have mentioned. Nor are they programming languages, except in certain special cases. They are, however, more structured than our everyday English. Because a formal design language is based upon a well-defined, documented set of rules, it is less subject to misinterpretation than other, more casual means of expression. It tends to be more directly translatable to a programming-language form.

Perhaps the best-known formal design languages are A Programming Language (APL) and a variation of it called APLGOL. APL is also a high-level programming language. Other formal design languages are the Viennese Definition Language (VDL), META IV, Syntax Definition Language (SDL), and Design Programming Language (DPL). Readers of this book who decide to use one or more of these languages should seek complete references dealing with them. (Some are listed at the end of this chapter.) We mention them to make you aware that such languages do exist and that extensive attention is being given to the development of design tools and methodologies.

Pseudo code, referred to by some computer professionals as a pseudo language or an informal design language, is rapidly gaining favor. It is most often used in expressing structured programming logic, and we discuss it in connection with that subject in Chapter 8. Though similar to some high-level programming languages (especially, PL/I), it does not impose strict rules such as one must follow when actually writing a program. Its primary function is to enable the programmer to express his ideas about program logic in a very natural, English-like form. He is free to concentrate on the solution algorithm rather than on the form and constraints within which it must be stated. The intended result is an unambiguous solution to the problem.

DOCUMENTATION

The top-down development of a program as described in this chapter is, at the same time, the continuation of another facet of the programmer's job: the top-down development of documentation. We have seen in this chapter that at the top level, the programmer should emphasize function and identify the inputs and outputs to each function. Likely forms of documentation at this level include structure charts and/or the visual table of contents and overview diagrams of a HIPO package. Working down from this level, the programmer develops lower-level HIPO diagrams, decision tables, and/or flowcharts. (The last two are discussed in detail in the next two chapters.) All such documentation can and should be included in the run manual being developed for the resultant program.

Some computer professionals suggest that pseudo code may supersede both flowcharts and decision tables, as well as narrative descriptions and any other forms of documentation commonly developed at this stage in program development. If entered as comments in program coding or retained on a separate but readily accessible computer file, pseudo code can be updated easily with computer help whenever the program logic is changed.

It is critical that design documentation be well-structured. A reader who wishes a specific level of detail should be able to obtain exactly the information he needs, no more and no less. Two common pitfalls in documenting are: providing too little information and providing too much. As a programmer, you should aim to be complete. Otherwise, your efforts may be of little value. On the other hand, providing too much information may totally obscure the critical portions of it. There is a tendency for the programmer, especially one who has spent many hours at his task or is extremely familiar with the subject area, to go too deeply into programming details. Providing a list of key variables and their uses is wise, but mentioning insignificant variables (for example, those used for intermediate storage of results) is unnecessary. Vital data structures should be explained, but unimportant or commonplace data structures and trivial algorithms should be ignored. Such details are a hindrance rather than a help; they serve merely as distractions.

A general guideline here is: Document (explain) the program design up to a point where the program coding itself and supporting comments can take over. You'll be glad you did.

QUESTIONS

Q1. What is an algorithm?

Q2. List at least six distinct ways of expressing an algorithm.

Q3. (a) Give a brief definition of top-down development. (b) What are the objectives of this approach?

Q4. (a) What does the acronym HIPO stand for? (b) Show why this acronym is appropriate for the design and documentation technique so identified.

Q5. List and explain three types of diagrams normally included in a HIPO package.

Q6. (a) Why is it important to avoid becoming engrossed in trivial details when designing a program? (b) How might one recognize when such a situation has occurred? (c) How might such a situation be avoided?

Q7. (a) Describe two different approaches to top-down coding. (b) Which do you prefer and why?

Q8. (a) Explain two alternative ways of organizing code on a program listing. (b) What are the advantages of each? (c) Which do you prefer and why?

Q9. (a) What is a program stub? (b) Why, when, and how are program stubs used?

Q10. List at least four advantages of top-down testing.

Q11. Give a brief definition of program modularity.

Q12. (a) What do you consider to be a reasonable restriction as to module size? (b) Give reasons to support your opinion.

Q13. Support or refute the statement "Global variables should not be used in a program."

Q14. Distinguish between data coupling and data interconnection.

Q15. Point out potential difficulties associated with providing either too much documentation or too little documentation (for maximum benefit here, select the situation most apt to occur in your case).

EXERCISES

E1. Refer to Figure 4-2. (a) What type of HIPO diagram is shown? (b) How many levels of hierarchy are depicted? (c) What are the subfunctions of the Obtain Inputs function?

E2. Look at Figure 4-3. (a) What function is designed and documented here? (b) What are its inputs? (c) What are its outputs? (d) What are the subfunctions of this function? (e) What processing is required if no matching master record is found? (f) What can you tell about the edit subfunction?

E3. Assume you have been directed to use HIPO to document the design of a corporate order-processing system. Identify factors that you would consider in deciding how many levels of diagrams were required.

E4. Obtain two program listings, one which shows wise use of labels and one which shows poor labeling techniques. Point out the good and bad practices you observe.

E5. Assume you have been given the task of developing installation standards to encourage modular programming. List the standards that you would suggest. (Be prepared to give arguments to support each one, as you might expect to do in such a situation.)

E6. Obtain a listing of a program prepared by you or by a classmate or coworker. Evaluate the program against the installation standards that you proposed in E5.

E7. Obtain samples of good and bad program design documentation. Point out the strong points and weak points of each.

E8. Calculation of gross pay requires an employee's time card, the payroll master file, and a pay rate table as input. An updated payroll master, gross pay file, and error messages describing invalid inputs are produced as output. An employee number, job code, and hours worked are read from the time card. The correct pay rate for the job code is extracted from the pay rate table. Gross pay includes both regular pay calculated as hours $\times$ rate (for hours less than or equal to 40) and overtime pay calculated as hours $\times$ rate $\times$ 1.5 (for hours greater than 40). Create a HIPO diagram for this function, one of several within an hourly payroll processing system.

REFERENCES

Chapin, Ned. *Computers: A Systems Approach.* New York: Van Nostrand Reinhold, 1971 (a comprehensive reference to the man-computer interface, hardware, software, and systems management).

Dijkstra, E. W. "The Structure of the THE Multiprogramming System," *Communications of the ACM* 11, 5 (May 1968): 341-46 (notion of levels of hierarchy of software modules generating abstract resources supported by lower levels and available to higher levels; e.g., levels of programs operate on files, vectors (sectors on disk), words, bytes, bits).

Geller, Dennis P. "How Many Directions is Top Down?" *Datamation* 22, 6 (June 1976): 109-12. See also "The Chief Programmer Team Administrator," by Lawrence H. Cooke, Jr., pp. 85-86; and "Structured Programming in COBOL," by Jan L. Mize, pp. 103-05.

HIPO — A Design Aid and Documentation Technique. IBM Corporation manual (GC20-1851). White Plains, N.Y., n.d.

IBM HIPO Template. IBM Corporation publication (GX20-1971). White Plains, N.Y., n.d.

IBM HIPO Worksheet. IBM Corporation publication (GX20-1970). White Plains, N.Y., n.d.

Inmon, Bill. "An Example of Structured Design," *Datamation* 22, 3 (Mar 1976): 82-86. See also "HIPO for Developing Specifications," by Martha Nyvall Jones, pp. 112ff.

Iverson, K. E. *A Programming Language.* New York: John Wiley & Sons, 1962 (an introduction to APL by one of its founders).

———. "APL in Exposition," Technical Report No. 320-3010, IBM, Philadelphia Scientific Center, Philadelphia, Pa., Jan 1972. See also "Introducing APL to Teachers," 320-3014 (July 1972), and "An Introduction to APL for Scientists and Engineers," 320-3019 (Mar 1973), by this author.

Katzan, Harry J. Jr., *Systems Design and Documentation. An Introduction to the HIPO Method.* New York: Van Nostrand Reinhold, 1976.

Maynard, Jeff. *Modular Programming.* Philadelphia: Auerbach, 1972.

Myers, Glenford J., "Characteristics of Composite Design," *Datamation* 19, 9 (Sept. 1973): 100-02.

———. *Reliable Software Through Composite Design.* New York: Petrocelli/Charter, 1975 (oriented toward experienced programmers and systems analysts).

Parnas, D. L. "A Technique for Software Module Specification with Examples," *Communications of the ACM* 15, 5 (May 1972): 330–36.

——. "On the Criteria to Be Used in Decomposing Systems into Modules," *Communications of the ACM* 15, 12 (Dec 1972): 1053–58.

Richardson, Daniel R. "The People Side of Top-Down," *Infosystems* 22, 7 (July 1975): 34–35.

Rigo, Joseph T. "How to Prepare Functional Specifications," *Datamation* 20, 5 (May 1974): 78–80.

Ross, Douglas, T., and John W. Brackett. "An Approach to Structured Analysis," *Computer Decisions* 8, 9 (Sept 1976): 40–44.

Stay, J. F. "HIPO and Integrated Program Design," *IBM Systems Journal* 15, 2 (June 1976): 143–54.

Wegner, Peter. "The Vienna Definition Language," *Computing Surveys* (ACM) 4, 1 (Mar 1972): 5–63.

Wirth, Niklaus. *Systematic Programming: An Introduction.* Englewood Cliffs, N.J.: Prentice-Hall, 1973 (introduces programming as the technique of constructing algorithms in a systematic manner). See also *Algorithms + Data Structures = Programs,*" by this author, Prentice-Hall, 1976, which emphasizes stepwise refinement of algorithms (especially, sorting and recursion).

Yourdon, Edward. *Techniques of Program Structure and Design.* Englewood Cliffs, N.J.: Prentice-Hall, 1975 (up-to-date coverage of top-down program design, modular programming, structured programming, testing, and debugging).

5

PROGRAM FLOWCHARTING

As most if not all readers of this book are aware by now, the computer is an extremely powerful, fast machine but it can do only what it is told to do, exactly as it is told to do it. It gets its directions from a stored program — the set of instructions, or solution algorithm, created by the programmer to tell the computer how to do its job.

One of the techniques that we can use in planning a program is program flowcharting. A *flowchart* is a pictorial representation that serves as a means of recording, analyzing, and communicating problem information. It shows a lot at a glance. Broad concepts and minor details, and their relationships to each other, are readily apparent. Sequences and relationships that are hard to extract from paragraphs of text become obvious when displayed on a flowchart. Even the symbols themselves have specific meanings that aid in interpretation of the solution algorithm.

TYPES OF FLOWCHARTS

In practice, two kinds of flowcharts are used in solution planning: *system flowcharts* and *program flowcharts*. A system flowchart shows the procedures involved in converting data on input media to data in output form. Emphasis is placed on the data flow into or out of a computer program, the forms of input, and the forms of output. In this respect, a system flowchart is similar to the HIPO lower-level diagrams described in Chapter 4. Unlike a HIPO diagram, however, a system flowchart makes no attempt to depict the function-oriented processing steps within a program. Whereas system and program flowcharts have been used in program planning for many years, HIPO diagrams are a relatively recent innovation. The programmer may choose to use either or both techniques. A system flowchart may be constructed by the

Figure 5-1   System flowchart for monthly billing

systems analyst as part of the problem definition; if not, it may be constructed by the programmer.

A simple system flowchart is shown in Figure 5-1. The *process symbol* (☐) tells us that a monthly billing program is to be written and executed; the *punched-card symbol* (☐) indicates that input (quantity and unit price) is to be entered on punched cards; and the *document symbol* (☐) indicates that output (amount due) is to be printed on a paper document. The direction of data flow is shown by *flowlines.*

We cannot tell by looking at Figure 5-1 whether multiplication, addition, subtraction, or a combination of these operations is needed to compute monthly bills. We cannot tell the order in which required operations must be performed. To provide this detailed information, the programmer constructs a program flowchart.

In contrast to a system flowchart, a program flowchart (also called a *block diagram* or *logic diagram*) shows the detailed processing steps within one computer program and the sequence in which those steps must be executed. (A system flowchart may show the flow of data through several programs, but each process symbol on a system flowchart represents one program.) To emphasize this distinction, a program flowchart showing the detailed processing steps in the monthly billing program and the system flowchart for the program are shown in Figure 5-2.

The program shown in Figure 5-2 controls the sequence of operations required to prepare a monthly statement for one customer. *Terminal symbols* (◯) show clearly the beginning and ending of the program. The computer performs reading and writing as well as calculations. Note that the process and flowline symbols are used on both system and program flowcharts. Specialized input/output symbols appear on the system flowchart, but the *generalized input/output symbol* (▱) is used on the program flowchart. As mentioned above, the major emphasis of a program flowchart is on the detailed operations performed on data, not on the media or devices used. Use of the specialized input/output symbols would tend to distract readers from its main purpose. Furthermore, modern EDP systems often permit devices to be assigned at program execution time, taking into account the devices available at that time. For these reasons, use of specialized input/output symbols on program flowcharts is not recommended. Either generalized or specialized input/output symbols may appear on system flowcharts. Because the system flowchart is intended to show the forms of input and output, use of specialized input/output symbols is usually preferred.

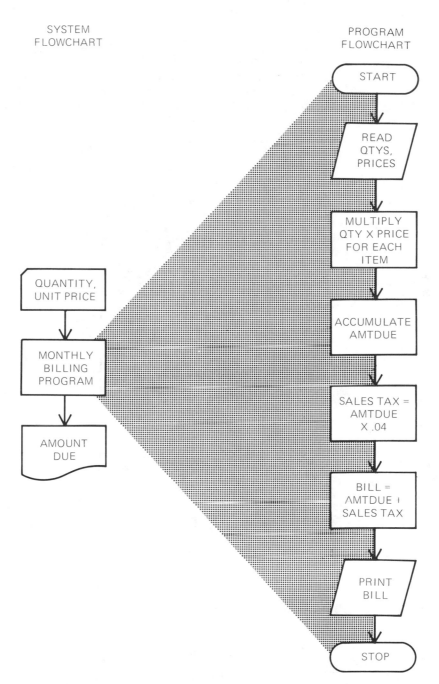

Figure 5–2   System and program flowcharts for monthly billing

BRANCHING OPERATIONS

The program flowchart in Figure 5-2 has one serious drawback: it shows how to compute the monthly statement for only one customer. Generally, a computer program is written to perform a particular operation or sequence of operations many times. To provide for this, a program flowchart can be

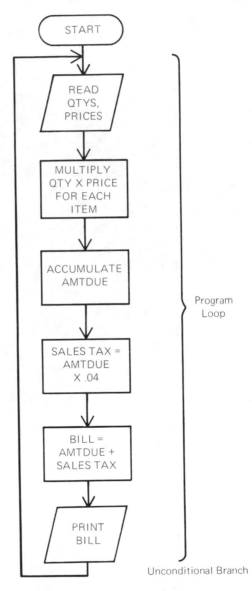

Figure 5-3   Using an unconditional branch to form a program loop

made to curve back on itself; that is, a sequence of processing steps can be executed repeatedly, on different data. In effect, a *program loop* is formed.

Stored-program instructions are usually executed in the sequence in which they are loaded into primary storage, but they do not have to be. Any one of several types of *branch* instructions can be used to cause the computer to branch, or transfer control, to an instruction other than the next one in sequence. The label of the alternate instruction is specified in the branch instruction.

Some branch instructions cause the computer to branch unconditionally; that is, it must go to the instruction whose label is specified. We modify the original plan for the monthly billing program to cause an *unconditional branch* (represented by flowlines joined at right angles) back to the beginning of the program to read input for another customer after each statement is printed, as shown in Figure 5–3.

Looking at Figure 5–3, we see that we need to do some additional planning. The flowchart does not handle the situation when there are no more cards (or no input at all) to be processed. Further, there is no longer a final step in the solution algorithm—we have not planned what makes program execution stop. So, we modify the flowchart again to specify a *conditional branch*, or decision-making step (represented by the *decision symbol* (◇) in Figure 5–4). Now the computer checks whether or not there are, indeed, cards to be read. If there are, the processing steps within the loop are executed. If there are not, the loop is exited and execution stops.

USES OF FLOWCHARTS

To the programmer, the program flowchart is an all-purpose tool. It is the program blueprint. In the initial stages of program development, he uses it as we have done—to lay out the solution algorithm. Later, it is a guide when coding. Both system and program flowcharts can also serve as valuable documentation. They are useful to programmers who are developing other modules of the program or of related programs. Computer operators who are managing the EDP-system console can refer to them before or during program execution. Both types of flowcharts usually contain explanatory material necessary for supervisory review or auditing purposes. They can be referred to by maintenance personnel when changes to the solution algorithm or its computer-program form of representation are required.

During design, coding, test, implementation, and operation (that is, "production use"), any changes made to the logic of the program should be reflected on the flowchart for that program. That is, the flowchart must always be an up-to-date indication of the solution algorithm. A lesson too often learned by experience is that a flowchart that is not up to date has little or no value.

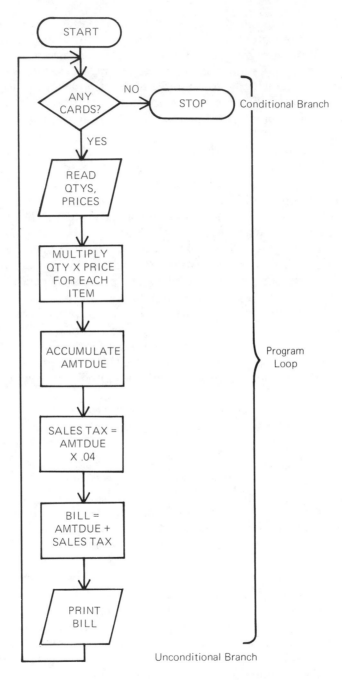

Figure 5–4   Exiting from a program loop by means of a conditional branch

Some readers of this book may be directing their efforts to writing all programs in a structured manner. As these readers may have discovered, a wide variety of flowcharting symbols and techniques designed especially for structured programming have been proposed. At this writing, however, none has been widely accepted or agreed upon. We shall not discuss any of them in this chapter. Rather, we shall direct our attention to the standard flowcharting symbols and techniques recommended by the *American National Standards Institute* (ANSI) and its international counterpart, the *International Standards Organization* (ISO). These standards are the result of much investigation and analysis of how flowcharts are created and used in common practice. They are summarized in Figure 5-5.

Sometimes a problem solution that involves complex logic can be developed most readily using the standardized flowcharting symbols and techniques discussed in this chapter. Once the required processing steps have been identified, they can be set up in structured form. Many existing programs are documented by flowcharts created according to standard methodologies. Whether or not the reader intends to make extensive use of flowcharting, this chapter should help him to develop his skill as a problem solver.

FLOWCHARTING TOOLS

A one-page program flowchart is shown in Figure 5-6. One flowcharting symbol we have not yet discussed appears on this flowchart. It is the *preparation symbol* (◯). This symbol shows a step that is executed before a sequence of operations in which the data affected by the preparation step is used. In this example, the preparation step sets COUNT to a value of zero. The programmer cannot assume primary-storage locations contain zeroes (or any other desired values) unless stored-program instructions have been executed to put them there.

To check your ability to read and understand the program flowchart in Figure 5-6, see whether or not you can answer these questions:

1. What is the first step carried out by the computer?
2. What happens when there are no more data values to process?
3. What will the value of COUNT be at that time?
4. What processing steps must be executed if the current value of X is greater than the current value of Y?
5. What happens if X is equal to Y? if X is less than Y?
6. If we assume punched-card input, how many data values should be punched into each card? What symbolic names are assigned to the primary-storage locations in which the values are to be stored?

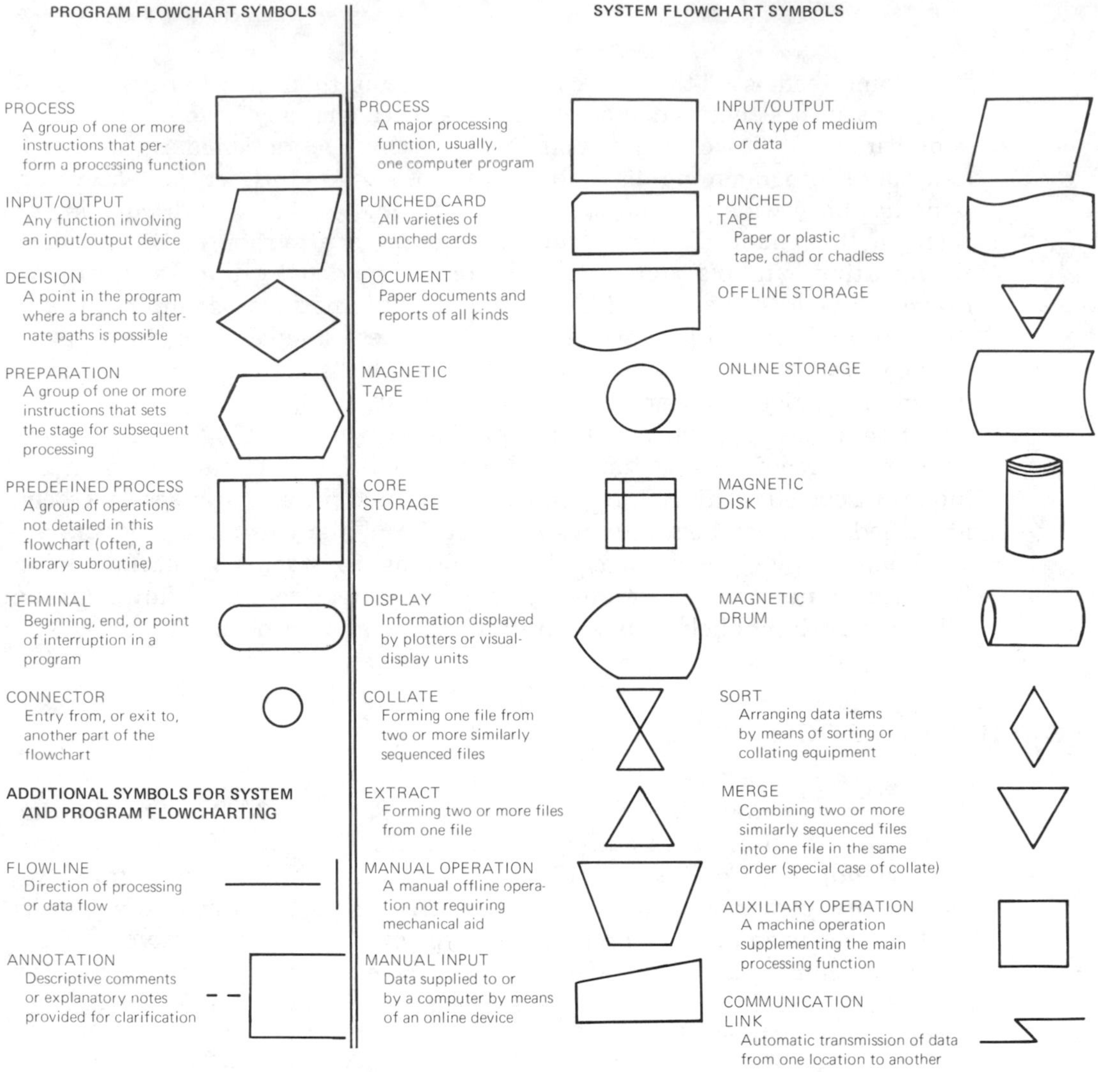

PROGRAM FLOWCHART SYMBOLS
PROCESS
A group of one or more instructions that perform a processing function
INPUT/OUTPUT
Any function involving an input/output device
DECISION
A point in the program where a branch to alternate paths is possible
PREPARATION
A group of one or more instructions that sets the stage for subsequent processing
PREDEFINED PROCESS
A group of operations not detailed in this flowchart (often, a library subroutine)
TERMINAL
Beginning, end, or point of interruption in a program
CONNECTOR
Entry from, or exit to, another part of the flowchart
ADDITIONAL SYMBOLS FOR SYSTEM AND PROGRAM FLOWCHARTING
FLOWLINE
Direction of processing or data flow
ANNOTATION
Descriptive comments or explanatory notes provided for clarification
SYSTEM FLOWCHART SYMBOLS
PROCESS
A major processing function, usually, one computer program
PUNCHED CARD
All varieties of punched cards
DOCUMENT
Paper documents and reports of all kinds
MAGNETIC TAPE
CORE STORAGE
DISPLAY
Information displayed by plotters or visual-display units
COLLATE
Forming one file from two or more similarly sequenced files
EXTRACT
Forming two or more files from one file
MANUAL OPERATION
A manual offline operation not requiring mechanical aid
MANUAL INPUT
Data supplied to or by a computer by means of an online device
INPUT/OUTPUT
Any type of medium or data
PUNCHED TAPE
Paper or plastic tape, chad or chadless
OFFLINE STORAGE
ONLINE STORAGE
MAGNETIC DISK
MAGNETIC DRUM
SORT
Arranging data items by means of sorting or collating equipment
MERGE
Combining two or more similarly sequenced files into one file in the same order (special case of collate)
AUXILIARY OPERATION
A machine operation supplementing the main processing function
COMMUNICATION LINK
Automatic transmission of data from one location to another

Figure 5–5 System and program flowcharting symbols

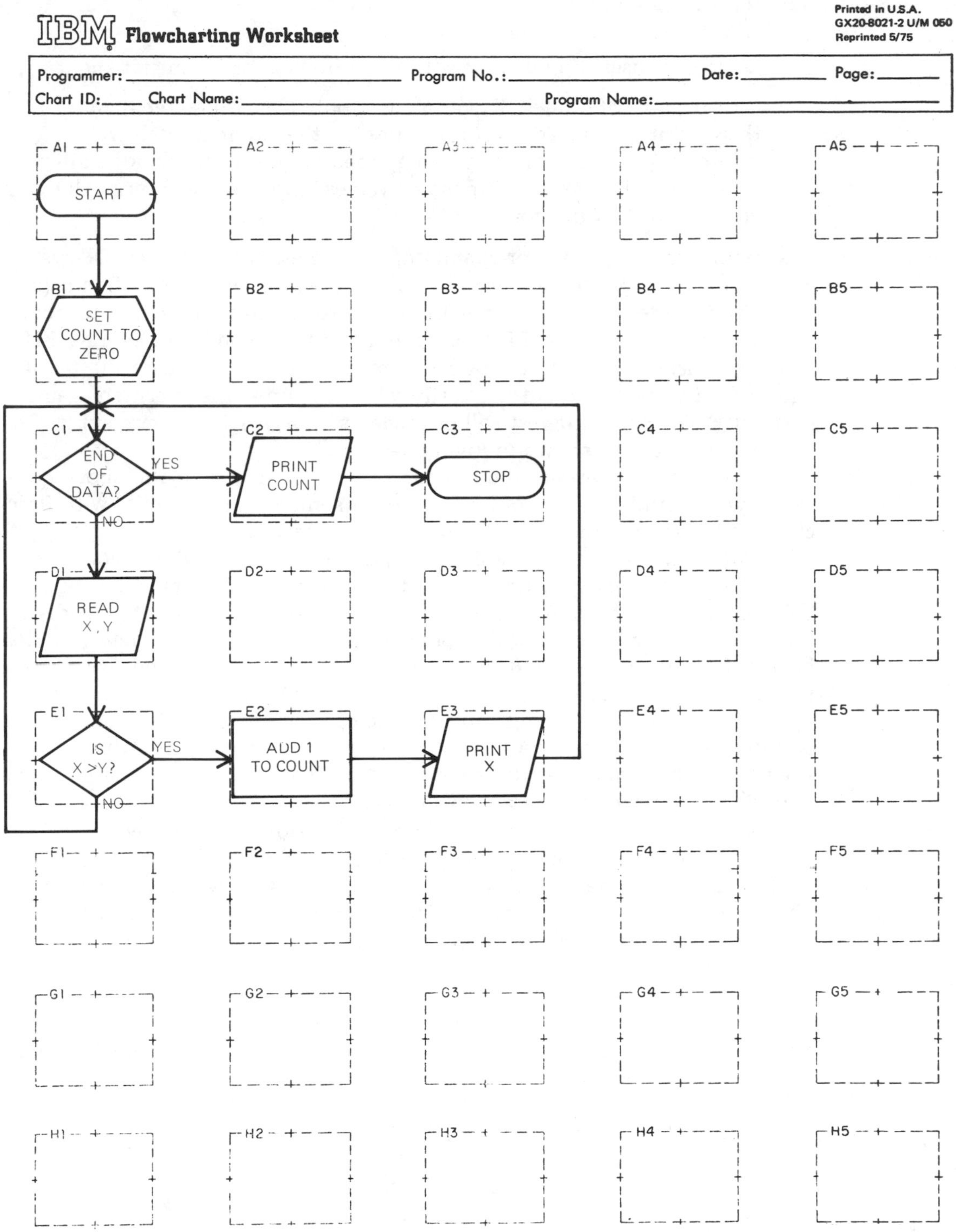

Programmer: _____ Program No.: _____ Date: _____ Page: _____

Chart ID: _____ Chart Name: _____ Program Name: _____

Figure 5-6 Program flowchart for processing X, Y values

Your responses should agree with the following problem statement:

"Read pairs of values, X and Y, as input. If X is greater than Y, then print X and add 1 to a count of the number of X values printed. If X is not greater than Y, then neither printing nor addition is required. When all pairs of values have been read, print the current value of the count and stop."

With some high-level programming languages, and in some EDP-system environments, the programmer need not code a specific end-of-data (also called end-of-file) test together with every read operation seeking to obtain input. For example, the PL/I programmer can include an ON ENDFILE statement near the beginning of a program or module to cause the test for end-of-data to be made automatically whenever a read is executed against a particular file. Since the test will be made, it is essential to document it. One way of doing so is as shown in Figure 5-6.

If you are uncertain about your responses to any of the above questions, you should consult your instructor or someone else familiar with flowcharting before continuing your study of flowcharting.

The flowchart in Figure 5-6 is superimposed on a *flowcharting worksheet*. Forms of this type are designed to assist programmers in placing symbols on flowcharts. In full size, the 11" × 16-1/2" worksheet provides an arrangement of 50 blocks with alphabetic and numeric coordinates: the ten horizontal rows are lettered from top (A) to bottom (K); the five vertical rows are numbered from left to right, 1 to 5. The blocks are aids for squaring up flowlines and maintaining uniform spacing between symbols. They provide coordinates, for example, A2 or K4, that can be referred to elsewhere on the flowchart. The worksheet itself is printed in light-blue ink so that its guidelines do not appear on photographic copies.

As Figure 5-6 indicates, the normal direction of data flow on a flowchart is from top to bottom and from left to right. When normal direction applies, flowlines may or may not be supplemented by *arrowheads*. If the direction of flow of any flowline is not top to bottom or left to right, an arrowhead must be used. More than one arrowhead may be used on a flowline if necessary for clarity.

Flowlines may cross. If they have no logical interrelation, no arrowheads should appear near their intersection. Two flowlines may join to form one line. In this case, a logical union or junction occurs in the flow. One arrowhead is usually advisable.

Three flowlines may join another flowline at a junction point. The resulting four flowlines are referred to as colinear in pairs. (The adjective *colinear* means in the same straight line.) One colinear pair must have opposing arrowheads near the junction point as shown below. A third arrowhead may be required for clarity.

Another tool usually provided for the programmer's use is a *flowcharting template*, a plastic or metallic card which contains flowcharting symbols as cutout forms. The programmer can easily trace the outlines of the symbols as needed on both system and program flowcharts. Use of such templates encourages uniformity in program flowcharting. This in turn provides for better communication between a programmer and others who refer to his flowcharts. The templates generally comply with the recommended standards for flowcharting symbols developed by ANSI and ISO.

MORE ABOUT PROGRAM LOOPS

In Figures 5-3, 5-4, and 5-5, we saw how an unconditional branch can cause a program flowchart to curve back on itself, so that a program loop is formed. In Figures 5-4 and 5-6, the loop is exited when there are no more data values to process. Sometimes, to solve a problem correctly, it is necessary to execute a program loop a certain number of times (rather than simply until there is no more input). One way to achieve this is to select one primary-storage location to be used as a *counter* or *index*.

As an example, consider the program flowchart in Figure 5-7. This program is to read 100 values as input, sum the values using the *accumulator method*, and print the total as output. At the start of processing, both the primary-storage location used as a counter (COUNT) and the one used as an accumulator (SUM) must be set to zeros. Then the program loop is entered the first time. The first input value is read and added to the contents of the accumulator. Then a value of 1 is added to the counter. Its value is tested immediately at the decision-making step. If the counter is equal to 100 (which it is not, the first time, of course), we have summed 100 values as required, so the loop is exited. Otherwise, the computer is directed to branch back to the beginning of the loop to read another input value. The processing steps within the loop are executed again and again until 100 values have been summed. Then the accumulated total is printed, and program execution is terminated.

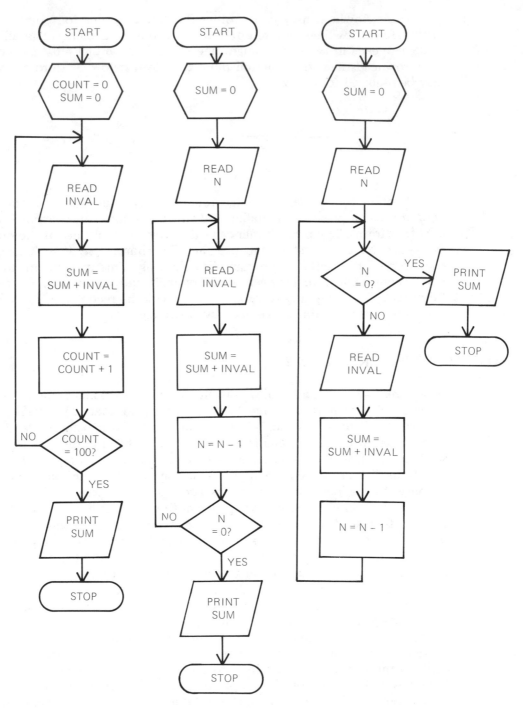

Figure 5-7 Program flowchart for summing 100 values

Figure 5-8 Program flowchart for summing N values

Figure 5-9 Program logic permitting a loop not to be executed at all

PROGRAMMING FOR FLEXIBILITY

Designing a program to provide flexibility was identified in Chapter 4 as a way to work toward program modularity. We discussed the use of symbolic names for both data items and I/O devices, and pointed out that developing a very specific implementation of a very specific algorithm may not be desirable. It is appropriate to mention flexibility again here, noting especially the looping considerations within a solution algorithm.

Sometimes it is impossible to know exactly how many times a program loop should be executed when the program is flowcharted. For example, suppose that a program is to compute and print the total number of points a student has earned on homework assignments. Individual scores are to be entered as input and accumulated by means of a program loop. The number of individual scores might not have been determined when the program was first planned. Furthermore, it might be advantageous to use the same program again to compute total points earned for another student who has a different number of scores. Such a program could even be reused to compute totals for other students the next term. Thus, program flexibility is desirable.

One way to provide this flexibility is to indicate the number of scores that must be added by submitting that number as a special data value preceding the set of scores. Such an approach is flowcharted in Figure 5-8. The program loop shown in this flowchart will be executed N times.

A program loop in which an index or counter is used is often called an *index loop*. Generally, in using an index loop, four distinct steps are involved:

- Initializing the loop index to a specific value
- Carrying out the main processing within the loop
- Modifying the value of the loop index
- Testing the current value of the loop index

The program flowcharts we have discussed thus far have shown these steps executed in this order. This sequence works well, provided that we can assume the processing steps within the loop are to be executed at least once. If we cannot make this assumption (that is, if a loop-control value of zero must be allowed for), the test of the loop index should be placed near the beginning of the loop as in Figure 5-9. You should compare Figures 5-8 and 5-9 to see how the program logic differs and understand when this difference is significant.

In some high-level programming languages, conditional branches or tests are programmed as IF statements. Unconditional branches are GO TO statements. Some languages permit the steps of initializing an index, modifying it, and testing it to be set up by means of a single DO statement. The programmer who uses such a statement must be sure that he understands the order in which these steps will be performed. For example, most FORTRAN implementations set up initialization, modification, and test steps in that order, so a program loop controlled by a FORTRAN DO statement is always executed at least once (like the loop in Figure 5–8). The FORTRAN programmer who flowcharts at this detailed level using ANSI standards should document the logic set up by each DO statement in his program, as shown in Figure 5–8.

In contrast to FORTRAN, PL/I implementations usually perform initialization, test, and modification in that order in a loop controlled by a DO statement. This means that a PL/I DO loop will not be executed at all if the exit test is satisfied when the loop is encountered during execution. The logic set up by a PL/I DO statement is like the loop processing in Figure 5–9.

BASIC-language programmers may use FOR and NEXT statements to control loops. COBOL programmers have PERFORM. The programmer who uses either of these languages should become familiar with the loop-control mechanisms of the implementation available before he takes advantage of these capabilities.

Another point to remember when using a single loop-control statement is to avoid making assumptions about what the value of the loop index will be after the loop is exited. It may or may not be the value that caused the exit to occur.

ADVANCED DECISION MAKING

Not uncommonly, in business data-processing applications, such as insurance claim processing or automobile parts handling, large numbers of records are kept for reference purposes on one or more *master files.* Current activities or transactions to be applied to, or which require data from, those records are grouped to form a *transaction file.*

As an example, one page of a program flowchart for a program that processes stock-status transactions is shown in Figure 5–10. Each transaction record contains a transaction number and a one-digit code indicating the type of activity to be applied against what data item, or field, in the matching master record.

Only the portion of the program flowchart that shows activity identification and subsequent updating is illustrated in Figure 5–10. Assume that this portion of the flowchart appears on page 3 of a 15-page flowchart. For each transaction, the number of required comparisons depends on the code field of the transaction record. As many as five comparisons (decision-making steps) may be required.

The same processing logic is shown in Figure 5–11, but it is described in a much more understandable form. By the simple use of *parallel flowlines*, the same possible outcomes are documented. Generally, when this flowcharting technique is used, the first test to be made should be shown by the left-most flowline on the flowchart.

Connector symbols (⟜○ , ⚲) are used on these flowcharts to denote exit to, or entry from, another part of the flowchart. When a flowline extends to a connector symbol, as do the flowlines to all connector symbols containing Al on these flowcharts, the symbol shows *exit* to another part of the flowchart. In our case, the next processing step is represented by whatever appears on the flowcharting-worksheet block with coordinates Al on page 5 of the flowchart. In a similar manner, the connector symbol containing B3 in Figure 5-11 shows *entry* to this page of the flowchart from a block on page 2 of the flowchart. Connector symbols may also be used to avoid excessive intersecting of flowlines within one page of a flowchart as do the symbols containing D2 in Figure 5-11. Connector symbols not accompanied by page references refer to corresponding connector symbols on the same page of the flowchart.

The *predefined process symbol* (⎕) is the programmer's way of referring to one or more operations specified in detail elsewhere, such as in a reference manual or on a different flowchart (but not on another part of the same flowchart or set of flowcharts). The printing inside the symbol summarizes the operations performed. In this case, an error routine to *log* (document) input that cannot be processed is carried out.

The *annotation symbol* (- -[ ) is used by the programmer to include valuable information that will not fit inside other flowcharting symbols. This symbol is often called an annotation flag. It is connected to the step it documents by a broken line. We can tell from Figure 5-11 that tests for the code values 1, 2, 3, and 4 are represented by the decision symbol that is flagged.

Cross references point out the correspondence between steps on a program flowchart and statements in the program described. These references take the form of statement numbers or symbolic names that are used to identify statements in the program. ANSI recommends that a cross reference to a statement be placed to the upper right of the corresponding flowcharting symbol, as in Figures 5-10 and 5-11. (See RECPT, ORDER, etc.) By adding cross references to a flowchart, the programmer helps others to follow the depicted logic in the resultant program.

UPDATING A SEQUENTIAL FILE

Because updating of records stored previously on sequential master files is a commonly required data-processing function, a general approach that can often be used is summarized in Figure 5-12. One master file and one transaction file are read as input. Records in each file are arranged in ascending sequence according to a certain *control field*. It may contain item number, customer number, or any similar entry common to records in both files. The following situations may be encountered when applying transactions to the master file:

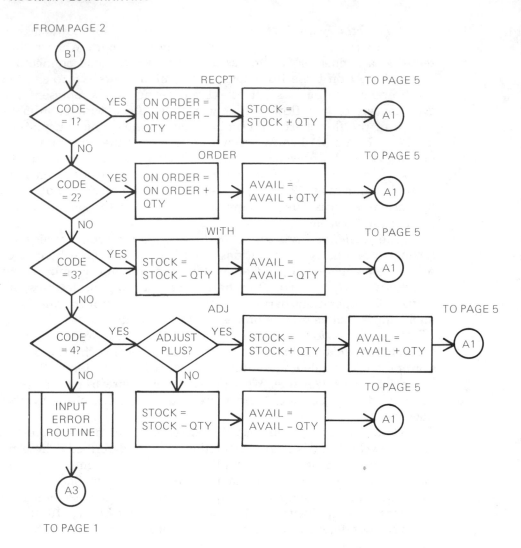

Figure 5-10   Testing a code value to determine activity required

1. One or more transactions may match a single master record.
2. There may be no transactions for a master record.
3. There may be transactions that do not match any master record; these are either errors or new additions to the master file.

Look first at the preparation symbols on the program flowchart. These symbols represent changing the contents of one or more primary-storage locations or registers used as a *program switch.* If the switch is set to 1s, it is interpreted as being ON, and a branch occurs. If the switch is set to 0s, it is interpreted as being OFF, and no branch occurs.

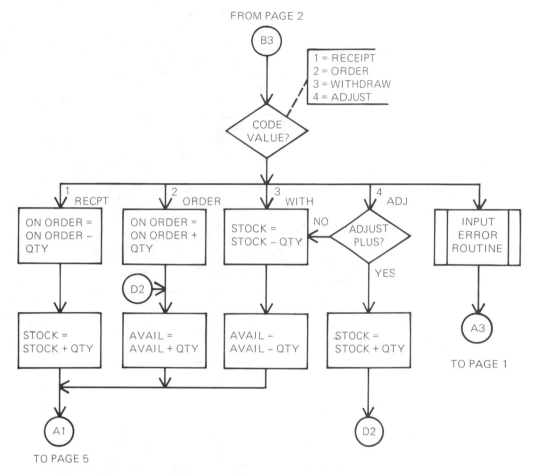

Figure 5–11   An alternative way of flowcharting successive tests of a value

The program flowchart in Figure 5–12 shows that the program switch is set OFF. Then one master record is read. Since the switch is OFF, a transaction record is read. The control field of the transaction record is compared against the control field of the master. If it is equal, the master record is changed as directed by the content of the transaction record. A second transaction is read.

If the control field of the second transaction is higher than the first, it is, of course, not to be applied against the current master record. So the current master is written to the output file, and the program switch is set ON. Then a branch is made to the beginning of the program loop. A new master record is read. Because the switch is ON, a new transaction is not read. Instead, the computer branches to the decision-making step to compare the new master record and the second transaction, which was read in previously. As shown on the flowchart, the switch is set OFF before the compare occurs. Comparison operations continue for each new record placed in storage.

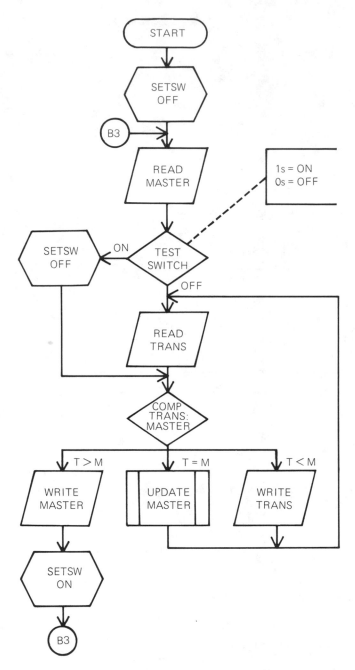

Figure 5-12   Processing transaction and master files

If a transaction is lower than a master, either an error has occurred or a new addition is to be made to the master file. In any case, a new addition need not be made at this time; an unmatched transaction is simply written out on another output file. For example, the file may be a printed listing of unmatched transactions to be checked manually after the processing run. Transactions in error can be corrected or discarded. All valid transactions can then be added to the master file in another processing run. This check helps to prevent additions of invalid data to the master file.

In some programs, additions may be made to the master file at this time. In such cases, the input/output symbol is replaced by a predefined process symbol referring to a routine appearing elsewhere, or by a series of symbols showing how a record is added to the master file. The program logic should also provide for the printing of a *change register*, which shows all changes made to the master file, for checking purposes.

MODULAR PROGRAM FLOWCHARTING

In Chapter 4, we discussed top-down development. We saw how the major function of a program can be identified first, then its subfunctions, and so on, down to lower levels of detail. This approach can be followed when flowcharting. The programmer establishes the main line of program logic on a very high-level, overview flowchart. Then he extracts large segments and describes them in detail on supplementary program flowcharts. This is like drawing a set of increasingly detailed maps — starting with a general all-inclusive map, then enlarging sections of it on succeeding maps, each showing greater detail. The technique is called *modular program flowcharting*.

Modular program flowcharting emphasizes the program logic, component routines, and subroutines; it helps to point out segments of code (modules) that can be written independently, then combined to form the executable program. The *striping convention* is often used. Striping a flowchart means that a more detailed representation of the function is to be found elsewhere in the same set of flowcharts (thus, it differs from a predefined process symbol, which refers to documentation not contained on a particular flowchart). The striping convention is applied as follows:

1. A horizontal line is drawn within and near the top of the striped symbol.
2. All paths of the detailed representation of the function start and end with terminal symbols.
3. An identifier is placed both above the stripe in the striped symbol and in the entry terminal symbol of the detailed representation.

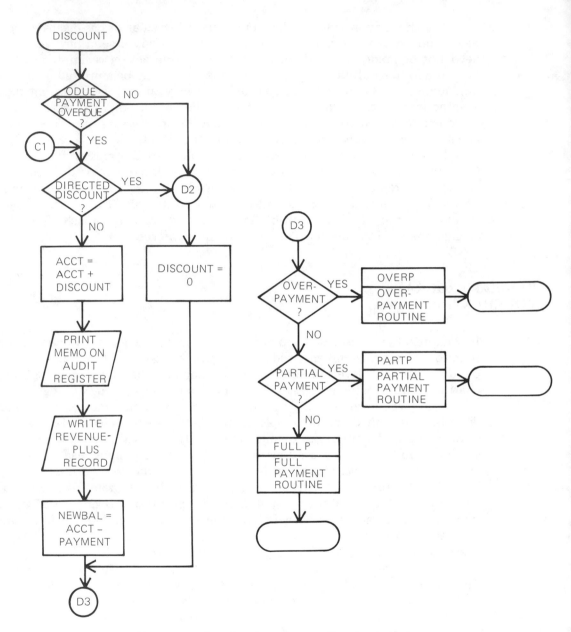

Figure 5-13 Modular program flowcharting — intermediate-level chart

Figures 5-13 and 5-14 illustrate the technique of modular program flowcharting. Both flowcharts represent program logic within a customer billing program. Figure 5-13 is an expansion of a striped symbol on a higher-level flowchart. Figure 5-14 is an expansion of the striped symbol appearing

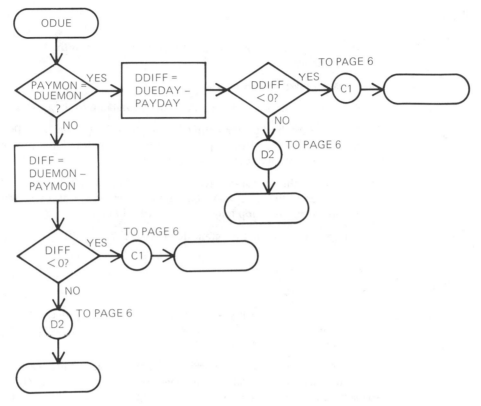

Figure 5-14   Modular program flowcharting — lowest-level chart

as the second symbol on the flowchart in Figure 5-13. Since Figure 5-14 is the final level for this set of flowcharts, no symbols on this flowchart are striped.

Modular program flowcharting enables the programmer to concentrate on the primary control logic and major functions of a program during initial stages of program planning. His pattern of thought is not bogged down by having to chart specific details of each required function immediately. The details can be flowcharted later on a lower-level flowchart.

Generally, each level of a program flowchart is valuable. Managers of departments using computer-generated output, individual users, internal and external auditors, data-processing management, operations personnel, systems analysts, and other programmers may need to refer to the flowcharts. Each audience has a "need to know" at a different level of detail. Thus, modular program flowcharting satisfies not only the programmer's needs but also the needs of personnel doing system planning, writing related programs, or using the program.

QUESTIONS

Q1. (a) Name two types of flowcharts. (b) Distinguish between the two, noting similarities and differences.

Q2. List at least five uses of flowcharts.

Q3. Describe two flowcharting aids that are usually available to the programmer.

Q4. (a) What is meant by "programming for flexibility"? (b) Describe flexible and inflexible techniques for setting up program loops. (c) Describe a problem situation where a flexible program-loop capability is required.

Q5. List and explain the four steps involved in an index loop, in order such that: (a) the processing steps within the loop will always be executed at least once, and (b) the processing steps within the loop may not be executed at all.

Q6. What is meant by "modular program flowcharting"?

EXERCISES

E1. Draw each of the following flowcharting symbols: (a) process, (b) input/output, (c) decision, (d) terminal, (d) flowline, (f) connector, (g) predefined process, (h) annotation, and (i) preparation.

E2. Which of the symbols that you drew for E1 should be used for each of the following steps? (a) entry of data on punched cards to an inventory-control program, (b) setting a counter to zero before entering a program loop, (c) adding amount owed to account balance in an accounts-receivable program, (d) determining whether a value is greater than, less than, or equal to zero.

E3. Look at the flowchart in Figure 5-4. Would it have been equally acceptable to put the decision-making step at the bottom of the flowchart in place of the unconditional branch? If not, why not?

E4. Refer to Figure 5-11 (or 5-10) to determine what actions should occur in each of the following problem situations: (a) A transaction record contains a code value of 2. (b) A transaction record contains a code value of 4.

E5. Modify the problem flowchart in Figure 5-6 to reflect the following changes in the problem statement: "If X is not greater than Y, then add X to Y and print their sum. Add 1 to a count of the number of sums printed. When all pairs of values have been read, print the number of X values printed and the number of sums printed and stop." (Assume the X greater than Y action remains unchanged.)

E6. Modify the program flowchart in Figure 5-8 to print out a student's average score on homework assignments rather than the total points earned.

E7. Now construct a flowchart for a program to print out the average score for each student in a class. Program execution should terminate when there are no more student scores to process.

E8. The flowchart in Figure 5-12 is a high-level flowchart. It does not show the details of logic required for end-of-file processing. Modify the flowchart to recognize end of file when it occurs on each file, and to process remaining records on either file, if end-of-file is encountered on the other file first. Program execution should terminate when all records on both files have been processed.

E9. Prepare a program flowchart for each of the following problem situations.

(a) Create a multiplication table for 30 pairs of values read as input. For each pair, the values multiplied and their product should be written as output.

(b) Read a value for C. Then compute and print out the sum of the 10 numbers, $1, 1+C, 1+2*C, 1+3*C, \ldots, 1+9*C$.

(c) Reception offices in a newly constructed medical center are to be furnished according to plans submitted by an interior decorator. The costs of all suggested furnishings are listed in a data source. To aid in project cost estimation, the sum of all individual costs exceeding $20.00 is to be determined. The end-of-file dummy cost is 0.

(d) Read employee time-card records, each of which shows name and hours worked for one employee. Assume the current wage rate is $3.55 per hour. For hours less than or equal to 40, compute pay as rate times hours. For hours beyond 40, compute pay as 1.5 times rate times hours. Each employee's name and pay should be printed on a Department Wage Report. If an employee has worked more than 40 hours, his name and the number of hours beyond 40 should be printed on a Department Overtime Report. When all employee time-card records have been processed, print a count of the number of records processed on the Department Wage Report and terminate processing.

(e) Cards from insurance applicants contain applicant number, name, age, and a 1-character code (M or F) indicating whether the applicant is male or female. Three insurance rates have been established and can be carried as constants (RATE1, RATE2, RATE3) in a program designed to determine what insurance rate each applicant should be charged and prepare a new-account report. If the applicant is male, 25 years or under, print applicant number, name, and RATE3. If the applicant is male and over 25, or if female and 25 or under, print applicant number, name, and RATE2. If the applicant is female and over 25, print applicant number, name, and RATE1. A special data card containing nines in its 6-position applicant-number field is the last card in the input deck and should cause program execution to be terminated.

(f) The fee for the first hour of parking at an airport parking lot is 50 cents. An additional 50 cents is due if a car is parked in the lot for up to 3 hours. A total of $2.00 is due for any car parked for more than 3 hours, up to 6 hours. An additional $2.00 is due if a car remains for more than 6 hours but not more than 24 hours. Three dollars are due for each day or portion of a day thereafter, to a maximum of 7 days. Each car is identified by a 6-digit car number which is to be provided as input together with its total parking time (in hours and minutes) to a program that provides car number and amount due tickets as output. Any violation (illegally parked car) is to be logged on an exception report. A ticket indicating car number and ILLEGAL PARKING; SEE ATTENDANT is to be printed as well. An input value of 999999 for car number is an end-of-file indicator.

E10. Look at the flowchart you constructed in response to E9d. What happens if no employee time cards are provided as input? If you have not provided for this condition, modify the program flowchart to do so.

E11. Look at the flowchart you constructed in response to E9e. What happens if an input card does not contain M or F? Or if no age is indicated? If you have not provided for the possibility of invalid input, modify the flowchart to do so.

*E12. Have your flowcharts for the problem statements in E9 (including any changes as a result of E10 or E11) verified (i.e., "desk checked") by an instructor or a co-worker. Then use the flowcharts as guides to coding as you write programs to carry out the processing steps specified.

REFERENCES

Bohl, Marilyn. *Flowcharting Techniques*. Chicago: Science Research Associates, 1971 (a tutorial that introduces standard flowcharting symbols and usage as it shows how to use flowcharting as a tool in problem solving).

Chapin, Ned. "Flowcharting with the ANSI Standard: A Tutorial," *Computing Surveys* (ACM) 2, 2 (June 1970): 119-46.

Farina, Mario. *Flowcharting*. Englewood Cliffs, N.J.: Prentice-Hall, 1970 (a tutorial closely related to the BASIC programming language).

IBM Flowcharting Template. IBM Corporation publication (GX20-8020) White Plains, N.Y., n.d.

IBM Flowcharting Worksheet. IBM Corporation publication (GX20-8021). White Plains, N.Y., n.d.

Silver, Gerald A., and Joan B. *Computer Algorithms and Flowcharting*. New York: Mc-Graw-Hill, 1975 (presents an overview of the programming cycle, teaches flowcharting and basic programming techniques (e.g., branching and looping), and then applies these in business data-processing situations).

6

DECISION TABLES

Tables are a familiar, widely used way of representing and communicating information. When we buy groceries and other items at the local supermarket, the clerk at the checkout counter refers to a table that shows fresh fruits and vegetables and the price per pound for each; he or she refers to another table that shows incremental price ranges and corresponding sales tax amounts. Airlines use tables that show destinations and distances, or destinations and fares. Insurance agents, buyers for large department stores, shipping clerks — indeed, all of us — depend on tabular forms of information when carrying out daily activities.

What's good about tables? They are an easy-to-follow means of communication. We read across, or over and down, often without even realizing we are doing so. They are an effective way of extracting details that tend to be lost or buried if included in paragraphs of text. They are concise; we need not wade through lots of excess verbiage to obtain the exact information we need. They help to insure that all aspects of a situation are covered. If there's a "hole" in the table (say, no price for Grade A Large eggs) or an entry that's missing (say, no listing at all for size 12), it's obvious; usually, someone is triggered into action, to supply or obtain complete information.

For much the same reasons, tables can be an effective tool in program development. The chief programmer, a systems analyst, or a team programmer assigned to a particular part of a project may set up one or more tables when planning a solution algorithm. Each table serves as a guide during program coding. It is meaningful to both technical and nontechnical personnel — users for whom the program (solution algorithm) is being developed, management with overall responsibility for the project, auditors who must verify that company policies and procedures are being carried out as claimed, programmers who must understand the program later for maintenance purposes, and so on. A table used in this way is known as a *decision table*. The purpose of this chapter is to explain how to read decision tables and how to construct them. We look at the kinds of decision tables that can be built and the kinds of situations for which they are useful.

DEPICTING PROGRAM LOGIC

Suppose we are to write a module to compute major-medical, family-dental-plan, and withholding-tax deductions, each based on total number of dependents, as a part of weekly payroll processing. We could lay out the required logic by drawing a program flowchart. The flowchart would begin with a long sequence of decision blocks: one for each possible number of dependents. We might decide to use the striping convention (explained in Chapter 5) to refer to routines described on subsequent pages. (See Figure 6-1a.) If we used any other approach, numerous connector symbols would be required (Figure 6-1b). In either case, the flowchart would be difficult to follow.

By contrast, a decision table would simply show the possible numbers of dependents as a series of *conditions*. The processing steps needed to compute the appropriate deductions would be listed as *actions*. It is generally true that when there are few different types of input (or output) that must be dealt with, there are correspondingly few decision-making steps and a relatively large number of straightforward processing steps. Flowcharts work well to depict this kind of logic. When there are many different types of conditions of input (or output), there are many possible control paths that must be planned for. Decision tables are especially useful when this kind of processing is required.

DECISION TABLE FORMAT

As shown in Figure 6-2, a decision table is divided into four sections. The upper left portion (called the *condition stub*) shows the conditions that are to be considered in reaching a decision. The lower left portion (called the *action stub*) shows the actions to be taken when any of the given sets of conditions is present. As a first step in constructing a decision table, the programmer extracts all conditions and actions set forth in the problem statement. He completes the left half of the decision table accordingly.

Conditions and actions are joined by an "if . . . then" relationship. That is, we read the logic set up in a decision table as follows: "IF this (condition) exists, THEN perform this (action)." The *condition entries* in the upper right portion of the decision table and the *action entries* in the lower right portion illustrate clearly each *if/then rule* to be followed. To understand a rule, we read *vertically* the column that one set of condition entries and action entries forms. The number of the rule appears at the top of the column. More than

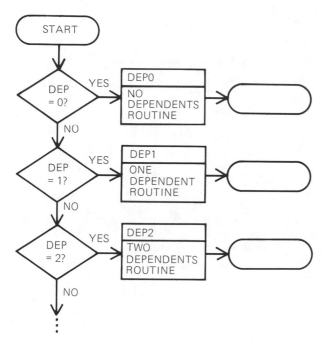

(a) Use of the striping convention

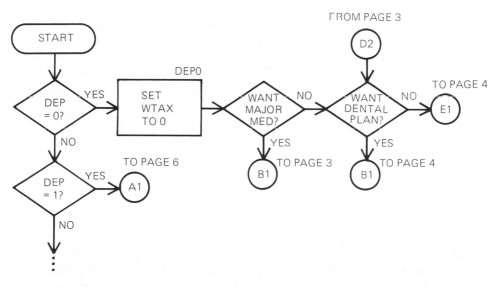

(b) Connectors to subsequent processing steps

Figure 6–1   Flowcharting decision-making logic

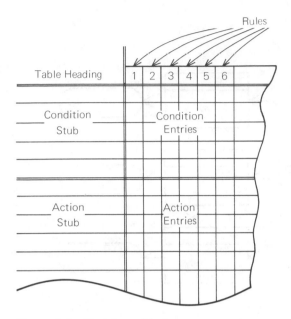

Figure 6-2   Decision table format

one condition may apply in a rule, and more than one action may be required if the applicable condition (or conditions) exists. That is, both multiple condition entries and multiple action entries for a rule are possible.

Whether we realize it or not, most of us use decision-table logic daily; we do so whenever we decide what actions to take on the basis of conditions that we observe. If it's raining, then we wear raincoats or carry umbrellas. If the grass is getting too long, then we mow it. If our favorite football team scores a touchdown, then we jump up and down, hug one another, and yell. Making a decision and then acting accordingly is a natural part of our lives.

AND PROBLEM STATEMENT

The decision table in Figure 6-3 shows the logic of a familiar situation: deciding whether or not to stop for gasoline at the next gas station. Two conditions affect the decision, and there are two possible actions. We might state the problem this way:

"*If* I have less than one-fourth of a tank of gas *and* the gasoline costs less than 61.9¢ per gallon, *then* I will stop for gas. *Otherwise*, I will continue to the next station."

The *and* in this problem statement indicates that both conditions stated in the problem must be present before the "stop for gas" action takes place.

A problem statement in which more than one condition must be present before a particular action takes place is called an *AND problem statement.* When any or all of the conditions of an AND problem statement are not met, an alternative action must be taken. Look for the word *otherwise,* or its implied presence, as a clue. In this situation, the alternative action is "continue to the next station."

	Buying Gasoline	Rules			
		1	2	3	4
IF (condition)	Less than ¼ tank of gas	Y	Y	N	N
	Less than 61.9¢ per gal. cost	N	Y	Y	N
THEN (action)	Stop for gas		X		
	Continue to next station	X		X	X

Figure 6-3   Decision table for AND problem statement

To check your ability to read and understand this kind of decision table, look at Figure 6-4. It shows a plan for determining the appropriate pay rate for hourly employees. See whether or not you can answer these questions:

1. How many conditions affect the decision to be made? What are they?
2. How many possible actions are there? What are they?
3. If a year has passed since a particular employee last received an hourly increase and he earns less than $3.00 per hour, then what action should be taken? Which decision-table rule applies?
4. If a year has passed since an employee last received an hourly increase and he earns more than $3.00 per hour, then what action should be taken? Which decision-table rule applies?

	Hourly Pay Rate	Rules			
		1	2	3	4
IF (condition)	1 year since last hourly increase	Y	Y	N	N
	Pay rate less than $3.00 per hour	Y	N	Y	N
THEN (action)	Increase pay rate by 25¢	X			
	Carry pay rate forward unchanged		X	X	X

Figure 6-4   Calculating hourly pay rate

5. If only six months have passed since an employee last received an increase and he earns more than $3.00 per hour, then what action should be taken? Which decision-table rule applies?

6. If only six months have passed since an employee last received an increase and he earns less than $3.00 per hour, then what action should be taken? Which decision-table rule applies?

Your responses should agree with the following problem statement:

"If a year or more has passed since an employee last received an hourly increase *and* the employee earns less than $3.00 per hour, *then* his hourly pay rate should be increased by 25¢. *Otherwise*, his hourly pay rate should be carried forward to the next pay-period unchanged."

If you are uncertain about your responses to any of the above questions, you should consult your instructor or someone else familiar with decision tables before continuing your study of this chapter.

OR PROBLEM STATEMENT

Determining hourly pay rate is, of course, only one of many decisions to be made during payroll processing. Consider, for example, the following portion of a problem statement pertaining to weekly time-card data:

"If an employee's time card indicates that he or she worked less than ten hours during the past week, *or* that he or she was late more than once, *or* that he or she was absent on the day before a holiday, *then* the employee's name should be deleted from the payroll list. *Otherwise*, the employee's payroll check should be printed."

This is an *OR problem statement*. Three conditions are identified, but any *one* of the three conditions will prompt a certain action. If an employee worked less than ten hours, his or her name should be deleted from the payroll list, irrespective of whether or not he or she was late more than once or absent on the day before a holiday, and so on. Since it is possible that none of the three conditions will be present for a particular employee, an alternative (otherwise) action is also specified.

The decision table in Figure 6–5 shows the logic within this problem statement. For each of the three possible conditions, the condition entry in a column may be Y for yes or N for no. Statistics formulas show that three conditions, each of which has two alternatives, generate 2^3 ($2 \times 2 \times 2$), or 8, possible combinations of conditions. That is, there are 8 rules to be set up. In general, given N conditions, there are 2^N possible combinations.

Time Card Data		Rules							
		1	2	3	4	5	6	7	8
IF (condition)	Worked less than 10 hours	Y	Y	Y	Y	N	N	N	N
	Late more than once	Y	Y	N	N	Y	Y	N	N
	Absent before a holiday	Y	N	Y	N	Y	N	Y	N
THEN (action)	Delete name from payroll list	X	X	X	X	X	X	X	
	Print payroll check								X

Figure 6-5   Decision table for OR problem statement

We recognize here a potential difficulty with decision tables: Their possible size and complexity grows exponentially. If there are 4 conditions, there are 2^4 or 16 possible combinations, 5 leads to 32, 6 leads to 64, and so on. Few programmers could be expected to undertake enthusiastically, or even willingly, the task of setting up a decision table with 16, 32, or 64 columns. Setting up correctly 16, 32, or 64 control paths in a program corresponding to such a decision table might be next to impossible.

COLLAPSING A DECISION TABLE

Fortunately, the very act of constructing a decision table helps the programmer to figure out what logic is actually required in a solution algorithm. A decision table doesn't have to show every possible combination of yes and no condition entries that could exist in the table; it has to show only the basic combinations of conditions necessary to determine which actions to take in solving a problem.

Given the OR problem statement set forth in Figure 6-5, the presence of any one of three possible conditions is sufficient to cause an employee's name to be deleted from the payroll list, so a Y in any one of three condition-entry spaces for a rule is a determining factor. The other condition entries for the rule do not make any difference, so we can just leave the spaces for those entries blank. If, for example, we have Y as a condition entry for "Worked less than ten hours," we care not whether we have YYY (rule 1), YYN (rule 2), YNY (3), or YNN (4). Our action is the same in all such cases, so Y-blank-blank suffices. (See rule 1 in Figure 6-6.) Similarly, a required logic path on a program flowchart or a corresponding sequence of instructions need not test for the second and third conditions if the results of a test for the first condition are positive. We can, in effect, *collapse* the decision table, combining rules 1, 2, 3, and 4 into 1.

Continuing in the same manner, if we have N for our first condition, but we have Y for the second condition ("Late more than once"), we care

Time Card Data	Rules			
	1	2	3	4
IF (condition)				
Worked less than 10 hours	Y			N
Late more than once		Y		N
Absent before a holiday			Y	N
THEN (action)				
Delete name from payroll list	X	X	X	
Print payroll check				X

Figure 6-6   A collapsed decision table

not whether we have NYN or NYY, so we combine rules 5 and 6 of Figure 6-5 into rule 2 of Figure 6-6. Checking back to our original problem statement reminds us that if we know we have Y for the second condition, we don't care whether we have Y or N for the first (though our reasoning has led us to N here); blank-Y-blank suffices. Rules 3 and 4 of Figure 6-6 are rules 7 and 8 of our original table.

Some programmers prefer to place dashes where we have simply left blank spaces in the condition-entry section of a decision table. Y means yes, N means no, and a dash (-) means don't care. The presence of a dash is a definite indication that the possible entries for that space were considered. A blank space could be an oversight.

The relationship among the rules in a decision table is one of mutual exclusiveness; that is, any one rule specifies a particular combination of conditions, and no other rule may specify exactly that same combination of conditions or a totally containable subset. (For example, YY-blank and YYY cannot both be specified.) Otherwise, a redundancy or an inconsistency exists in the decision table. To avoid problems of either type, each rule must be unique in its condition portion.

Loan Processing	Rules				
	1	2	3	4	5
IF (condition)					
Credit rating excellent	Y	Y	Y	N	E L S E
Net worth ≥ $100,000	Y	Y	N	N	
Annual income ≥ $25,000	Y	N	N	N	
THEN (action)					
Approve long-term loan	X	X			
Approve short-term loan	X	X	X		
Reject application				X	
Investigate					X

Figure 6-7   Use of the ELSE rule

THE ELSE RULE

A catchall condition occasionally employed in constructing decision tables is the *ELSE rule*. There can be at most one ELSE rule per decision table. If used, it appears in the extreme right column of the table, as shown in Figure 6-7. The ELSE rule says simply: If a combination of conditions that does not match any of the combinations stated explicitly in this decision table occurs, then take the actions specified in the action stub of this ELSE rule.

Use of the ELSE rule is advantageous in that it is another means of collapsing a decision table; the programmer does not have to show all possible combinations of conditions that may apply. However, in eliminating the need for a fully detailed outline, the ELSE rule tends to permit the introduction of logical errors. (For example, combinations of conditions may not be specified for which the ELSE rule really doesn't apply.) It also tends to hide any redundancy errors in the table. Consequently, it should be seldom — and very carefully — used.

	Accounts Receivable Processing	Rules		
		1	2	3
IF (condition)	X < 0	Y		
	X = 0		Y	
	X > 0			Y
THEN (action)	Compute credit amount	X		
	Compute debit amount			X
	Calculate amount owed	X		X
	Print statement	X	X	X
	Read next input	X	X	X

Figure 6-8   A limited-entry decision table

KINDS OF DECISION TABLES

A decision table in which condition entries are limited to Y, N, or blank (or dash) is called, appropriately, a *limited-entry decision table*. Another example of this kind of table is shown in Figure 6-8. We see that three possible conditions are listed in the condition-stub section: $X < 0$, $X = 0$, and $X > 0$.

The same conditions can be shown in a slightly different fashion in an *extended-entry decision table*. (See Figure 6-9.) An extended-entry decision table permits the conditions listed in the condition-stub section of a table to be *extended* into the condition-entry (upper right) section of the table. The

Accounts Receivable Processing	Rules		
	1	2	3
Value of X	<0	=0	>0
Compute credit amount	X		
Compute debit amount			X
Calculate amount owed	X		X
Print statement	X	X	X
Read next input	X	X	X

IF (condition)

THEN (action)

Figure 6-9   An extended-entry decision table

condition-stub section identifies the elements to be tested. The condition-entry section defines values for those elements in absolute or relative terms. Absolute entries are simply numerals such as 5, 100, or 1000; relative entries often include relational symbols as do those shown in Figure 6-9. Looking again at Figure 6-9, what actions should be taken if the value of X is less than 0? If the value of X is 26?

Although the logic described in a decision table is independent of the order in which rules are stated, it is helpful to list the conditions for a rule in the sequence in which they are to be checked for in program coding. Actions indicated by Xs for a rule may take place in the order specified, but this is not a requirement of decision-table construction, nor can it be assumed. If a certain order is required within a rule in the table, numbers should be used instead of Xs as action entries to indicate sequence. In any case, the final conceptual (meaning here, not written) row of a decision table is usually a specification to re-enter the table (begin testing the conditions again). A GO TO specification (explained below) may be employed for one or more rules of a decision table to direct a transfer of control to another table within a decision table set. For such a rule, the final conceptual row (the re-enter the table specification) is, in effect, not marked with an action entry.

Sometimes it is convenient to construct a *mixed-entry decision table*. As the name implies, a mixed-entry table contains some condition rows with limited entries and some condition rows with extended entries. This is permissible. In Figure 6-10, the first row has a limited-entry format, while the remaining rows have an extended-entry format. Note that this table also demonstrates a convenient way in which value ranges can be specified. An important guideline that must be followed when constructing a mixed-entry decision table is that each row of the table must be entirely limited or entirely extended; formats cannot be mixed within one condition specification.

As we have seen, the total number of possible rules can be calculated rather easily for a limited-entry decision table. Each additional row in the condition portion of the table doubles the number of possible decision rules.

Salesman's Commission Table	Rules				
	1	2	3	4	5
IF (condition)					
With firm 1 year	N	Y	Y	Y	Y
Units sold		<400	≥400	≥1000	≥5000
Units sold			<1000	<5000	
THEN (action)					
1% commission rate	X	X			
2% commission rate			X		
2-½% commission rate				X	
3% commission rate					X
$1000 bonus					X

Figure 6-10   A mixed-entry decision table

For extended-entry and mixed-entry tables, computing the total number of possible rules is more difficult. It involves multiplying the total for the rules thus far by the number of possible conditions permitted in the row. Thus, an extended entry permitting three conditions (say, $>$, $=$, and $<$) triples the number of possible rules. Somewhat in contradiction to this fact, in actual practice, use of extended-entry format is often a means of collapsing a decision table; we specify fewer rules rather than more.

DECISION TABLE SETS

As we have indicated, a primary objective in using decision tables is to present the logic within a solution algorithm in a clear, concise, and easy-to-follow manner. Obviously, small tables (like the ones we have discussed) are much easier to read and comprehend than larger tables involving many possible conditions and many combinations of those conditions. To present the logic within a program involving complex decision making, many variables, or many data relationships, use of several decision tables is usually advisable. Each table within the decision table set is labeled by a unique name or number for reference purposes.

The discipline imposed upon the programmer in separating conditions and actions, and in covering every possible useful combination of conditions in a separate, mutually exclusive rule before beginning to code, leads to program modularity. The development of a set of manageable-size decision tables covering all of the logic within a program further extends this modularity. A complete set of decision tables can serve as a very effective guideline for the application of structured-programming techniques. We discuss these techniques at length in Chapter 8.

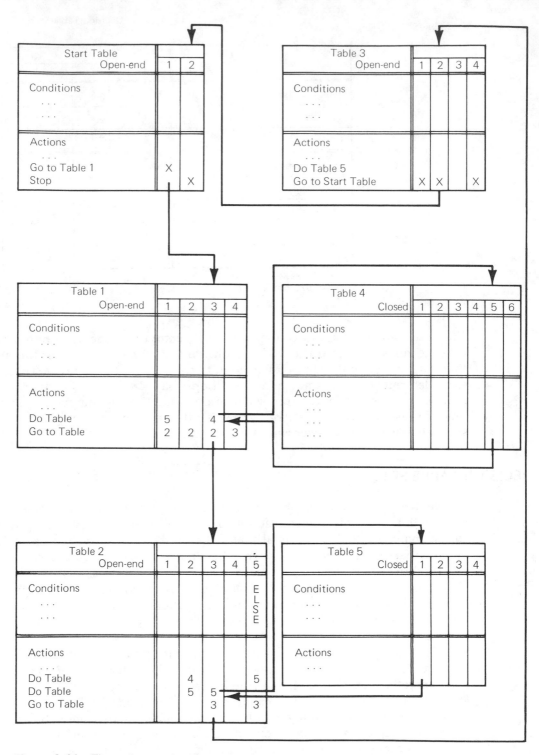

Figure 6-11 Flow of control within a decision table set

When constructing a set of decision tables, the main line of program logic is described in what are known as *open-end tables*. Each open-end table passes control to the next open-end table in succession by means of a *GO TO specification*. It represent sequential or straightline coding.

A set of conditions and actions, generally, common to two or more open-end tables, is described in a *closed-end table*. Each closed-end table is entered from another table by means of a *DO specification*. After an appropriate rule in the closed-end table has been determined and acted on, control is returned to the point of reference in the table from which control was transferred. In effect, a closed-end table represents a separate program module or a subroutine.

Each table in a decision table set is classified as open-end or closed as shown in Figure 6-11. When limited-entry decision table format is used, the name or number of the table to which control is transferred is written as part of the GO TO or DO specification in the action-stub section of the table (Figure 6-11, Start Table and Table 3). When the extended-entry decision table format is used, the table name or number appears in the action-entries section of the table (Figure 6-11, Tables 1 and 2).

No special return instruction is needed in a closed table because the term *Closed* in the table header indicates that the return is to occur. A single table may include both GO TO and DO specifications, and multiple instances of each. When both are used, all DO specifications should be listed ahead of the GO TOs. Any number of tables can refer to a given closed table. An open-end table cannot be entered and exited by way of the same table.

Figure 6-11 shows one possible flow of program control through a program whose logic is described by a set of six decision tables. For ease of reading, some action-stub and condition-stub items in the tables are not shown. You should assume that they are other GO TO or DO specifications or pertain to other (sequential) processing steps within the solution algorithm.

We see that Start Table is an open-end table. It passes control to another open-end table, Table 1, when rule 1 is acted on. If rule 3 in Table 1 is selected (because the particular combination of condition entries stated in rule 3 applies), control is transferred to Table 4. A rule in Table 4 is selected and acted on, and control is returned to Table 1. The last action entry in rule 3 causes a direct transfer of control to Table 2. Any one of the five rules in Table 2 is selected (we have assumed rule 3). Eventually, control is transferred to Table 3. From there control returns to Start Table where, at some point, processing is terminated.

SAMPLE PROBLEM

To pull together and apply some of the techniques we've discussed, we look now at the problem statement in Figure 6-12a. It deals with sales order processing. The programmer has identified conditions and actions. They are flagged by solid underscores and broken underscores, respectively.

(a) Problem statement

Obtain the next sales order. If the quantity ordered for a particular item does not exceed the order limit for that item, move the quantity-ordered amount to the quantity-shipped field. Update the master inventory file accordingly. Of course, the customer's credit rating must be OK and there must be sufficient quantity on hand of the item to fill the order.

When the quantity ordered for an item exceeds the order limit for that item, reject the order for that particular item. When the customer's credit rating is not OK, reject the entire order. In either case, print notice of the rejection on an exception report.

If the quantity ordered for an item is within the limit for that item and the customer's credit rating is OK, but there is insufficient quantity on hand of the item to fill the order, back-order processing should be performed. The next item on the sales order should be processed in the usual fashion.

When all items listed on a sales order have been processed, the next sales order should be read. When all orders have been read, processing should be terminated.

(b) List of conditions and actions from problem statement

C1 Quantity ordered does not exceed order limit
C2 Customer's credit rating is OK
C3 Sufficient quantity on hand to fill order
C4 Quantity ordered exceeds order limit
C5 Customer's credit rating is not OK
C6 Quantity ordered is within the limit
C7 Customer's credit rating is OK
C8 Insufficient quantity on hand of the item
C9 All items listed on sales order have been processed
C10 All orders have been read

A1 Obtain next sales order
A2 Move quantity-ordered to quantity-shipped
A3 Update master inventory file
A4 Reject order for item
A5 Reject entire order
A6 Print notice of rejection on exception report
A7 Do back-order processing
A8 Process next item on sales order
A9 Read next sales order
A10 Terminate processing

Figure 6–12 Extracting conditions and actions of a sample problem

IBM®

SYSTEM Sales Order Processing DECISION-TABLE WORKSHEET

Page 1 of 3

Line .... entered from .... & ....
Line .... entered from .... & ....
Line .... entered from .... & ....

Analyst H. Johnson
Date 7/26/78

Line .... entered from .... & ....
Line .... entered from .... & ....
Line .... entered from .... & ....

GX28-1630-1 U/M 025*
Printed in U.S.A.
*No. of sheets per pad
may vary slightly.

Sales Order Table	Open-end	1	2	3	4	5	6
All orders read		Y	N	N	N	N	N
All items on order read		Y	N	N	N	N	N
Credit rating OK				N	Y	Y	Y
Qty ordered ≤ limit					Y	N	Y
Qty on hand ≥ qty ordered						Y	N
Obtain next sales order		X	X				
Obtain next item			X	X	X		
Reject entire order				X			
Reject order for item						X	
Print rejection notice					X	X	
Do Back Order Table							X
Move qty-ordered to qty-shipped						X	
Do Inventory Update Table					X		
Stop		X					

Figure 6–13   Using a decision-table worksheet to lay out program logic

Note that the problem statement describes situations serially; it repeats both conditions and actions. The next step in constructing a decision table is to list the actions and conditions — to separate them out so that we can see and analyze them clearly, as in Figure 6-12b.

In a decision table, each condition or action is listed only once. The opposite (negative) form of a condition or action is not listed. We develop the conditions and actions by consolidating similar or repetitious portions of the problem statement, and ignoring the opposites of those we select. A tool we have not mentioned thus far, but one that is very useful at this point, is a *decision-table worksheet*. We list the conditions and actions needed in the decision table on the worksheet, as shown in Figure 6-13.

A double vertical rule is marked on the form to separate the left half of the decision table from the right half. We add double horizontal lines where they are appropriate for the table we are constructing, and we number the rules that we set up. Our table is a limited-entry open-end decision table. Control is transferred from this table to a Back-Order Table when back-order processing is needed. It is transferred to an Inventory Update Table when updating of the master inventory file is required. These are, of course, closed decision tables that cause control to be returned to this table after appropriate processing has been accomplished.

We have here, therefore, the basic plan for a modular program. The Sales Order Table shows the main line of program logic. It calls upon other program modules to do back-order and master-file processing. They may call other modules, say, for error-condition and input/output processing.

QUESTIONS

Q1. (a) Distinguish between problem situations where flowcharts are apt to be most useful and those especially suitable for decision tables. (b) Give examples of each.

Q2. Distinguish between AND and OR problem statements.

Q3. (a) List and explain three types of decision tables. (b) Describe a problem situation where each type of decision table is most useful.

Q4. Describe three techniques for collapsing decision tables.

Q5. (a) Why do decision tables lead to modular programs? (b) Based on what we have learned thus far, what other steps might you take to insure that the resulting program will indeed be modular?

Q6. Explain the following types of errors, to be guarded against in decision-table construction: (a) redundancy, (b) inconsistency, (c) incompleteness.

EXERCISES

E1. Refer to Figure 6-4 to determine what actions should occur in each of the following problem situations: (a) An employee currently earns $2.68 per hour, having received a 12¢ per hour raise two months ago. (b) An employee who received his or her last raise 16 months ago now earns $3.00 per hour.

E2. Refer to Figure 6–10 to determine what actions should occur in each of the following problem situations: (a) John Clap, an employee with 12 years of service, has sold 616 units. (b) Martha Jones has sold 216 units during her first six months of employment. (c) Clarence Dobbs, who has been with the firm for a year, has sold exactly 1000 units.

E3. Still using Figure 6–10, answer the following questions: (a) How does an employee qualify for a $1000 bonus? (b) How long must an employee have been with the firm to have the opportunity to earn 3% commission? (c) What else besides length of service determines eligibility for a 3% commission rate?

E4. (a) Rewrite the OR problem statement on page 94 of this chapter, so that it becomes an AND problem statement. (b) Construct a decision table showing the logic that you specified in (a) above.

E5. Modify the decision table in Figure 6–10 to reflect the following changes in the problem statement: "A salesman's commission rate is based solely on number of units sold. Each employee is entitled to a $500 bonus when the number of units he or she has sold first equals or exceeds 500." (Assume the rates/units sold and $1000 bonus qualifications remain unchanged.)

E6. Prepare a decision table for each of the following problem situations: (a) If $A < B$, $A + B = C$. If $A = B$, $C = 0$. IF $A > B$, $A \times B = C$. (b) If the quantity on hand for part 6A31 falls below the minimum stock level, check to see whether the part is obsolete. If it is not, determine the reorder quantity established for the part and issue an order for it. If part 6A31 is obsolete, print the part name and current stock level on an inventory exception report. (c) Column 80 of each employee time card, submitted weekly, contains either a 1 or a 2, indicating salaried or hourly payroll, respectively. If 1, the employee's gross pay is simply extracted from the salaried payroll master file. If 2, the number of hours that the employee worked is read from the employee time card, the hourly pay rate is extracted from the hourly payroll master file, and regular pay (for hours ≤ 40) is computed as hours $\times$ rate. If the employee worked overtime, overtime pay (for hours > 40) is computed as hours $\times$ rate $\times$ 1.5. Gross pay equals regular pay + overtime pay. If the overtime hours exceed 8, the employee's name and total hours worked are printed on an exception report. (d) An 8-page advertising circular is to be mailed to each charge-account customer who opened his or her account at the local branch within the past 90 days, lives within 20 miles of the branch, or actioned his or her account (credit or debit) within the past 30 days. If the customer has both charged and paid at least $1000 against the account during the year, he or she is to receive a second circular giving advance notice of a 2-day pre-sale special on large household appliances.

E7. Construct a program flowchart depicting the logic of the problem statement in either E6c or E6d above.

E8. Compare your work for projects E6c (or E6d) and E7 above. Which approach to solution planning was more convenient for you in the particular problem situation? Why? Which layout of the program logic do you prefer? Why?

*E9. Using either the decision table of E6c (or E6d) or the program flowchart of E7 as a guide, write a sequence of programming-language statements to perform the processing steps required.

REFERENCES

Gildersleeve, Thomas R. *Decision Tables and Their Practical Applications in Data Processing.* Englewood Cliffs, N.J.: Prentice-Hall, 1971. *IBM Decision-Table Worksheet.* IBM Corporation publication (GX28–1630). White Plains, N.Y., n.d.

London, Keith R. *Decision Tables.* Princeton: Auerbach, 1972 (the classic in this field).

McDaniel, Herman. *An Introduction to Decision Logic Tables.* New York: John Wiley & Sons, 1968.

Montalbano, Michael. *Decision Tables.* Chicago: Science Research Associates, 1974 (a relatively sophisticated discourse on decision tables, for those seeking in-depth coverage of this topic).

Myers, H. J. "Compiling Optimized Code from Decision Tables," *IBM Journal of Research and Development* 16, 5 (Sept 1972): 489–503 (describes the general methodology for automated decision-table processing).

Pollack, Solomon R., Harry T. Hicks, Jr., and William J. Harrison. *Decision Tables: Theory and Practice.* New York: Wiley-Interscience, 1971 (contains a comprehensive decision-table bibliography).

Pooch, Udo W. "Translation of Decision Tables," *Computing Surveys* (ACM) 6, 2 (June 1974): 125–33 (includes a decision-table bibliography of 108 references).

7

WRITING THE PROGRAM

After the programmer is satisfied that all processing has been planned, with all alternatives and exceptions provided for, the next step is to write the program. In some cases, the programmer may give the solution algorithm and the tools he has developed (for example, flowcharts or decision tables) to another person who works as a coder. (Since writing the program is, in effect, stating the algorithm in a particular language, or code, *programming* may also be called *coding*. A programmer may and usually does work as a coder. A coder is expected to represent the algorithm in coded form, but he does not have full responsibility for all of the steps in the program-development cycle.) If the programming language to be used has not been selected, that selection must be made at this time. As noted in Chapter 2, instructions can be written at any of several levels, ranging from machine language to high-level programming languages. Ultimately, what the programmer writes must be understood by the computer; that is, stored-program instructions must be in machine-readable form.

AVAILABLE LANGUAGES

Literally hundreds of languages have been developed for use in writing programs. Each language is a set of symbols with attached meanings, explicitly defined to permit unambiguous communication with computers. Only a few are widely used. Usually, one assembler program is provided for each type of computer, and programs can be written for that computer in the assembler language that the assembler program is designed to translate. Because assembler languages are tied closely to machine capabilities, assembler languages for two different types of computers are not the same. They may be very

Language	Sample Statements	Special Characteristics

FORTRAN (Formula Translator)	DIMENSION UNTPR (500), TPRC (500)
	
	  60 READ (5, 100) A,B,C
	100 FORMAT (2F3.1,F6.4)
	     DO 200 I=1,K,INC
	     TPRC(I) = UNTPR(I) * UNTNO
	200 CONTINUE
	     S = (A + B)/(C – D)**3
	
	     GO TO 300
	
	250 IF (LIM.NE.20) GO TO 600
	
	900 STOP
		(1) oldest high-level language (mid 1950s) and first to be implemented widely
		(2) algebraic-like language well suited to problems involving numerical computation
		(3) includes a wide variety of mathematical and service subroutines built into the language itself
		(4) simple enough to be used in problem solving by other than professional programmers
		(5) because certain I/O operations and certain operations on nonnumeric data cannot be expressed, not well suited for file maintenance, editing of data, or production of documents
		(6) standardized by ANSI since 1966
		(7) student-oriented version of the language and compiler, WATFIV, developed for use in a learning environment

COBOL (Common Business-Oriented Language)	DATA DIVISION.
	FD FILE-1
	     RECORDING MODE IS F
	     BLOCK CONTAINS 50 TO 125 CHARACTERS
	
	1 DATA-RECORD.
	    02 RECORD-IDENTIFICATION.
	      03 RECORD-CODE, PICTURE XX.
	
	PROCEDURE DIVISION.
	    READ WORK-FILE; AT END GO TO END-RUN.
	    MULTIPLY AMOUNT BY RATE, GIVING TOTAL, ROUNDED.
	    MOVE SPACES TO BILL-LINE-1.
	    WRITE OUTPUT-LINE AFTER ADVANCING 1.
		(1) introduced in late 1950s, with widespread usage strongly encouraged by the federal government
		(2) particularly applicable to business data-processing problems
		(3) can be used to process alphabetic and numeric data and to designate all types of I/O operations
		(4) English-like, permitting programs to be constructed of sentence-like statements grouped in paragraphs, sections, and divisions (Identification, Environment, Data, and Procedure)
		(5) imposes rather inflexible coding disciplines, so not suitable for the inexperienced user who wants to write programs to solve his own problems
		(6) self-documenting (few additional comments required for explanatory purposes)
		(7) standardized by ANSI since 1968
		(8) the major programming language for today's business applications

BASIC (Beginners' All-purpose Symbolic Instruction Code)	10 DIM A(20), B(4,3) 20 PRINT "ENTER TEMP" 30 INPUT F 40 LET C = (F – 32) * 5/9 50 PRINT "CENTIGRADE:" C 60 REM MATRIX OPERATION 70 MAT Z = X – Y	(1) developed at Dartmouth College in the 1960s for students to use in solving simple problems (2) designed primarily for conversational interaction with the computer from a remote terminal (3) similar to FORTRAN in many respects, and, like FORTRAN, well suited to numerical problem solving (4) simple to learn and easy to use, because of ordinary English words and familiar mathematical symbols

Figure 7-1 Significant characteristics of common high-level languages

dissimilar. Assembler-language programs written for one type of computer cannot generally be executed without change on others.

High-level programming languages are frequently subdivided into two categories: *procedure-oriented languages* and *problem-oriented languages.* Procedure-oriented languages are general-purpose languages designed to facilitate expression of a solution algorithm in terms of procedural, or algorithmic, steps. Popular examples are FORTRAN, COBOL, PL/I, BASIC, and APL. Since these are the languages you are most apt to encounter, their primary characteristics are summarized in Figure 7-1. Representative statements in the languages are also shown, to indicate their general formats and

Language	Sample Statements	Special Characteristics
BASIC (continued)	160 FOR Q = 1 TO 12 170 LET T = T + P(K,Q) 180 NEXT Q 570 IF N < 100 THEN 30 990 END	(5) includes common mathematical functions and operations readily performed on 2 x 2 arrays, or matrices (6) produces a standard-form output, generally acceptable to the problem solver (7) enhanced in later versions, which gain function but lose some simplicity (8) a common language of the minicomputer and small computer, as well as of the time-sharing environment
APL (A Programming Language)	A←1 3 5 7 +/A V←40 x □ C←ι6 3 2 ρ C →45 **Note:** These statements assign a 4-component vector to A; add the values of A and print their sum; request input from user, multiply the input by 40, and assign result to V; generate a vector of integers from 1 to 6 and assign it to C; create a 3 X 2 matrix from C and print it; and transfer control to statement 45.	(1) first described by K.E. Iverson in the early 1960s, implemented in part at IBM's T.J. Watson Research Center in 1966, and since offered commercially as a language program product and for use in time-sharing environments (2) designed to permit users to specify complex algorithms (not necessarily mathematical in nature) succinctly (3) like BASIC, well suited for interactive problem solving (4) includes a powerful set of operators and dynamic features for specifying types and shapes of data (5) difficult to learn and to understand because of complex notation (6) requires a special keyboard supporting the rather large, unusual APL character set (7) somewhat slow to win acceptance but enthusiastically proclaimed by its supporters

PL/I (Programming Language I)	BILL: PROCEDURE OPTIONS (MAIN);
	      DCL RATE DEC FIXED (3,2),
	          (DATE, TIME) CHAR (6);
	
	LB0: GET LIST (NAME, RATE, DATE, TIME);
	      IF TIME = 40 THEN
	          IRATE = RATE;
	      ELSE DO;
	          IRATE = RATE/2 + .05;
	          SW = '1'B;
	          END;
	      NET = GROS – FIT – FICA – DEDUCT;
	      /* THIS IS A COMMENT */
	LB1: PUT EDIT (NAME, NET) (A(9),F(6,2));
	
	      END BILL;
		(1) developed in 1960s, for use on IBM's System/360 computers
		(2) multipurpose language to be used by programmers at all levels for all types of problems
		(3) very powerful: includes many features not available in other commonly used languages and a wide variety of built-in functions
		(4) extensive and sophisticated, but modular in design so that programmers need learn only the features that meet their immediate problem-solving needs
		(5) block-structured language, so more suitable to structured programming than other commonly used languages
		(6) flexible, permitting much freedom in coding
		(7) standardization efforts in the 1970s led by ANSI and the European Computer Manufacturers Association
		(8) student-oriented version of the language and compiler, PL/C, developed for use in a learning environment

Figure 7-1   (Continued)

some available statement types. Use of these languages is especially prevalent where algebraic problems must be dealt with, and in business data-processing environments.

Problem-oriented languages are designed to facilitate solutions to particular types of problems. The programmer who uses one of these languages does not specify the procedural steps to be followed in solving the problem. Instead, he specifies characteristics of the input data, output requirements, and other parameters of the problem to be solved. An example is RPG, which we discussed in Chapter 2. It provides for convenient file updating and generation of printed reports. Other examples are APT (Automatic Programmed Tool) and ADAPT (Advanced Automatic Programmed Tool), special-purpose languages for describing functions of numerically controlled equipment such as milling machines and other machine tools.

SNOBOL is a special-purpose language designed specifically for string-handling. It has a powerful set of operators for processing sequences of characters rather than numeric values. SNOBOL is most often used, therefore, where text must be manipulated—for example in such applications as language translation, question answering, and automatic abstracting services.

LISP is another of the more common special-purpose languages. It is designed specifically for *list-p*rocessing. Since the data elements handled by a LISP program are linked by means of pointers, the sequence in which they are processed (logical sequence) need not be the same as their physical sequence in storage. A language offering this capability is particularly well suited to problems that involve few arithmetic operations but numerous logical operations or any kind of operation to be performed recursively (that is, where one execution of an operation calls for another execution of the same operation, and so on, repetitively). The greatest strength of LISP lies in the area of handling symbolic expressions derived from mathematics. List-processing languages are also used in the area of work known as artificial intelligence, where emphasis is placed on determining whether or not computers can be used to solve problems that seem to require imagination, intuition, or intelligence when they are solved by humans. Examples here are solving puzzles, playing chess or checkers, analyzing grammar and translating statements of one language into another, proving mathematical theorems, and the like.

Other special-purpose languages that should be mentioned are SIMSCRIPT and GPSS. They are leading examples of simulation languages, designed to facilitate simulation, or modeling, by means of computers. For example, the flight of a rocket lifting a satellite into orbit can be simulated. By varying certain parameters, the effects of external forces such as gravity, wind velocity, and air density can be studied. The simulation provides an indication of what the performance of the rocket—its direction of movement, acceleration, and so on—will be when the simulated conditions are encountered in a real environment.

Perhaps the most important point to be grasped at this time is that the list of available programming languages is a long one. Obviously, a programmer cannot be expected to know all of them. As pointed out in the next section, however, it is vitally important that the language selected for a programming task be well suited to the problem that must be solved.

SELECTING A LANGUAGE

One question that might be raised at this time is why so many programming languages have been developed. Or, to put it another way, why concern ourselves with the fact that so many programming languages are available? Within one program-development environment, or for one type of computer, why not use the same language for all programs?

Perhaps the simplest answer to this question is that each language has its advantages, but it also has its limitations. In actual practice, a number of factors should be taken into account when selecting an appropriate language for a problem-solving task. These include:

- the execution-time requirements that will be imposed on the program
- the time and money required to develop the program in a particular programming language
- the availability of particular languages
- the primary characteristics of the languages available
- the type of problem to be solved

The execution-time requirements of a program are considerations that emphasize the speed with which a program written in a particular language can be executed and the amount of storage space that will be required for the program during execution. Under most circumstances, if two programmers of equal talent were to write programs to solve the same problem, one using an assembler language and the other a high-level programming language, the program written in assembler language would execute faster and occupy less storage. Because assembler-language instructions correspond very closely to machine operations, the programmer can specify exactly what is to be done, using a minimal number of processing steps. In contrast, the sequence of machine-language instructions corresponding to a single high-level-language statement tends to be more general in nature, may include tests and other instructions needed in some cases but not in others, and so on — in short, is not necessarily the most efficient code for every problem situation. Further, some machine operations may be either not available or not easily programmed in a given high-level language. A programmer who uses the language cannot readily take advantage of these machine capabilities.

In most cases, the systems software for a computer is written in the assembler language of that computer. Many of the routines are executed repetitively by many users, for many types of jobs, so fast execution is essential. Some, notably all or portions of the operating-system monitor, are resident in primary storage even when not being executed, so minimal use of storage is desirable.

The second language-selection criterion listed above is basically a question of the cost of program preparation. One of the major drawbacks of assembler language is the amount of time and effort required for coding. More instructions must be written to accomplish a given function when using an assembler language than are required when using a high-level language. More rules must be followed, and more details dealt with, so programming errors are more likely to occur. Because assembler-language programs are not easy to understand, the programmer must make extensive use of comments, for the benefit of others who must read and understand the coding, and for himself when he refers to the program at a later time. Any required alteration of an assembler-language program may necessitate extensive rewriting. If the nature of a program is such that it is likely to be revised from time to time, use of a high-level language is particularly advisable.

The question of language availability is primarily concerned with whether or not a language-processor program has been developed for the EDP system in use, to translate the programmer's coding into machine-language form. If such a program is not currently installed but can be obtained from a computer manufacturer or software development firm, the cost of obtaining it should be weighed against the benefits of being able to use the particular language in programming.

Another aspect of language availability is whether or not the programmer assigned to the problem-solving task is familiar with the particular language under consideration. If not, the training costs and the ease of adapting to the language should be estimated. The time required for such training and adjustment should be factored into the selection process.

A third aspect of availability deals with not only right now but later: Is a change in EDP-system hardware anticipated during the expected lifetime of the program? Because high-level programming languages are designed to be machine-independent, a program written in one of these languages is not necessarily restricted to one computer type. It may be possible to take the program in its high-level-language form and have it translated again, using an appropriate language-processor program designed for the new computer. The language processor will make use of the new EDP-system's features and develop a program in the machine language of the new computer. Some modification of the original program may be necessary, but the programming effort will be much less than that which would be required to rewrite it.

The trend in programming is clearly away from machine-oriented languages to high-level languages. We have seen in this section that there are significant differences between assembler languages and high-level languages. The previous section pointed out that there are also significant differences among high-level languages. In deciding which language to use, the programmer should look at both the primary characteristics of the languages available and the type of problem to be solved. The fundamental question here is: Which of the available languages is best suited to the problem?

As Figure 7–1 indicates, for example, FORTRAN is well suited to problems involving numerical computation. It is relatively easy to learn, but specifying certain operations to be performed on nonnumeric data is difficult. And FORTRAN cannot be used at all for some types of I/O operations. COBOL was primarily designed for, and is well suited to, business data-processing problems. Its English-like structure is advantageous in that programs tend to be self-documenting, but disadvantageous to the extent that programs become wordy, lengthy, or require excessive amounts of time for translation. If a business data-processing problem involves only simple calculations and requires numerous printed reports as output, RPG or MARK IV (both of which were discussed in Chapter 2) may be an appropriate choice. The programmer should remember also to consider applications packages. Some examples of this type of software were listed in Chapter 2.

As this discussion indicates, choosing the best language for a particular problem-solving task can be a difficult assignment. It must not be taken lightly. If a good choice is made, the resultant program is likely to be written in a reasonable amount of time, require a reasonable amount of storage, and execute at a reasonable speed; we can expect a satisfactory solution to the problem. If a poor choice is made, programming time, storage use, and execution speed may be excessive. The program may never perform as intended and may fail to provide an acceptable solution to the problem.

PROGRAM CODING

Writing a program is the process of expressing a solution algorithm (as shown on a program flowchart or decision table, or stated in another design language) in programming-language form. This process is a rigorous one in that the programmer must follow very specific rules. He can use only characters from a certain allowable character set; he must use periods or semicolons (depending on the language) as delimiters; he must specify parameters of a statement in a certain positional order; and so on.

For most programming languages, *language reference manuals* and *coding forms* are available for the programmer's use. The familiar adage, "if all else fails, read the directions," is a guideline that should be applied before programming as well as after. It is usually easier to write a statement correctly the first time than to find an error in the statement and correct it later. Even an experienced programmer can profit from reading and re-reading language documentation. Otherwise, many useful constructs of the language may be forgotten. For example, why write a sequence of instructions to test for end of file if including the keyword END on an input statement will serve the same purpose? What data conversions must be provided for by program coding? What conversions are handled automatically by routines built into the language itself?

Before writing statements about how input data will be received, the programmer should refer to the *layout specifications* for that data. (We discussed such layouts in Chapter 3.) Before writing statements about how output will be returned, he should refer to any applicable printer spacing charts or other output layouts. Depending on the level of detail specified in the design-language representation of the solution algorithm, the coding of the processing steps needed to create the output from the input is relatively straightforward. Figure 7-2 shows one example of the transition from program flowchart to programming-language statements. In this case, the statements make up a simple FORTRAN edit program.

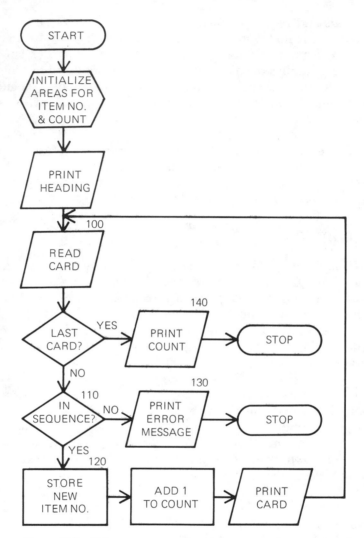

Figure 7-2 Using a program flowchart as a guide to coding (part 1)

In most if not all instances, there is no one correct way to write a program, just as there is no one correct way to solve a problem. Different programmers will develop different sequences of instructions to perform a given series of operations, just as they will develop different solution algorithms for a problem. These differences arise because there are usually several ways to arrange the logical sequences of operations needed, and alternative ways of coding some of the sequences. It is not necessarily true, however, that any combination of statements that provides the required output is acceptable. When using COBOL or FORTRAN, for example, the programmer must

FORTRAN Coding Form

```
      INTEGER ITEM, DES(4), DES2, QTY, KITEM, KNT
      REAL AVC, SALEP
 1    FORMAT(' ITEM NO.     DESCRIPTION        COST   PRICE   QUAN',/)
 2    FORMAT(I6,4A4,A2,2F5.2,I3)
 3    FORMAT(' ',1X,I6,3X,4A4,A2,2X,F6.2,2X,F6.2,2X,I3)
 4    FORMAT('0ITEM NO. OUT OF SEQUENCE. NO =',I6)
 5    FORMAT('0NO. CARDS = ',I3)
      KITEM=0
      KNT=0
C     PRINT HEADING FOR REPORT
      WRITE (3,1)
C     READ CARD
100   READ(1,2)ITEM, DES, DES2, AVC, SALEP, QTY
C     CHECK FOR END OF FILE
      IF(ITEM-999999)110,140,110
C     DO SEQUENCE CHECK
110   IF(ITEM-KITEM)130,130,120
120   KITEM=ITEM
C     UPDATE COUNT OF CARDS
      KNT=KNT+1
C     PRINT CARD JUST READ
      WRITE(3,3)ITEM, DES, DES2, AVC, SALEP, QTY
      GO TO 100
C     OUT OF SEQUENCE ERROR MESSAGE
```

FORTRAN Coding Form

```
130   WRITE(3,4) ITEM
      STOP
C     TOTAL NUMBER OF CARDS MESSAGE
140   WRITE(3,5) KNT
      STOP
      END
```

This FORTRAN edit program accepts inventory-control cards as input.
It sequence-checks the cards, which are to be in ascending order
by item number. An out-of-sequence condition causes program
termination. If a card is read in correct sequence, the card is counted
and its contents are printed so that they can be checked manually
if calculations in subsequent computer runs fail to balance. A
card containing 999999 as an item number is recognized as the
last card. The accumulated count of input cards is printed
as a control total, and processing is terminated.

Figure 7-2 (continued)

know the functions of the statements that he codes. The more familiar he is with the language, the better equipped he is to devise simple sequences of statements that perform operations as fast as possible, using a minimal amount of storage. A skilled programmer is aware of the number and kinds of machine-language instructions likely to be generated by the language-processor program for the various types of statements, and how long they are apt to take to execute. Then, when there are alternative ways of coding, he can make intelligent choices. Such a programmer can develop quality code.

BATCH PROCESSING

In a typical program-development environment, after a program has been written on coding forms, it is forwarded to a central computer operations group for keypunching. One card is punched for each line of code on the form. The resultant deck of cards is the programmer's source-program deck (*source deck*, for short). A wise programmer *"desk checks"* the source deck at this point, either by studying the printing at the tops of the punched cards or by having the contents of the cards listed on the printer for verification. He eliminates errors by punching new cards to replace erroneous cards.

Next, the programmer (or the programming librarian, in a chief programmer team environment) submits the source deck to the EDP system for translation to machine-language form. He may have the machine-language instructions punched into cards, thereby creating an object-program deck (*object deck*) that can be read back into primary storage at a later time. Alternatively, or in addition, he may want the machine-language program written to magnetic tape or disk for subsequent use. To tell the computer how to handle a job, the programmer prepares one or more job-control statements. They are keypunched to form a set of job-control cards. The cards are forwarded with the source deck to the computer for processing.

In some program-development environments, the programmer may have to prepare only a single job-control statement to cause a prewritten sequence of job-control statements, known as a *cataloged procedure*, to be read into storage from a system library to direct subsequent processing. Generally, other programmers are also submitting jobs to be run. When the job definitions are collected, then forwarded to the computer as an input job stream, the computer can execute one job after another with little or no operator intervention. This approach is called *stacked-job processing*, *batched-job processing*, or simply *batch processing*. It helps to maximize the amount of useful work that an EDP system can do.

In contrast to programming languages, there are no machine-independent or standard forms of job-control language. The formats of job-control statements and the information they must provide are determined by the designers of the operating-system software that processes them. What works well at one installation may be partially correct or totally unacceptable at another. As we pointed out earlier, each programmer must become familiar with the JCL requirements at his installation. Most computer operations groups provide *job-control-language reference manuals* or *user's guides* unique to the installation or developed by the supplier of the operating-system software in use. Figure 7–3 is included here as a representative example of an input job stream, selected from among the wide range of available alternatives to help you visualize what is required.

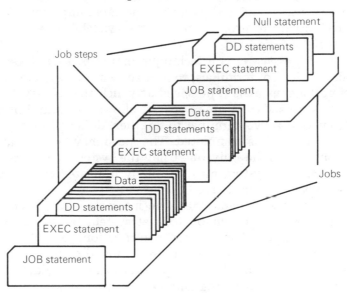

Figure 7–3   Stacked-job processing

INTERACTIVE PROCESSING

Though batch processing can, and usually does, help to make effective use of computer processing time, it may not help the programmer to make effective use of programming time. Suppose, for example, the programmer submits a job, then waits for an hour, or even several hours, or until the next day to receive results, only to discover that a trivial error in a job-control statement prevented the job from being run at all, or that a now-obvious error in program coding prevented the program from producing output. He must make the required corrections, then resubmit the job, only to wait again for results.

When *interactive-processing* capabilities are available, the programmer communicates more directly with the EDP system. He enters program statements into storage from a direct-input device such as a typewriter-like printer-keyboard or a visual-display unit with a keyboard attachment. The statements that are entered are displayed on the device (terminal) as they are entered, so that obvious errors can be corrected immediately. After the complete program has been entered, one or more *system commands* of a *terminal command language* (also called *operator command language*) can be entered to cause translation, or translation and execution, to occur. In most cases, the programmer is notified of job failure or successful job completion immediately. If necessary, he can make corrections from the terminal and re-submit the job. After the program has been successfully translated, he may run it several times, but with different inputs, for debugging and testing pur-poses. Studies have shown that the most important factor in increasing the productivity of programmers is the availability of interactive debugging and testing facilities.

Time sharing is a technique that allows a number of EDP-system users, at a variety of terminals, to interact with the system on what appears to be a simultaneous basis. The speed at which the EDP-system components — both hardware and software — operate allows the central processing unit to switch from one active terminal to another, doing all or a part of each user's job, until all work is completed. The speed may be so great that each user acts as though he is the only one using the system. The purpose for which one per-son uses the system may be totally unrelated to that of others. But the sys-tem resources are shared by all.

The user programmer who interacts with the computer via a time-shar-ing system must sign on to that system by means of a sign-on, or log-on, command, specifying a user identification. (See Figure 7-4.) For additional security (that is, protection from unauthorized use), a user password may also be required. After the systems software validates the user identification and password, the programmer can proceed with a job. He may write a new program, or he may enter a system command to retrieve from storage a pro-gram that was begun or completed previously. As noted for batch-processing job-control statements, a wide variation exists in the formats and contents of system commands of a terminal command language. Generally, they are described in a *terminal operator's guide*. The programmer must become familiar with the commands available.

Applications programs developed interactively may be written in any of several programming languages. If the programs are to be run in the interac-tive environment upon completion, BASIC and APL are likely choices. Figure 7-4 shows how a simple BASIC-language program might be created in a typical time-sharing environment. In addition to BASIC statements, system commands entered by the terminal user and system responses (underlined) are displayed. Brief explanations of some printouts are given at the right.

It is also possible to write a program in, say, COBOL, FORTRAN, or PL/I, from a terminal. It can be tested from the terminal by initiating various executions upon different inputs. The fully checked-out program can be stored on a system library, thereby making it available for execution when re-ferred to from a batch-processing input job stream or an interactive terminal.

```
LOGIN:  USERID
PASSWORD:                            For security, what user enters is not
LANGUAGE:  BASIC                     displayed at terminal.
OLD OR NEW:  NEW: TEMP               Identifies new program as TEMP.
READY


100   PRINT "FAHRENHEIT";
110   INPUT F
120   LET C = (F − 32) * 5/9
130   PRINT "CENTIGRADE:" C
140   PRINT
150   GO TO 110 ←←←100              Backspacing 3 times deletes 110.


LIST  150                            Lists statement to insure that correction worked.
150    GO TO 100
READY


160   END


RUN                                 Translates BASIC program to machine language
                                     and initiates its execution.

TEMP   18:28   MAY 28, 1978


FAHRENHEIT?   212                    BASIC INPUT statement causes question mark
CENTIGRADE:   100                    to be displayed and program to halt for input
                                     of value for F from terminal.

FAHRENHEIT?   98.6
CENTIGRADE:   37


FAHRENHEIT?   STOP                   BASIC STOP statement is entered to cause
STOP                                 program termination.


RUNNING TIME:  00.7 SECS.


READY


SAVE                                 Stores program as TEMP.
READY
```

Figure 7-4   Entering a BASIC program at a terminal

PROGRAMMING DETAILS

To write a program is to pay attention to details. As noted in Chapter 1, the computer is a powerful, fast machine, but it acts only according to directions. All actions that it is to take must be specified by systems software or an applications program. All conditions that can occur during processing must be provided for. All potential causes of error must be recognized and dealt with. Even "impossible" situations that cannot happen (but will) must be taken into account. In a typical business data-processing application, input and output considerations require a great deal of time and attention.

_____ 1. The amounts and types of storage required for data and instructions within the program.

_____ 2. The formats of data on the input medium (the transaction file).

_____ 3. Checking of input to identify data that is incorrect (for example, not numeric or not within expected ranges) and therefore cannot be processed.

_____ 4. Availability and formats of reference data, such as constants, tables, and files (including master files).

_____ 5. Any conversions, such as from the decimal number system to binary and from binary to decimal, that must be handled by the program.

_____ 6. Availability of other software such as routines and subroutines that have been used and tested in other programs and that may be used advantageously in this program.

_____ 7. Automatic monitoring performed by operating-system software to ascertain that required input and output devices are connected and available for operation.

_____ 8. "Housekeeping" procedures that (a) preset indicators, switches, and registers, (b) clear primary storage and set locations to specific values if needed, (c) write messages to the computer operator, and (d) check labels on volumes and files.

_____ 9. Requirements for precision and accuracy, both in intermediate calculations and in final results, or output.

_____ 10. The formats of output data with provisions, if required, for later conversion to punched cards, printed reports, or displays.

_____ 11. Methods of verifying the correctness of the problem-solving method (set of instructions, or solution algorithm) and the validity of output.

_____ 12. Ability to restart the EDP system and this program in case of unscheduled interruptions or error conditions.

Figure 7–5 Checklist for program planning

To minimize the likelihood of programming errors, or simply to be able to refer to a "memory jogger," many programmers build and refer to programming checklists during the design stage, when writing code, and during checkout of the design and of the resultant code. Such a checklist is shown in Figure 7-5. Some or all of the points in the checklist must be considered when preparing even the simplest program. We have touched on some of them briefly. Others will be mentioned later. As you gain experience with a particular language, you will probably want to add items to the list. In doing so, you will create for yourself an invaluable aid to correct programming.

COMMENTS

Source-program statements consist of characters combined in very specific ways to tell the computer how to solve a problem. *Comments* also consist of characters, but they do not tell the computer anything. Comments are not translated to machine language by the language-processor program that converts the programmer's coding to executable form. They are printed out, along with the source-program statements, on the listing produced as one output of the translation process. Their function is to provide information for humans who must read and understand the program.

Are comments necessary? We can make an analogy between comments and the printing that may or may not appear at the tops of punched cards. The computer does not need the printing; it reads the coded character patterns represented by the holes punched in the cards. But we as humans would much rather determine the card content by reading the printing than by figuring out what is represented by the holes.

As another example, consider the program in Figure 7-6. Can you tell what it does? A similar program, documented by informative comments, is shown in Figure 7-7. Few if any persons would prefer to work with the program in Figure 7-6. The comments are one very important reason why.

The technique used to incorporate comments in a program depends on the programming language in use. PL/I is liberal in this respect, allowing comments enclosed by the character pairs /* and */ to be placed alone on coding lines, following statements on lines, and even within statements on lines if the programmer feels such comments are necessary (Figure 7-7 shows

```
MYPROG: PROC OPTIONS (MAIN);
DCL A DEC FIXED (11,4);
DO I = 9 TO 60 BY 3;
A = 3.1416*I*I*12;
PUT LIST (I*2, A);
END;
END;
```

Figure 7-6   A "bare-bones" program

PL/I). The FORTRAN programmer identifies a comment by placing a C in the first position of the coding line that holds the comment. The BASIC programmer writes REM as the first three characters of each comment line. Because COBOL statements resemble familiar English, a COBOL program is not apt to require extensive commenting. In common practice, an asterisk in position 7 of a coding line identifies a comment in a COBOL program.

```
CYLVOL:  PROC OPTIONS (MAIN);
/* THIS PROGRAM COMPUTES AND PRINTS A TABLE OF CYLINDER VOLUMES.
    CYLS ARE 12 IN DEEP, FROM 18 IN TO 10 FEET WIDE.              */
            DCL VOL REAL DEC FIXED (11,4);    /* CYLINDER VOLUME   */
            DCL R REAL BIN FIXED (15);        /* CYLINDER RADIUS   */
            PUT LIST ('TABLE OF VOLUMES');
            PUT SKIP (3);
            DO R = 9 TO 60 BY 3;
              VOL = (3.1416*R*R)*12;
              PUT LIST (R*2, VOL);
              PUT SKIP;
            END;
            PUT SKIP (2);
            PUT LIST ('END OF JOB');
            END;
```

Figure 7-7   An example of good program documentation

Comments tend to be valuable program documentation because they are so readily available as part of the program. However, they are not an end unto themselves, nor are they good just because they are present. Important points to remember are given below.

1. Use comments to introduce each major function, or section of code. This helps to convey the logical structure of the program.

2. Use comments to explain the data on which the program operates. These explanations are most valuable when placed near the data definitions (see the DECLARE (DCL) statements in Figure 7-7).

3. Make sure comments and code agree. Considerations here are that the comments must be up to date, technically correct, and complete. Perhaps not so obvious is the consideration that the code itself must be correct. A segment of code will not direct the computer in a certain way just because a comment says it does.

4. Avoid redundancies. Comments should convey new information; they should not just echo the code. For example, few persons would find the following comment helpful:

```
C        READ AND PRINT VALUES OF A AND B
         READ (5,400) A, B
         WRITE (6,400) A, B
```

5. Do not overuse comments. A comment takes your time to write it, printer time to print it, and storage space in the computer and on data-recording media. If a program is overly cluttered and lengthened by comments, a reader may become discouraged or not even try to wade through it. There are no absolutes as to how many comments are appropriate. Certainly, a rule such as "one comment per every three lines of code" is ridiculous. A guideline such as "one comment per section (of a COBOL program)" may be helpful for new programmers. In actual fact, comments should be provided on an as-needed basis.

6. Use comments to help readers over difficult segments of code or in potential trouble spots. For example, the programmer who uses a sophisticated sorting technique or develops a complex but essential conversion routine should comment it thoroughly. Any use of global variables should be flagged by comments. If a programmer elects to use nonstandard features of a programming language, say, FORTRAN, that are handled correctly by a particular FORTRAN compiler but may not be recognized at all by another, each use of such features should be preceded by comments. This helps to insure that the nonstandard features can be identified easily and removed or replaced by alternative coding as necessary if the program is to be translated by other than the originally intended compiler.

7. Make sure comments are understandable. The programmer should avoid computer jargon, overuse of acronyms, and uncommon or "homemade" abbreviations. Comments written simply as personal notes may provide little help to other readers of the code. Therefore, the comments should be developed with the potential readers in mind. If comments are very difficult to write, it may be that the code itself is poor. Here, the guideline is: Don't comment bad code — rewrite it.

OTHER GOOD PROGRAMMING PRACTICES

A point that may be obvious to the reader by this time is that the programmer can learn much by studying examples. That is why we make frequent use of examples in this book. Indeed, complete books have been written about the goods and bads in examples of programming style.* The program-

---

*See Kernighan and Plauger, *The Elements of Programming Style*, developed as a study of "real" programs.

mer who studies program listings of well-documented code produced by skilled programmers can learn much about coding from them. To emphasize this point further, we need only list some additional good programming practices evident in Figure 7-7. (There are more, which we discuss below.) The reader will benefit by noticing the programming practices used in examples throughout this text and in other programs.

- Use parentheses in arithmetic expressions even when they are believed not to be essential. Such parentheses are the programmer's way of making certain that the intended order of expression evaluation will be followed by the compiler during translation. They also help others to read and understand the code. The compiler will not be bothered by syntatically correct but unnecessary parentheses.

- Document program output. It should be self-explanatory. Even if the programming specifications do not dictate that report titles or column headings be displayed on printed results, for example, the programmer should plan and provide for them.

- Document successful completion of program execution. A positive indicator such as END OF JOB printed at the conclusion of program output affirms that no difficulties sufficient to warrant abnormal termination were encountered during execution. It also assures the output recipient that complete results were provided.

PROLOGS

In some program-development environments, comments are being replaced or supplemented by *prologs*. A prolog is (as the term infers) placed at the beginning of each module or program under development. Installation standards are agreed upon, detailing the content, order, and format of information contained therein.

Entries commonly included in a prolog are module name, descriptive title, function, date of initial completion, and responsible programmer. Additional entries indicate external references, dependencies, restrictions, and so on. Some programmers include pseudo code within their prologs to describe sections of program logic that may be difficult for others to follow. (We discussed pseudo code under "Other Design Languages" in Chapter 4 and will see it again in Chapter 8.) If changes are made to a module, the reason for each change, date, and responsible programmer should be noted in the prolog.

A representative prolog is shown as an example in Figure 7-8. The prolog introduces an I/O module that performs message-routing functions when called to do so by other program modules.

```
* * * * * * * * * * * * * * * * * * * * * * * * * * * * * * * * * * * * * * * * * * * * * *
*                                                                                         *
*   MODULE NAME: RMSGPROC                                                                 *
*                                                                                         *
*   DESCRIPTIVE TITLE: REMOTE MESSAGE HANDLER                                             *
*                                                                                         *
*   FUNCTION: THIS MODULE ACCEPTS A MESSAGE TO BE ROUTED TO A REMOTE                      *
*   TERMINAL AS INPUT AND ROUTES THE MESSAGE TO A REMOTE TERMINAL QUEUE.                  *
*   A CARRIER RETURN IS APPENDED TO THE END OF THE MESSAGE.                               *
*                                                                                         *
*   DATE: 08/20/76                                                                        *
*                                                                                         *
*   RESPONSIBLE PROGRAMMER: H. R. DURAND                                                  *
*                                                                                         *
*   EXTERNAL REFERENCES —                                                                 *
*                                                                                         *
*     MODULES CALLED: NONE.                                                               *
*                                                                                         *
*     MACROS USED:      GETM — TO OBTAIN INTERNAL MESSAGE NUMBER                          *
*                                                                                         *
*     DATA AREAS:       MSGPOOL — CONTAINS INTERNAL MESSAGE NUMBERS                       *
*                                                                                         *
*                       TERMQUE — POOL OF FIFO QUEUE ACTIVITY INDICATORS                  *
*                                                                                         *
*                       BUFPOOL — I/O BUFFER POOL                                         *
*                                                                                         *
*   DEPENDENCIES: NONE.                                                                   *
*                                                                                         *
*   RESTRICTIONS:  NO MESSAGE CAN EXCEED 64 CHARACTERS. MESSAGES THAT ARE                 *
*                  TOO LONG WILL BE TRUNCATED ON THE RIGHT.                               *
*                                                                                         *
*                  THE MESSAGE TEXT AREA MUST BEGIN ON A FULL WORD                        *
*                  BOUNDARY.                                                              *
*                                                                                         *
*   LINKAGE CONVENTIONS —                                                                 *
*                                                                                         *
*     AT ENTRY, R12 CONTAINS RETURN ADDRESS.                                              *
*               R14 CONTAINS ADDRESS OF MESSAGE TEXT AREA.                                *
*     AT EXIT, R12 AND R14 ARE SAME AS AT ENTRY.                                          *
*               R15 CONTAINS RETURN CODE, AS FOLLOWS:                                     *
*                   0 — MESSAGE ROUTED                                                    *
*                   2 — INVALID CHARACTER IN MESSAGE TEXT                                 *
*                   4 — TERMINAL QUEUE NOT AVAILABLE                                      *
*                   8 — TERMINAL QUEUE NOT AVAILABLE: RETRY                               *
*                                                                                         *
*   CHANGE ACTIVITY:                                                                      *
*                                                                                         *
*     EXPAND MAXIMUM MESSAGE LENGTH TO 64, 02/02/78, M. M. LANCER                         *
*                                                                                         *
* * * * * * * * * * * * * * * * * * * * * * * * * * * * * * * * * * * * * * * * * * * * * *
```

Figure 7–8   A module prolog

OTHER INTERNAL PROGRAM
DOCUMENTATION

There is perhaps at least some truth to the statement, "The better the code, the less the need for comments." Putting it another way, we ask: What techniques can be used to make a program self-documenting? Our goal is not simply to minimize the need for comments but rather to maximize the usefulness of the program.

Choosing Names for Variables

A basic, easily applied but vitally important programming technique is the use of meaningful names for variables. A wisely chosen variable name is an invaluable mnemonic (memory aid) for the programmer and for others who must understand the code.

Looking back at Figure 7-6, we see that two variable names are used: A and I. The names do not tell us much. In contrast, we might suspect that the names VOL and R in Figure 7-7 are clues to meanings. The comments confirm our suspicions: they tell us that VOL and R stand for cylinder volume and cylinder radius, respectively. Since these names are now meaningful to us, we should be able to remember how they are used as we examine this (or even a much longer) program.

Another technique worth remembering here is: Choose variable names that will not be confused. It is not the computer we need to worry about, but rather the humans again: the programmer, a keypunch operator, a co-worker who checks the program logic by reading the program listing, or another programmer responsible for modifications at a later time. What is the likelihood that NOS will be confused with NO5, or COP with CØP, if both members of such similar pairs are used in a program? Too often, the letter S looks like the numeral 5, the letter L looks like the numeral 1, 2 looks like Z, and so on. Whether the letter O or the numeral 0 is slashed when writing code varies, not only from one installation to another but also from programmer to programmer within the same environment. Many programmers find it safest to avoid using numerals in variable names altogether. Other error-prone usages to be avoided are:

- names that differ only by one letter; BKAR and BPAR
- names that differ only at the end; VALU and VALUM
- names that are commonly misspelled in ordinary English; RECEIPT, DEBIT, VOLUME
- names that sound alike; PADE and PAID
- names that have similar meanings; INPUT and INVAL

- names that have ordinary meanings differing from their program usage; TRUE (say, for total revenue under escrow) or MARY (for maximum amount received yearly).

In general, the free interspersing of blanks in variable names is unwise, even if the language-processor program allows it (as do most FORTRAN compilers). On the other hand, separator characters such as the hyphen in COBOL (IN-RATE) and the break character in PL/I (IN_RATE) can be very effective guides to understanding. It is also wise not to use key words of the programming language as variable names, even if they are not reserved words, according to strict rules of the language. In COBOL, key words are generally reserved words, but PL/I permits even statement verbs such as DECLARE and WRITE to be chosen as identifiers.

Use of Declaratives

Another point to be made about variable names is that it is good programming practice to declare them. In FORTRAN, unless explicity stated otherwise, any variable whose name begins with I, J, K, L, M, or N is assumed to be of type INTEGER; a variable whose name begins with any other letter is assumed to be of type REAL. Strictly speaking, if the programmer is satisfied with the assumption that a compiler will make (called a *default*) on the basis of a variable name, he need not explicitly declare that name in a program. But if he fails to do so, other readers of the program have no easy way to determine which variable names are used and for what purposes.

In PL/I, the situation is more complex and there are more pitfalls. For example, a PL/I variable name may carry with it defaults for scope, storage class, type, mode, base, scale, and precision attributes. But the programmer who attempts to take advantage of these defaults has much to remember. If a name does not appear in any DECLARE statement, it is assumed to be arithmetic (type). Further, if it begins with one of the letters from I through N, it is assumed to be real (mode), binary (base), fixed-point (scale). However, if a name beginning with one of the letters from I through N does appear in a DECLARE statement and any arithmetic attributes other than base (but not base) are specified for it, it is assumed to be decimal. In either case, if no precision attribute is specified, the default precision value depends on the compiler in use.

Unfortunately, the programmer who believes he remembers defaults may not remember them accurately. (Many programmers agree that specifying all attributes for a data item is at least as easy, if not easier, than remembering what happens when some or all of them are not specified.) A reader who is not well-versed in PL/I can hardly be expected to remember all defaults. And good programmers write with potential readers of their code, including themselves, in mind.

Program Formats

Another observable difference between the programs in Figures 7–6 and 7–7 is that in the latter, attention has been given to program format. The physical layout of a program can and should help the reader to understand its logical structure. An advantage of many high-level programming languages is that they are *free-format languages*. This means that they do not require strict column positioning of the source-program text, permit any number of blanks wherever one blank is permitted (or ignore blanks altogether), permit a single statement to be split over several lines, and so on. The programmer who uses these languages can employ indention, alignment, and spacing in ways that help others to read and understand the code.

```
C              THIS PROGRAM READS THE NUMBERS OF PARTS AND THEIR COLORS.
C              IT COUNTS PARTS OF FOUR SPECIFIC COLORS, RECOGNIZES A
C              ZERO PART NUMBER AS AN END-OF-FILE INDICATOR, AND
C              PRINTS THE COUNT FOR EACH COLOR.
C
               INTEGER PART, COLOR, EOFC, COL(4), COUNT(4)
               DATA COL(1), COL(2), /'BLA', 'RED'/
               DATA COL(3), COL(4), /'BLU', 'YEL'/
               DATA EOFC /'0000'/
C
               DO 20 I = 1,4
                  COUNT(I) = 0
        20     CONTINUE
        90     READ (5,100) PART, COLOR
       100     FORMAT (A4, 5X, A3)
               IF (PART.EQ.EOFC) GO TO 290
                  DO 120 I = 1,4
                     IF (COLOR.NE.COL(I)) GO TO 120
                        COUNT(I) = COUNT(I) + 1
                        GO TO 90
       120        CONTINUE
C
C              LIST PARTS OF OTHER COLORS
C
       190     WRITE (6,200) PART, COLOR
       200     FORMAT (' PART ', A4, ' IS ', A3)
               GO TO 90
C
C              ALL INPUT HAS BEEN PROCESSED
C
       290     WRITE (6,300) (COL(I), COUNT(I), I = 1,4)
       300     FORMAT (6X, A3, 4X, I6)
               STOP
               END
```

Figure 7–9   Use of indentions, blank lines, and comments to document logical structure

Consider as another example the FORTRAN coding in Figure 7–9. Here we see additional program formatting conventions in use. Data declaration and initialization statements and comment lines are separated from other program statements by blank lines, which contain only C in position 1. Statements at the same logical level are aligned on the same left margin position. Inner blocks of code such as nested loops formed by inner DO statements are indented further. A 3-position indention per logical level is common. Generally, the text on comment lines follows the indention of the section of code it describes.

For clarity and ease of maintenance, a separate CONTINUE statement can be included as the closing statement of each DO loop in a FORTRAN program, whether or not the program logic and rules of FORTRAN programming actually require it. (See Figure 7–9.) These CONTINUE statements help to emphasize logical structure. They add very little to program compilation time and nothing to program execution time. The same can be said of END statements for DO groups or loops, BEGIN blocks, and PROCEDURE blocks in a PL/I program.

```
PROGA: PROC OPTIONS (MAIN); L1: GET DATA (A,B,C,D); E = B*D/12;
F = C – E; G = B – F; PUT DATA (A,B,E,F,G); GO TO L1; END;
```

Figure 7–10   Use of string format for a PL/I program

```
MORTCALC:      PROCEDURE OPTIONS (MAIN);
/* THIS PROGRAM COMPUTES INTEREST AND PRINCIPAL            */
/* PAYMENTS ON A LOAN.                                     */
/*                                                         */
               DCL MORNUM  CHAR (06),
                   OBAL     DEC FIXED (9,2),
                   PAYMT    DEC FIXED (9,2),
                   RATE     DEC FIXED (3),
                   CHARGE   DEC FIXED (9,2),
                   PRIN     DEC FIXED (9,2),
                   NBAL     DEC FIXED (9,2);
               ON ENDFILE GO TO LASTCARD;
/*                                                         */
NEXTCARD:      GET DATA (MORNUM, OBAL, PAYMT, RATE);
               CHARGE = OBAL * RATE/12;
               PRIN    = PAYMT – CHARGE;
               NBAL    = OBAL – PRIN;
               PUT DATA (MORNUM, OBAL, CHARGE, PRIN, NBAL);
               GO TO NEXTCARD;
/*                                                         */
/* END OF INPUT                                            */
/*                                                         */
LASTCARD:      PUT LIST ('END OF JOB') SKIP (3);
               END;
```

Figure 7–11   A qualitative representation of the solution algorithm

If a statement is to be continued on two or more coding lines, the second and succeeding lines of the continued statement should be indented further than the first line. Generally, any number of spaces may be employed for the indention, provided that (1) the level of indention for continuation is different from that used for logical indentions, and (2) the same uniform level is employed consistently to indicate continuation wherever it occurs throughout the program.

Some high-level languages, notably PL/I, permit multiple statements to be written on a single coding line as shown in Figure 7-10. Obviously, indiscriminate use of this capability tends to mask program statements. It makes program maintenance difficult or inconvenient when changes to statements, reorderings, or insertions are required. A more readable program is shown in Figure 7-11. We can see clearly that the principal and interest payments on a mortgage loan are being calculated and printed out.

VIRTUAL ENVIRONMENTS

As stated in Chapter 2, at least some parts of the major operating-system control program are resident in primary storage whenever an EDP system is in use. Applications programs are loaded into primary storage as needed to solve specific user problems. In some systems, two or more applications programs may be resident in primary storage at the same time. Since the CPU can execute only one instruction at a time, simultaneous execution of instructions from different programs is not possible. However, the CPU can execute instructions from one program, then instructions from another program, then instructions from the first program again, and so on. This type of processing is called *concurrent* processing. The system is said to have *multiprogramming* capabilities.

Programs that run concurrently in an EDP system compete for available resources. Not uncommonly, the primary-storage space available within the system is a limiting factor. It determines not only the number of programs that can be active but also the amount of data that can be kept in primary storage for their use. Virtual-storage capabilities, which we mentioned briefly in Chapter 2, have been developed to help remove or eliminate this limitation.

The term *virtual* means "not in actual fact." It follows that *virtual storage* means storage that does not in actual fact exist. Fundamentally, virtual-storage capabilities give the programmer the illusion of a primary storage with characteristics different from those of the underlying physical storage. Generally, the significant difference is that the virtual storage is much larger. The EDP system itself maintains this illusion through a combination of hardware and software techniques. Each instruction of a program must be resident in primary storage before it can be executed, but not all parts of a program have to be resident in primary storage at any given time. The system keeps some portion of an executing program in primary storage, but other portions of the program may be on secondary storage only. Through the virtual-storage addressing schemes and structured organization of storage space, both instructions and data can be loaded into primary storage very quickly when referred to by other instructions executed within the program.

There are various ways of implementing virtual-storage capabilities. The principal methods are *segmentation*, in which each program's address space (range of storage locations referenced by the program) is split into variable-size blocks (segments), and *paging*, in which physical storage space is divided into fixed-size physical blocks (page frames) and programs and data are divided into blocks (pages) of the same size. Thus, one page of information can be loaded into one page frame.

Segmentation involves breaking a program into logically separable units. For example, one segment may be a subroutine; another may be a data area. If an executing program tries to reference a segment that is not in primary storage, the systems software intervenes and brings the segment into primary storage. Under paging, a program is broken into pages of uniform length. The length of the pages is determined by the characteristics of the hardware rather than by program logic. The page size may be very small, say, space for 256 characters, or very large, say, 2K or 4K (where K = 1024) bytes. (See Figure 7–12.)

A segmentation and paging system attempts to combine the best features of both segmentation and paging. Programs are first broken into logical segments by systems software. Each segment that exceeds the uniform page size is in turn broken into pages for loading and execution on the computer. The IBM System/370 virtual-storage operating systems (DOS/VS, OS/VS1, and OS/VS2) and the Multics operating system implemented on GE 645 computers are examples of segmentation and paging implementations.

The concept of virtual storage has been extended to include the concept of *virtual machines*, or virtual computer systems. Thus, several different complete configurations of computers can be simulated on a single EDP system. This concept relies heavily not only on hardware and software but also on firmware, or microprogramming, to tailor the basic operations of the computer in use. With virtual-machine capabilities, for example, fully checked-out programs can be run in one system environment, while programs under test are run in another. An operating system originally designed for another computer can be set up on a tailored virtual machine, and programs written to execute under that operating system can be run without change in the simulated environment. Meanwhile, programs originally developed for the computer in use can be run in another virtual machine on the computer at the same time.

An important question for the programmer to ask is: How does the knowledge that a program will be run in a virtual environment affect the design and coding of that program? One response is: Not excessively. Many of the details of virtual-storage manipulation are handled automatically by

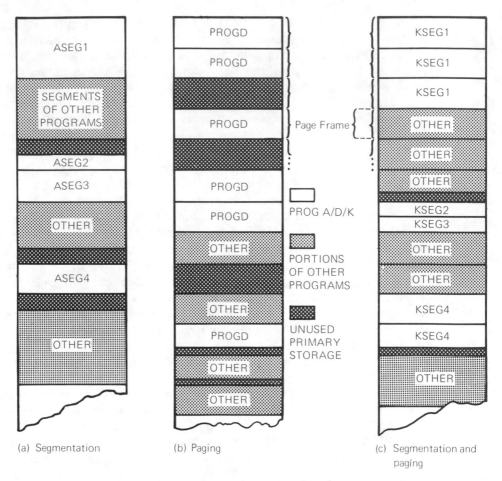

Figure 7-12   Systems techniques for implementing virtual storage

hardware and software within the EDP system; these details need not concern applications programmers. Since there is, for all practical purposes, no limit on program size, the programmer need not be overly concerned with whether a program is too large for the primary-storage space that will be available for it at execution time.

If the EDP system uses segmentation, programs should be designed and coded so that individual segments are neither too large nor too small. Segments that are too large take too much time when being moved to or from primary storage. Segments that are too small involve too many moves. But there is no absolute "too large" or "too small." What is acceptable in one EDP-system environment may not be acceptable in another. Programming practices must vary accordingly.

A program to be run in a system that uses paging should be coded so that its size is approximately a multiple of the fixed page size. Otherwise, a significant portion of the page frame holding the last page of the program will be wasted whenever that page occupies primary storage. Frequently exercised subroutines and the data they use should be grouped together, in the probable sequence of use, so that they fall within the same page or minimal number of pages. Error-handling and other exception-condition routines should be grouped apart from the main line of the program. When using a high-level programming language with subprogram capabilities, often-used subprograms should be positioned near the program that calls them. This increases the likelihood that when the calling program is loaded into storage, the subprograms will be loaded also. If a short subprogram is used only once or twice, it should be included as part of the program rather than called as a subprogram. A possible example here is a square root or log routine.

In general, programs to be run in a virtual environment should not be self-modifying; that is, they should not operate on their own instructions as data. Stored-program instructions that have not been modified can simply be overlaid when other stored-program instructions or data must be loaded into the primary-storage locations they occupy. If they have been modified, however, they must first be written out to virtual storage so that they are available in that form when next required. The more system processing of this type required, the slower the overall performance of the EDP system as seen by its users.

QUESTIONS

Q1. (a) Distinguish between the work of a programmer and that of a coder. (b) Which type of position is more interesting to you? Why?

Q2. (a) Distinguish between procedure-oriented languages and problem-oriented languages. (b) Give examples of each.

Q3. Discuss three aspects of language availability that must be considered when selecting an appropriate language for a programming task.

Q4. (a) Compare and contrast batch-processing and interactive-processing capabilities. (b) Suggest situations where each is more suitable.

Q5. What is a cataloged procedure?

Q6. Give examples of housekeeping procedures required in most programs.

Q7. Support or refute the statement, "The better the code, the less the need for comments."

Q8. What are some of the reasons why it is good programming practice to declare the variable names used in a program?

Q9. What advantages do free-format languages offer?

Q10. (a) Explain the terms *virtual storage* and *virtual machine*. (b) What advantages do these capabilities offer?

EXERCISES

E1. Suggest a language that is apt to be appropriate for each of the following applications. In doing so, give at least one reason for each choice. (a) modeling the business cycle to determine optimal ordering, reordering, and stock quantities, (b) an accounts-receivable system, (c) preparing telephone lists and extracting subsets of them for commercial use, (d) preparing weekly reports for management from an accounts payable file, (e) playing tic-tac-toe, (f) a sorting algorithm, and (g) solving systems of simultaneous linear equations.

E2. Assume that one of your responsibilities as chief programmer on a project to develop a medical information system is to recommend the programming language to be used. Make a list of the factors you would consider in language selection.

E3. List at least six types of documentation useful to the programmer when he begins to actually write a program.

*E4. (a) If a batch-processing system is available to you, prepare the job-control statements needed to compile and execute either a FORTRAN or a COBOL program. (b) If an interactive-processing system is available to you, list the system commands needed to gain access to the system, write a program, then compile and execute that program from a user terminal.

E5. Find a program you have written or one that is otherwise available to you. What evidence can you find that the programming points listed in Figure 7–5 were (or were not) considered in planning the program?

*E6. Find a program that is not well commented. Insert comments as needed to provide essential information about the program.

E7. (a) Are module prologs used in your program-development environment? (b) If so, what installation standards have been developed concerning them? (c) What changes, if any, would you recommend in the standards? (d) If no standards exist, what standards would you recommend? (e) If prologs are not used, summarize the arguments you might use to build a case for including them. (f) Assuming you are successful in E7e, what standards would you recommend?

*E8. Find a program which has no prolog. Create a prolog for it according to the guidelines you agreed to or proposed in E7 above.

E9. Obtain two program listings, one which shows wise use of variable names and one which shows poor naming practices. Point out the good and bad usages in each.

E10. List the assumptions that the COBOL, FORTRAN, or similar compiler available to you will make on the basis of variable names if you fail to declare variable names in your programs.

E11. Construct a list of formatting guidelines to be used in your program-development environment.

E12. What guidelines apply to programming for a virtual environment?

REFERENCES

Bulow, Knut. "Programming in Book Format," *Datamation* 20, 10 (Oct 1974): 85–86.

Chapin, Ned. *360/370 Programming in Assembly Language.* 2d ed. New York: McGraw-Hill, 1973 (covers assembler-language programming for System/360 and System/370, including operating-system-dependent I/O considerations).

Denning, P. J. "Virtual Memory," *Computing Surveys* (ACM) 2, 3 (Sept 1970): 153–89 (already a classic; the most comprehensive treatment of this subject available).

Dijkstra, E. W. "The Humble Programmer," *Communications of the ACM* 15, 10 (Oct 1972): 859–66 (an eloquent argument for simpler higher-level programming languages; 1972 ACM Turing Award Lecture).

Introduction to Virtual Storage in System/370 — Student Text. IBM Corporation manual (GR20-4260). White Plains, N.Y., n.d.

Kennedy, Michael, and Martin B. Solomen. *Ten Statement Fortran plus Fortran IV.* 2d ed. Englewood Cliffs, N.J.: Prentice-Hall, 1975 (shading is used effectively to bring out good programming practices; basic computer concepts, modular programming, and debugging are among topics covered in appendices).

Kernighan, Brian W., and P. J. Plauger. *The Elements of Programming Style.* New York: McGraw-Hill, 1974 (teaches good programming practices by showing "real" (PL/I and FORTRAN) programs, discussing their shortcomings, rewriting them in a better way, and drawing a general rule from each specific case).

_____ . "Programming Style: Examples and Counterexamples," *Computing Surveys* (ACM) 6, 4 (Dec 1974): 303–19. This issue is devoted to *programming* with additional articles "Guest Editor's Overview," by P. J. Denning; "Programming and Documenting Software Projects," by P. J. Brown; "On the Composition of Well-Structured Programs," by N. Wirth; "An Overview of Programming Practices," by J. M. Yohe; and "Structured Programming with Go To Statements," by D. E. Knuth (contains 102 references).

Knuth, D. E. *The Art of Computer Programming: Fundamental Algorithms.* Vol. 1. Reading, Mass.: Addison-Wesley, 1968 (the first volume of a series of sophisticated mathematical treatments of basic topics in computer science; already a classic).

Myers, G. J. "Composite Design Facilities of Six Programming Languages," *IBM Systems Journal* 15, 3 (Sept 1976): 212–24.

Pratt, Terrance W. *Programming Languages: Design and Implementation.* Englewood Cliffs, N.J.: Prentice-Hall, 1975 (emphasizes fundamental programming-language concepts and describes FORTRAN, ALGOL 60, COBOL, PL/I, LISP 1.5, SNOBOL4, and APL in terms of them).

Sammet, Jean E. *Programming Languages: History and Fundamentals.* Englewood Cliffs, N.J.: Prentice-Hall, 1969 (develops a detailed framework for comparing languages; then uses it to provide details on almost every high-level language developed up to 1969; a comprehensive, highly regarded reference work).

8

STRUCTURED PROGRAMMING

What is structured programming? A major technological advancement to be ranked with the development of subroutines, or high-level programming languages, or even the stored-program concept? A panacea to cure all programming ills? A road map to error-free code? A new set of rules and procedures that all programmers must follow? Or just a new name for techniques that good programmers have been using for years?

With little effort, we could probably find computer professionals who are willing to support or refute each of these claims. If the current level of interest, attention, and controversy is any indication, structured programming is indeed an idea whose time has come. As part of our very practical study of programming, it behooves us to explore this topic further.

HISTORICAL BACKGROUND

No one "invented" structured programming. A few people have, however, contributed significantly to its development. As early as 1965, Professor E. W. Dijkstra of the Netherlands suggested that the GOTO (or, GO TO) construct could be eliminated from programming languages. In 1968, in his now-famous "GOTO letter," he tried to show that programs written using a definite structuring technique were easier to write, read, and debug, and were more likely to be correct. He voiced some of his ideas about top-down systems design, which seemed to go hand-in-hand with structure in programming, in a paper presented at the First ACM Symposium on Operating Systems Principles. At about the same time, he attended the NATO-sponsored Software Engineering Conference and described some of his ideas in the 1969 issue of *Software Engineering Techniques.**

As long as the idea of imposing a structure in programming (i.e., structured programming) appeared to be a theoretical issue, few computer professionals paid much attention to it. But other significant events were happening elsewhere. At the same Software Engineering Conference at which Dijkstra presented his ideas on structured programming, Joel Aron of IBM described an experiment known as the "superprogrammer project." In this experiment, Dr. Harlan Mills and a team of coworkers undertook to do in six months what appeared to be a 30-person-year effort. New ideas in project organization were suggested, and top-down systems design and programming were emphasized. A follow-on project of a much larger scale was IBM's development of an information retrieval system for *The New York Times.* Now mentioned frequently in computer literature, this project was used as a proving ground for a new form of project organization and management: the chief programmer team concept, which we discussed in Chapter 3. This approach was closely twined with and directly related to the programming-technologies used in the project: top-down design and structured programming.

Structured programming can be viewed as the pulling together, or synthesization, of such ideas as program modularity and top-down design, and the concrete representation of them at the program-coding level. It is a manner of coding and organizing programs that makes them easier to understand, to test, and to modify. Results have demonstrated that, employed together with other improved programming technologies, it can lead to spectacular increases in programmer productivity and correspondingly spectacular decreases in the error rate of resultant code. Other projects within IBM and elsewhere have adopted the chief programmer team/top-down design/structured programming approach to program development. Universities, research organizations, and software development firms are striving to gain practical experience with structured programming.

GOTO-LESS PROGRAMMING

As we have just seen, when Professor Dijkstra first discussed structured programming, he spoke against the use of GOTO statements. In doing so, he used the phrase *GOTO statements* as a generic term meaning unconditional branches, or, stated more formally, unconditional transfers of control. Professor Dijkstra argued that the blatant use of GOTO statements resulted in

---

*Specific entries in the bibliography at the end of this chapter give publication information for the three writings of Professor Dijkstra referred to here. References to other writings elsewhere in the chapter are also explained further in the bibliography.

unnecessarily complex control paths leading to difficult debugging on the part of programmers. His suggestion was to avoid GOTO statements as much as possible.

As we will continue to see, structured programming is a *philosophy* of writing programs according to a certain set of rules in order to achieve a certain set of objectives. One *technique* that can be employed in doing so is the elimination of GOTO statements and the replacement of them by other well-structured branching and control statements. Unfortunately, upon first encounter, the implementation technique is much easier to understand than the underlying philosophy. Very often, there is a tendency to conclude that structured programming consists simply of eliminating GOTO statements. So let us look first at what is really behind this action.

One fundamental problem with the GOTO statement is that excessive use of this statement and of statement labels (symbolic names or statement numbers, identifying branch targets) is a hallmark of undisciplined design. We might well ask how carefully or thoroughly the programmer thought out the program logic before beginning to code. If he really planned the overall flow of program control beforehand, why should frequent, apparently random jumps be needed to get from where we are to where we should be next?

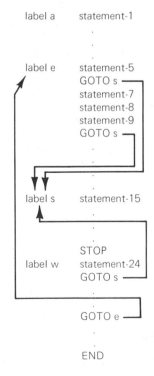

Figure 8-1   Flow of control in an unstructured program

The jumps in a program contribute significantly to its real or apparent complexity. And program complexity has been shown to be both a symptom and a cause of errors in code.

Another problem is that excessive use of GOTO statements tends to obscure the program logic, to hide it from those who must understand what the program does and how it does it (say, for testing or for changing or adding functions at a later time). Tracing the flow of program control is next to impossible if there are many potential paths from one point in a program to another. We know we are at statement-15 but did we get to here from statement-6 or statement-10 or statement-25? (See Figure 8-1.) Any attempt to understand the program listing is frustrated by the fact that we read the first few statements, jump ahead to a statement on page 10 and read a few more, turn back to a statement on page 3 and read a few more, and so on. After four or five maneuvers of this type, we have forgotten both where we started and why we are where we are. Even when such code appears to be correct, and even when we think we understand it, we cannot make a modification to the program at a certain point without having to worry about unintentional side effects on the program logic elsewhere. Our only safe course is to stand pat — to avoid the risk of introducing new errors into the code.

In contrast, when excessive, random use of GOTO statements is eliminated, there is a much better correspondence between what the programmer sees (the program listing) and what the computer is supposed to do (the programmer's statements translated, individual program modules linked together, and the resultant machine-language code loaded into primary storage and executed). This closer relationship between the static placement of statements and the dynamic flow of control during program execution can be very helpful when we are trying to understand the program. (See Figure 8-2.)

If a program is written using only the three basic patterns, or control structures, of structured programming (explained below), the program listing can literally be read from top to bottom, or from beginning to end — just like a book. There is no branching back to some preceding statement or otherwise jumping around to any of numerous points in the program. When we

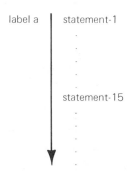

Figure 8-2   Flow of control in a structured program

get to statement-15 in the program listing, the computer has done what comes before and it has not done what comes after. This is generally not true for unstructured programs.

A key point to be grasped here is that to treat the elimination of GOTO statements as a major goal of structured programming is getting the matter backwards. The real situation is that when the basic patterns of structured programming are used correctly, there is no need for undisciplined, random use of GOTOs.

It is true, however, that not all common high-level programming languages provide control statements directly analogous to all the basic patterns of structured programming. With these, disciplined use of GOTOs is necessary to set up the control structures. (We say more about this later.) In addition, some programmers argue that there are occasional situations where considerations of efficiency or clarity dictate the use of GOTO statements. Some organizations have developed programming standards for their installations that permit use of GOTOs, but only in certain ways; for example, only to branch forward in code. In any case, the programmer should avoid unnecessary branches. Stated simply, a general guideline here is: If you feel you must use GOTO statements, use them sparingly.

BASIC CONTROL STRUCTURES

The theoretical framework for structured programming is usually traced to a paper by Bohm and Jacopini, initially published in Italian in 1965, then republished in English in the May 1966 *Communications of the ACM.* Their "structure theorem" is a proof that any algorithm can be expressed using only three basic building blocks: (1) a process box; (2) a binary decision mechanism, usually referred to as an if-then-else; and (3) a loop mechanism. (See Figure 8–3.) Note that each of these structures is characterized by a single point of entrance into the structure and a single point of exit from it. The process box may be thought of as a single statement or as a properly combined sequence of statements having only one entry and one exit. The if-then-else mechanism indicates that a test is made during execution and the outcome determines which of two alternative control paths is followed. The loop mechanism indicates that a test is made and, depending on the result of the test, either an immediate exit from the structure occurs or a set of one or more statements is executed and then the test is made again. The fact that the constructs in Figures 8–3b and 8–3c have only one entry and one exit is significant: they can themselves be thought of as process boxes.

The basic patterns of structured programming are:

SIMPLE SEQUENCE: Statements are executed in the order in which they appear, with control passing unconditionally from one statement to the next. This pattern is so simple that it hardly needs mentioning, but it is necessary for the construction of an algorithm. As we saw in Chapter 3, algorithmic problem solving is achieved via a series of steps carried out in the order specified.

IFTHENELSE: IF p THEN c ELSE d.

The condition p is tested. If p is true, the statement c is executed and the statement d is skipped. Otherwise, the statement c is skipped and the statement d is executed. Control passes to the next statement. This is, of course, the if-then-else mechanism of Figure 8–3b. Note that each "statement" may be a single state-

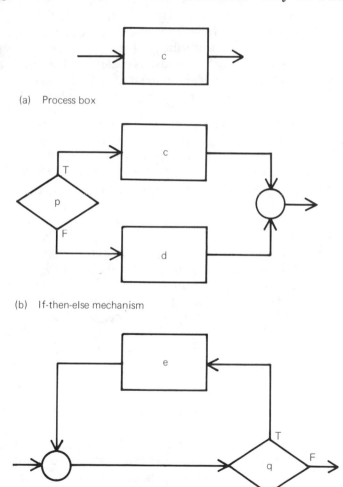

(a)   Process box

(b)   If-then-else mechanism

(c)   Loop mechanism

Figure 8–3   Basic building blocks

ment. It may also be a simple sequence of statements combined in some fashion to form a basic pattern that can be treated as a single statement. This is true for each of the patterns we shall discuss. We use the connector symbol as a collector in Figure 8–3b to emphasize that the IFTHENELSE pattern has only one entry and one exit. When used as a collector, this symbol always has two flowlines entering and one exit flowline.

DOWHILE: DO e WHILE q.

The condition q is tested. If q is true, the statement e is executed and control returns to the test of q. If q is false, then e is skipped and control passes to the next statement. This is the loop mechanism of Figure 8–3c. We have here a leading-decision loop: the test occurs immediately upon entering the loop and what follows within the loop is executed only if the tested condition is true. Therefore, the complete loop may never be executed. If the tested condition is false, the loop is exited immediately following the test.

Now that we have looked at these basic patterns, let us look again at the significance of the building block concept of Bohm and Jacopini. As we pointed out, each of the basic building blocks can be treated as a process box. This means that a block of statements forming one of the other constructs can be substituted wherever a process box, or single statement, can appear in a program. A block can consist of only a single statement, or it can consist of a sequence of single statements, or it can contain other blocks that in turn contain other blocks as part of their structure. We say that the contained structures are *nested*. (See Figure 8–4 for example.) A complete module or program can be built up in this way. The program itself can then be viewed as a single structure. A program having only one entry point and one exit point, and in which, for every structure, there exists a path from entry to exit which includes it, is called a *proper program*.

The reverse of this building-block process is also possible. That is, we can start with a single process box and break that box into a lower level of structures. Some or all of these component structures can be broken into still lower-level structures, and so on. We continue until we have reached the level of atomic (basic-building-block) structures: single statements, if-then-else mechanisms, and leading-decision loops — our SIMPLE SEQUENCE, IFTHENELSE, and DOWHILE. This is precisely the top-down design approach that we have already discussed. (See Chapter 4.)

Note also the relationship between the nested structure concept above and the modularity concept discussed in Chapter 4. A program that consists of only these basic building blocks is modular in the true sense. Any of the one-in/one-out constructs can be replaced by a functionally equivalent construct without affecting the rest of the program. And the concept of modularity is carried down to the lowest level possible within the program.

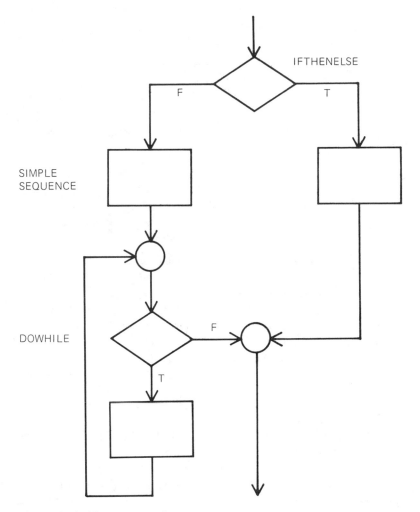

Figure 8-4   Nested control structures

PSEUDO CODE

Figure 8-5 shows a flowchart for a structured program that reads individual records from a card reader as input and writes the contents of the records to a printer as output. It assumes that a card containing only 9s has been placed as the last card in the input deck to serve as a special, or dummy, record indicating end-of-file.

The program in Figure 8-5 meets the structured program criterion of comprising only basic control structures. You should be able to detect several examples of SIMPLE SEQUENCE and one DOWHILE. Because the program has only one entry and one exit, we can call it a proper program.

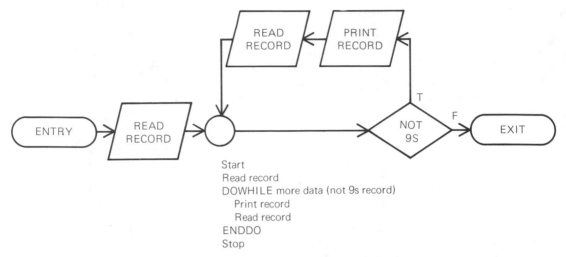

```
Start
Read record
DOWHILE more data (not 9s record)
   Print record
   Read record
ENDDO
Stop
```

Figure 8-5   A structured read-and-print program

Notice the correspondence between the program flowchart and the paragraph of text in Figure 8–5. The text is an informal method of expressing structured-programming logic, usually known as *pseudo code*. This pseudo code presents the logic of the program in an easy-to-read, top-to-bottom fashion. It is similar to some high-level programming languages (such as FORTRAN and PL/I), but it does not impose strict rules such as we must be willing to follow when actually writing a program. For emphasis and clarity, the key words of the DOWHILE pattern (DOWHILE and ENDDO) are written in uppercase letters. The lines describing functions within the DOWHILE pattern are indented three spaces from the left-hand margin.

Figure 8-6 depicts the logic of a program that reads input records. It adds 1 to a count for each record containing a code value of A, but subtracts 1 from that count for each record not containing A. When a special 9s record indicating end-of-file is encountered, the current value of the count is written as output. Then program execution is terminated.

It is not so easy to tell just by looking at this program flowchart whether or not it depicts a structured program. (Even an experienced programmer might draw such a flowchart, then wonder whether or not he had structured the program.) Therefore, pseudo code that describes the program logic is also shown in Figure 8-6. The pseudo code includes SIMPLE SEQUENCE constructs and a DOWHILE pattern containing two nested structures: an IF-THENELSE pattern and a SIMPLE SEQUENCE (the IFTHENELSE pattern followed by Read record). A general guideline here is that nesting of patterns to any number of levels is permissible, provided that each nested pattern is wholly contained within the control structure that includes it. (For example, the Add 1 to count step could be replaced by another IFTHENELSE pattern or a DOWHILE pattern if desired, and so on.)

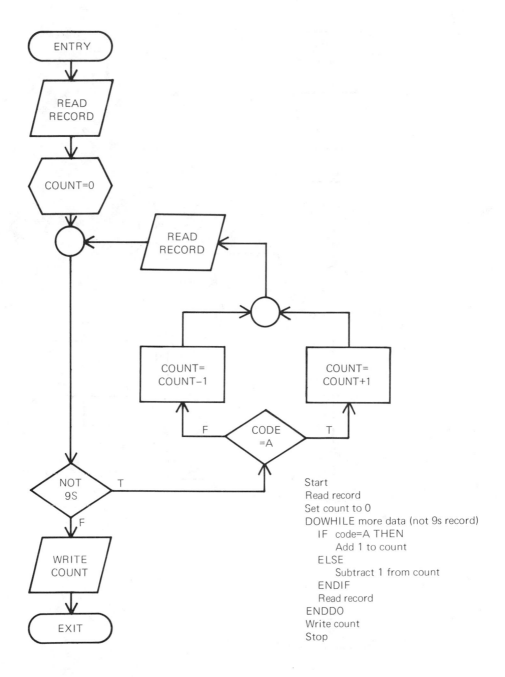

Figure 8-6 A structured program with nested IFTHENELSE and SIMPLE SEQUENCE patterns

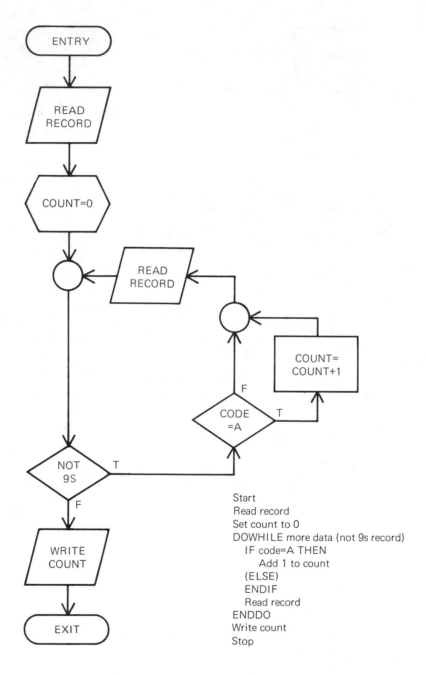

```
Start
Read record
Set count to 0
DOWHILE more data (not 9s record)
  IF code=A THEN
    Add 1 to count
  (ELSE)
  ENDIF
  Read record
ENDDO
Write count
Stop
```

Figure 8-7 A structured program with nested IFTHENELSE pattern having a null ELSE

Notice carefully the key words of the IFTHENELSE pattern. Notice also the levels of indention. Without indention we would not be able to see the nesting easily. As before, we read the pseudo code from top to bottom; there are no GOTO statements that cause us to jump about in the code.

Figure 8–7 shows another example of structured-programming logic. It introduces one new idea: the "no-function condition," usually called a *null ELSE*. When the tested condition of the IFTHENELSE pattern (CODE=A, in this case) is true, we follow the true (T) control path. When the tested condition is not true, no special alternative function is required. Thus, the false (F) control path goes directly to the collector closing the IFTHEN-ELSE. In pseudo code, the no-function condition is represented by enclosing the key word ELSE in parentheses.

ADDITIONAL, COMBINED CONTROL STRUCTURES

By now, we are at least beginning to "think structured." We have acquired some familiarity with the basic patterns, which are sufficient for any program. Because certain combinations of these basic patterns have proven to be especially useful, they are given special attention in most discussions of structured programming. One is the combination of SIMPLE SEQUENCE and DOWHILE known as a *DOUNTIL control structure.* (See Figure 8–8.)

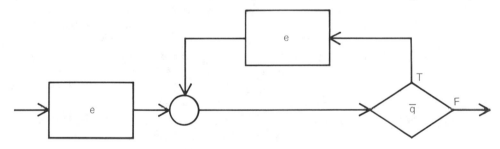

(a)   SIMPLE SEQUENCE and DOWHILE

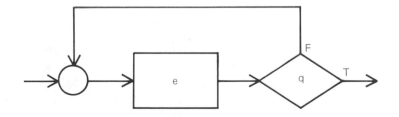

(b)   DOUNTIL

Figure 8–8   The logic of DOUNTIL

Part a in Figure 8–8 shows the program logic that we want to set up. It says: "do e once, then test for the condition not q (indicated by q with a line over it, or q̄). Continue to *do* e *while* the condition q̄ is true." Note that when the condition q̄ is false, we have not q̄—therefore, q! If you find this negative logic confusing, do not be discouraged. That is a common reaction. And it is precisely why many programmers prefer to abandon the construction in Figure 8–8, part a, in favor of the equivalent DOUNTIL control structure in part b. It says: "*do* e *until* the condition q is true."

When using this logic in an ordinary situation, we might say, for example, for part a: "Make one cheese sandwich. Continue to make (*do*) cheese sandwiches *while* you are *not* too tired to do so." Putting it another way for part b, we might say: "*After* you have made one cheese sandwich, continue to make (*do*) cheese sandwiches *until* you are too tired to do so."

A very important point to remember about the DOUNTIL control structure is that it sets up a trailing-decision loop. No matter what the outcome of the test within the loop, we *always* perform the function that precedes the test once before we even make the test. How many more times we perform the function depends on the outcomes of any successive tests, which are continued until the loop is exited when the tested condition is known to be true.

Now assume that we are to write a structured program to process accounts receivable. The status of any particular account may be: (1) has a credit balance, (2) neither long nor short (no action needed), (3) payment due, or (4) payment overdue. Try drawing a structured flowchart to show the testing for these conditions, using the control structures we have studied so far. Or, write pseudo code to set up the required program logic. Then compare your work with Figure 8–9, part a.

Maybe you did not include the OTHER routine. That is not critical to this discussion, but it is the kind of situation that most programmers soon learn to allow for (the case that can never happen, but does). You may have used a sequence of DOWHILE structures. That approach can work, but the IFTHENELSE is more appropriate, because DOWHILE provides for looping, which is unnecessary in this case. Also, with DOWHILE, once we have performed the routine required, we go on and check the conditions of any remaining DOWHILEs anyway—this also is unnecessary here.

Even though the nested IFTHENELSE structures seem to meet our needs in this example, if you used them you probably found them difficult to work with and had to proceed very carefully to avoid making errors. And what if there were 10, or even 100, possible conditions? Obviously, many pages of flowcharting, or an unmanageable number of pseudo code indentions, would be required. Therefore, we choose to replace the nested IFTHENELSE structures with a *CASE control structure.* (See Figure 8–9, part b.) CASE is really a generalization of the IFTHENELSE pattern, extending it from a two-valued to a multiple-valued operation. Now that we understand

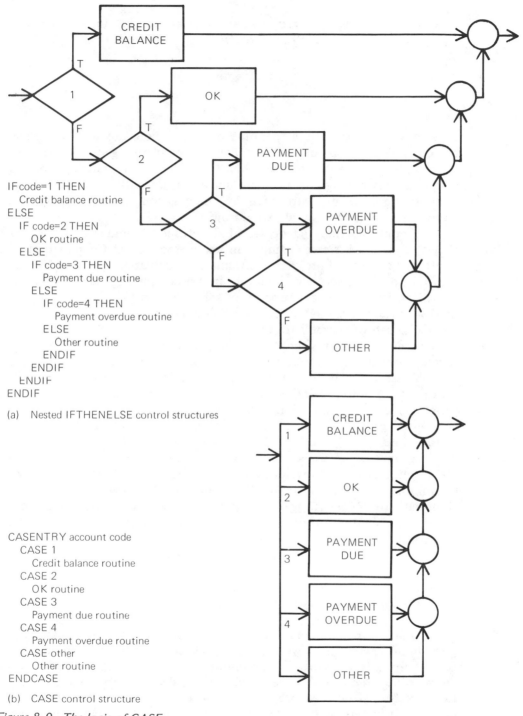

IF code=1 THEN
   Credit balance routine
ELSE
  IF code=2 THEN
    OK routine
  ELSE
   IF code=3 THEN
     Payment due routine
   ELSE
    IF code=4 THEN
      Payment overdue routine
    ELSE
     Other routine
    ENDIF
   ENDIF
  ENDIF
ENDIF

(a)   Nested IFTHENELSE control structures

CASENTRY account code
   CASE 1
     Credit balance routine
   CASE 2
     OK routine
   CASE 3
     Payment due routine
   CASE 4
     Payment overdue routine
   CASE other
     Other routine
ENDCASE

(b)   CASE control structure

Figure 8-9 The logic of CASE

how this structure is derived, we can use it in flowcharting or specify its key words (CASENTRY, CASE, and ENDCASE) as shown in part b when writing pseudo code.

FLOWCHARTING

This may be a good time to point out that there are wide differences of opinion regarding the use of flowcharts when planning structured programs. In this chapter, we have used ANSI standard flowcharting symbols as a means of visualizing the program logic set up within the structured-programming control structures. This approach is convenient, because it enables us to build upon what we already know.

In contrast, many advocates of structured programming have suggested that the standard flowcharting symbols introduced in Chapter 5 are inadequate for structured-program planning. A wide variety of new flowcharting symbols, devised especially for structured programming, have been proposed. At this writing, there is no one set of symbols that has gained widespread approval although some software-development groups have agreed upon particular sets of symbols for use at their installations.

Some advocates of improved programming technologies feel that structured programming is self-explanatory and need not be accompanied by flowcharts. These persons usually point out that a flowchart often fails to represent the current status of a program. Even flowcharts for structured programs can become cumbersome and unwieldly. If a person can write structured programs without flowcharting, he is encouraged to do so at some installations.

To many, the use of an informal language such as pseudo code is a viable alternative to flowcharting. The pseudo code is a means of technical communication at many levels, from managerial review to detailed specifications basic to actual writing of program statements. It permits the programmer to express required program logic unencumbered by programming-language rules and constraints, yet it can be stored in machine-readable form as comments or as part of the program prolog, for documentational purposes.

LANGUAGE IMPLEMENTATION

After a structured program has been planned, it must be expressed in a programming language. As we might expect, some programming languages are better suited to structured programming than others. Those in common use were defined, and most were standardized according to ANSI recommendations, before structured programming received widespread attention. A primary consideration therefore is whether or not programming-language statements directly analogous to the control structures we have described are available in a particular language. If not, they must be simulated; for example, the use of GOTO statements may be necessary to build appropriate DOWHILE or DOUNTIL patterns.

Most of you are apt to be writing programs in PL/I, COBOL, or FORTRAN, so we shall direct most of our attention here to these three languages. Computer professionals generally agree that, of these, PL/I is most suitable for structured programming. It is not unreasonable to expect that the definitions of these and other programming languages will be extended by language designers to include statements that directly facilitate structured programming. But ANSI-sponsored committee meetings, widespread distribution of proposals for review and comment, and formal approval procedures take a very long time. Some software development firms and individual computer users have developed precompiler compilers—language-processor programs that operate on programming-language statements directly analogous to the structured-programming control structures and generate standard programming-language statements in their place. A standard PL/I, COBOL, or FORTRAN compiler can then be used to translate the complete program (including the precompiler-generated statements) to machine-language form.

Our intent here is to suggest how structured programming can be done by using available implementations of these languages; it is not our intent to teach details of any particular language as such. For additional rules concerning the use of specific statements shown, the reader is referred to available programming-language texts or language references manuals.

PL/I

Statements directly analogous to the three basic patterns of structured programming are available in the PL/I programming language. An example of the most fundamental—SIMPLE SEQUENCE—is:

```
GET LIST (ITEM,MIN,QTY,PRICE);
VALUE = QTY * PRICE;
```

This is, of course, the straightforward execution of one statement after another. The general form of this construct in PL/I is:

```
statement-A;
statement-B;
```

Look now at the table in Figure 8-10. The structured-programming control structures are listed and represented in pseudo code in the leftmost column of this table. Analogous general forms for PL/I are shown in the second column from the left, beginning with SIMPLE SEQUENCE as we have

Pseudo Code	PL/I

```
SIMPLE SEQUENCE                          statement-A;
   A                                     statement-B;
   B

IFTHENELSE                               IF p THEN
   IF p THEN                                statement-A;
      A                                  ELSE
   ELSE                                     statement-B;
      B
   ENDIF


DOWHILE                                  DO WHILE (p);
   DOWHILE p                                statement-F;
      F                                  END;
   ENDDO


                                         DCL TESTVAR BIT(1);
DOUNTIL                                  TESTVAR = '1'B;
   DOUNTIL p                             DO WHILE (TESTVAR);
      F                                     statement-F;
   ENDDO                                    IF p THEN
                                               TESTVAR = '0'B;
                                            ELSE;
                                         END;

CASE                                     DCL CASE (1:N) LABEL INITIAL
   CASENTRY selection                       (CASE1,CASE2,...,CASEN),
      CASE 1                                CASE_MAX FIXED BIN(15) INITIAL(N);
         Case-1 function                 ON CONDITION (CASE_RANGE)
      CASE 2                                on-unit action;
         Case-2 function
                                         CASE_INDEX = integer-expression;
         .                               IF CASE_INDEX < 1 |CASE_INDEX > CASE_MAX THEN
                                            SIGNAL CONDITION (CASE_RANGE);
         .                               ELSE;
      CASE n                             GO TO CASE (CASE_INDEX);
         Case-n function
   ENDCASE                               CASE1: DO;
                                               Case-1 function ;
                                               GO TO END_CASE;
                                            END;
                                         CASE2: DO;
                                               Case-2 function ;

                                               .

                                               .
                                         CASEN: DO;
                                               Case-n function ;
                                               GO TO END_CASE;
                                            END;
                                         END_CASE:;
```

Figure 8-10 How to use commonly available programming languages to do structured programming

COBOL	FORTRAN
statement-A. statement-B.	statement-A statement-B

IF p
   statement-A
ELSE
   statement-B.
	IF (not p) GO TO 200
	       statement-A
	       GO TO 210
	200 CONTINUE
	       statement-B
	210 CONTINUE

PERFORM F
   UNTIL not p.
	400 CONTINUE
	       IF (not p) GO TO 500
	       statement-F
	       GO TO 400
	500 CONTINUE

PERFORM F.
PERFORM F
   UNTIL p.
	550 CONTINUE
	       statement-F
	       IF (not p) GO TO 550

PERFORM CASE-PARA THRU CASE-END.
   .
   .
   .
   CASE-PARA.
     GO TO CASE1,CASE2,. . .,CASEN
      DEPENDING ON identifier.
     Exception routine.
     GO TO CASE-END.
CASE1.
  Case-1 function.
  GO TO CASE-END.
CASE2.
  Case-2 function.
    .
    .
    .
CASEN.
  Case-n function.
  GO TO CASE-END.
CASE-END.
  EXIT.
	GO TO (s1,s2,. . .,sn), variable
	     Exception routine
	     GO TO 900
	s1 CONTINUE
	     Case-1 function
	     GO TO 900
	s2 CONTINUE
	     Case-2 function
	     .
	     .
	     .
	sn CONTINUE
	     Case-n function
	     GO TO 900
	900 CONTINUE

Figure 8-10   (Continued)

just discussed it. You can refer to this table as we continue our discussion of structured programming and later as a general guideline when writing structured code.

The IFTHENELSE pattern is readily expressed in PL/I. For example, suppose that *if* a counter (COUNT) is less than 10, *then* we want to add current charge (CCHG) to current balance (CBAL); otherwise (*else*) we want to ignore CCHG at present and simply divide CBAL by 10. We write:

```
IF COUNT < 10 THEN
    CBAL = CBAL + CCHG;
ELSE
    CBAL = CBAL / 10;
```

The general form of this construct in PL/I is:

```
IF p THEN
    statement-A;
ELSE
    statement-B;
```

One of the reasons why PL/I is especially well suited to structured programming is that it supports the building block concept in a very effective fashion. Either statement-A or statement-B above, or both, can be a simple statement as we have shown, or a group of statements headed by a DO or BEGIN statement that causes the entire group of statements to be treated as a block. For example, suppose that *if* COUNT is less than 10, *then* we want to add CCHG to CBAL and increase the value of COUNT by 1; otherwise (*else*) we want to divide CBAL by 10, just as we did before. We write:

```
IF COUNT < 10 THEN
    DO;                              ⎫
        CBAL = CBAL + CCHG;          ⎬  statement-A
        COUNT = COUNT +1;            ⎪
    END;                             ⎭
ELSE
    CBAL = CBAL / 10;                ⎫  statement-B
                                     ⎭
```

To set up a DOWHILE pattern in PL/I we use a DO statement containing a WHILE clause. For example, to add CCHG to CBAL and increase COUNT by 1 *while* COUNT is less than 10, we write:

```
DO WHILE (COUNT < 10);
    CBAL = CBAL + CCHG;
    COUNT = COUNT + 1;
END;
```

A statement directly analogous to the DOUNTIL pattern is not available in PL/I, so we simulate it. Remember that we need a trailing-decision loop effect—the required function is to be executed at least once. To add HRS to TIME at least once and continue doing so *until* TIME exceeds LIMIT, we can write:

```
TIME = TIME + HRS;
DO WHILE (TIME ≤ LIMIT);
    TIME = TIME + HRS;
END;
```

To see what is really happening here, look back at Figure 8-8. The condition we are looking for is TIME > LIMIT, but in our simulation we must test for TIME ≤ LIMIT to get the overall logic required.

Another way of simulating DOUNTIL involves use of a bit-string variable. We set the variable to a value of binary 1 just before entering the loop. Then we execute the loop repeatedly until after we ourselves have deliberately set the same variable to binary 0 because we know that the condition we are looking for exists (that is, our tested-for condition is true). For example:

```
DCL TESTVAR BIT(1);
    .
    .
    .
TESTVAR = '1'B;
DO WHILE (TESTVAR);
    TIME = TIME + HRS;
    IF TIME > LIMIT THEN
        TESTVAR = '0'B;
    ELSE;
END;
```

Here, we use the fact that the expression WHILE (TESTVAR) in the DO statement has the effect of WHILE (TESTVAR = '1'B). An advantage of simulating DOUNTIL in this way is that it permits us to state the condition we are really looking for (TIME > LIMIT) in its actual form instead of having to express negative, or inverse, logic (TIME ≤ LIMIT). Once the programmer or a reader of such code becomes familiar with the bit-string-variable simulation technique, this form of representation may appear to be a more direct expression of what is really happening in the program. (It is a good idea to document any use of a bit-string variable in this way in the prolog for the code.)

The CASE pattern is not directly available in PL/I, so we simulate it. One way of doing so involves use of a special PL/I data type, the label variable, and of GOTO statements in a predefined structural form. For ease of explanation, we shall use the accounts-receivable situation described earlier. (See Figure 8-9.)

```
        DCL  CASE(1:4)  LABEL INITIAL (CASE1,CASE2,CASE3,CASE4),
            CASE_MAX  FIXED BIN(15)  INITIAL(4);
    ON  CONDITION  (CASE_RANGE)
            other routine;
            GOTO END_CASE;
            .
            .
            .
        CASE_INDEX = INPUTVAL;
        IF CASE_INDEX < 1 | CASE_INDEX > CASE_MAX THEN
            SIGNAL CONDITION (CASE_RANGE);
        ELSE;
        GOTO CASE(CASE_INDEX);
CASE1: DO;
            credit balance routine;
            GOTO END_CASE;
        END;
CASE2: DO;
            ok routine;
            GOTO END_CASE;
        END;
CASE3: DO;
            payment due routine;
            GOTO END_CASE;
        END;
CASE4: DO;
            payment overdue routine;
            GOTO END_CASE;
        END;
END_CASE:;
```

Whether the subscript of the CASE label variable is set to 1, 2, 3, or 4, or to another value, determines which alternative function routine is branched to when the GOTO CASE(CASE_INDEX) statement is encountered during program execution.

The reader who is familiar with PL/I may have already noticed that the last GOTO END_CASE statement in this example appears to be extraneous. What if the GOTO statement were removed? Whenever the CASE4 code was executed, the statement identified by the label END_CASE (in this example, a null statement) would be encountered next anyway. But the proposed removal of the GOTO is precisely the type of "refinement" that must be avoided when writing a structured program! Remember that an important goal of structured programming is modularity. And one benefit of modularity is the ability to modify a program at any point without causing unanticipated side effects on the program logic elsewhere. Here, the DO groups could be rearranged, another function (DO group) could be added following CASE4, or whatever, to respond to changing requirements of the problem situation. It is essential to set up every structure in its complete form so that all parts of the program are truly modular.

COBOL

There exists today, in the business data-processing environment, widespread interest in whether or not the COBOL programming language can be used to write structured programs. Some proponents of structured programming are quick to point out that COBOL does not support the concept of block structure; others argue that although it is not always possible or convenient to code a group of statements in sequence (*in-line*) and treat them as a block at that point during program execution, they can be branched to and executed as a block (*out-of-line*) by means of a PERFORM statement. (We say more about this below.) While some computer professionals claim that use of COBOL for structured programming is not only inconvenient but also leads to inefficient code, others insist that they are writing structured programs in COBOL and experiencing tremendous benefits in terms of greater programmer productivity and reduced testing costs. Let us see what is involved.

In COBOL, the language implementation techniques for structured programming are primarily concerned with the Procedure Division and pertain to setting up the basic control structures. A COBOL example of SIMPLE SEQUENCE is:

```
MOVE  TOTAL-LINE  TO  PRINT-AREA.
WRITE  PRINT-AREA  AFTER  ADVANCING  3  LINES.
```

As the third column from the left in Figure 8–10 indicates, the general form of this construct in COBOL is:

```
statement-A.
statement-B.
```

The IFTHENELSE pattern can be represented directly in COBOL. Suppose that *if* a counter (COUNT) is less than 10, *then* we want to add current charge (CCHG) to current balance (CBAL); otherwise (*else*) we want to ignore CCHG at present and simply divide CBAL by 10. We write:

```
IF COUNT < 10
    ADD CCHG TO CBAL
ELSE
    DIVIDE 10 INTO CBAL.
```

The general form of the IFTHENELSE construct in COBOL is shown by the second entry in the third column from the left in Figure 8–10. Either statement-A or statement-B, or both, can be a single statement as we have shown or a sequence of statements. In either case, according to the rules of COBOL, it can include another IF statement. But, to avoid program complexity, it is preferable to use a PERFORM statement referring to a paragraph containing any (otherwise nested) IF or other sequence of statements whenever the readability of the program would be impaired by the use of in-line code.

There is no COBOL statement directly analogous to the DOWHILE pattern. Therefore, to set up a DOWHILE in COBOL, we use a PERFORM statement with an UNTIL clause. When the PERFORM statement is encountered during program execution, the condition specified in the UNTIL clause is tested for immediately. A branch occurs until (unless) the tested-for condition is true. We must deal with negative, or inverse, logic to set up the logic we really want, so careful attention is required. As an example, assume we want to add CCHG to CBAL and increase the value of COUNT by 1 *while* COUNT is less than 10. We write:

```
PERFORM PAR1
    UNTIL COUNT ⩾ 10.
    .
    .
    .
PAR1.
    ADD CCHG TO CBAL.
    ADD 1 TO COUNT.
```

The DOUNTIL pattern must also be simulated. We need to do a function until a tested-for condition is known to be true. Because this construct represents a trailing-decision loop, the function is always executed at least once. (If you need to review the logic of the DOUNTIL pattern, look back at Figure 8–8.)

To add HRS to TIME at least once and continue doing so *until* TIME exceeds LIMIT, we can use a SIMPLE SEQUENCE and a DOWHILE pattern as follows:

```
PERFORM  TIMECALC.
PERFORM  TIMECALC
    UNTIL  TIME >  LIMIT.
    .
    .
    .
TIMECALC.
    ADD  HRS  TO  TIME.
```

This example is simple, but it illustrates one very important point: in the COBOL simulation of DOUNTIL, the implementation logic is straightforward; there is no need for negative, or inverse, logic representation.

The CASE control structure can be simulated in COBOL through use of a GO TO statement with a DEPENDING ON clause. The key to maintaining structure is that each procedure named in the GO TO DEPENDING ON statement concludes with another GO TO statement branching to a common collector node. Once again, we refer to the accounts-receivable situation described in Figure 8-9 as an example. The COBOL simulation of this example is shown below.

```
    PERFORM CASE-PARA THRU CASE-END.
    .
    .
    .
CASE-PARA.
    GO TO CASE1, CASE2, CASE3, CASE4 DEPENDING ON INPUTVAL.
    other routine.
    GO TO CASE-END.
CASE1.
    credit balance routine.
    GO TO CASE-END.
CASE2.
    ok routine.
    GO TO CASE-END.
CASE3.
    payment due routine.
    GO TO CASE-END.
CASE4.
    payment overdue routine.
    GO TO CASE-END.
CASE-END.
    EXIT.
```

To encourage high-quality error-free coding, some COBOL users have established installation standards governing the use of COBOL language features in their particular programming environments. Some of these standards pertain to the use of comments and the formatting of source-program text, which we discussed at length in Chapter 7. Others pertain directly to executable constructs. Representative guidelines are:

1. Do not use ALTER statements. A program should not modify itself.
2. (a) Do not use nested IF statements; *or*

(b) Use nested IF statements sparingly and never beyond a nesting level of 3.

Nested control structures are permitted in structured programming, but COBOL nested IF statements are apt to be coded incorrectly. Even when coded correctly, they are difficult to understand and their presence increases the likelihood that errors will be made when program modifications are required.

3. Do not PERFORM more than one paragraph in any single PER-FORM statement except in implementing the CASE control structure. This means that a statement such as PERFORM PARA-A THRU PARA-B is permissible only when PARA-A contains a GO TO DEPENDING ON statement and PARA-B is essentially a null paragraph (EXIT) marking the end of the CASE control structure.

4. A paragraph may be entered only at the top and may be exited only at the end. That is, only one point of entry and one point of exit (as specified) are allowed. At some installations, this standard is imposed at the section level, with transfer of control to a section permitted only via a PERFORM statement referencing the section as a whole, and transfer of control from the section effected by executing an EXIT statement as the last paragraph. No other section can PERFORM a paragraph within the section or branch via a GO TO to some point within it. Conversely, no GO TO statement within the section can branch to a point outside it.

5. (a) Do not use GO TO statements except in implementing the CASE control structure; *or*
(b) Avoid GO TO statements as much as possible; if a GO TO statement is used, it must transfer control to a point physically beyond the GO TO statement in the program listing; *or*
(c) Avoid GO TO statements as much as possible; if a GO TO statement is used, it can transfer control to the exit of the paragraph containing it or occur within a conditional statement that transfers control to the beginning of the paragraph.

FORTRAN

The FORTRAN programming language is not well-suited to structured programming. At first glance, it may appear to be, because both IF and DO statements are available in the language. But let us take a closer look.

There is no concept of block structure in FORTRAN; that is, it is not possible to group statements and treat them as one statement. This means that we have to use GO TO statements to jump around groups of statements if we wish to simulate blocks. Structured programming is essentially anti-GO TO, but the FORTRAN language as currently defined encourages the use of GO TO statements of various kinds. Much self-discipline is required on the part of the programmer not to use them extensively. Because there is no support of block structure, many computer professionals argue that the GO TO statement is *the* (only) way of getting about in a FORTRAN program.

There are two types of IF statements in most FORTRAN implementations: arithmetic and logical. The arithmetic IF provides for selection of a branch target (a single statement, but not really a block of code) from among three alternatives. The only possible basis for selection is whether the arithmetic value of a specified expression is less than 0, equal to 0, or greater than 0. The logical IF statement permits a single statement to be executed or skipped. This is not sufficient for the IFTHENELSE control structure, although the fact that the single statement can be a GO TO statement is key to FORTRAN simulation of this and other control structures. Neither type of IF permits control structures to be nested. There is no capability to nest consecutive IF statements in a FORTRAN program.

The DOWHILE pattern of structured programming specifies that a condition is to be tested prior to executing a block of one or more statements, but most if not all FORTRAN compilers execute the statements in the range of a FORTRAN DO statement first and then test for the loop termination condition afterwards. This means the complete loop is always executed at least once. The fact that the FORTRAN DO loop is therefore a trailing-decision loop might lead us to expect that it is analogous to the DOUNTIL control structure. Unfortunately, it has many limitations. The only condition that can be tested for is whether a particular variable used as an index, or loop counter, has a particular value. The only operation that can be performed on that variable is to increase it by a fixed amount each time the loop is executed. Obviously, we may want to test for any of a great many other conditions when setting up the logic needed to solve a problem. In actual practice, the FORTRAN DO statement cannot be used effectively for other than control of iterative processing.

FORTRAN supports SIMPLE SEQUENCE in the same fashion as other programming languages. An example is:

```
READ (5,100) A, B, C, D
SUM = A + B
```

As the rightmost column in Figure 8–10 indicates, the general form of this construct in FORTRAN is:

```
statement-A
statement-B
```

The IFTHENELSE pattern cannot be represented directly in FORTRAN. Suppose that *if* a counter (COUNT) is less than 10, *then* we want to add CCHG to CBAL and increase the value of COUNT by 1; otherwise (*else*) we want to divide CBAL by 10 and subtract 1 from COUNT. We write:

```
      IF (COUNT.GE.10) GO TO 200
          CBAL = CBAL + CCHG          Then clause; coding for "false"
          COUNT = COUNT + 1           case of inverse logic, but "true"
          GO TO 300                   of actual problem
  200   CONTINUE
          CBAL = CBAL / 10            Else clause; coding for "true"
          COUNT = COUNT - 1           case of inverse logic, but "false"
  300   CONTINUE                      of actual problem
```

Because the then clause is supposed to represent the true condition, we must use negative, or inverse, logic to set up the construct we want. A branch to the else clause (beginning at statement 200) occurs when our inverse logic is true (and, therefore, the condition we are really interested in is false). The general form of this construct in FORTRAN is illustrated by the second entry in the rightmost column in Figure 8-10. Either statement-A or statement-B, or both, can be a single statement or a sequence of statements.

To simulate the DOWHILE pattern in FORTRAN use a logical IF statement and an unconditional GO TO. For example, to add CCHG to CBAL and increase COUNT by 2 *while* COUNT is less than MAXVAL, we write:

```
  400   CONTINUE
          IF (COUNT.GE.MAXVAL) GO TO 500
          CBAL = CBAL + CCHG          Body of loop; coding
          COUNT = COUNT + 2           for "false" case of in-
          GO TO 400                   verse logic, but "true"
  500   CONTINUE                      of actual problem
```

The condition we are really looking for is COUNT $<$ MAXVAL, but in our simulation we must test for COUNT $\geqslant$ MAXVAL to get the overall logic required.

Simulation of the DOUNTIL pattern also requires a logical IF statement and the use of inverse logic. Remember that we need a trailing-decision loop effect — the required function is to be executed at least once and may be executed several times. For example, to add HRS to TIME at least once and continue doing so until TIME exceeds LIMIT, we write:

```
  500   CONTINUE
          TIME = TIME + HRS  ◄──────────  Body of loop; coding for
          IF (TIME.LE.LIMIT) GO TO 500    "true" case of inverse logic,
                                          but "false" of actual problem
```

To see what is really happening here, look back at part a of Figure 8–8. The condition we are looking for is TIME > LIMIT, but in our simulation we must test for TIME ≤ LIMIT to get the overall logic required.

To simulate the CASE control structure in FORTRAN, we use a computed GO TO statement. The key to maintaining structure is that each section of code that may be branched to concludes with a simple GO TO statement branching to a common collector node. Once again, we refer to the accounts-receivable situation described in Figure 8-9 as an example. The FORTRAN simulation of this example is:

```
        GO TO (100,200,300,400), INVAL
        other routine
        GO TO 500
100 CONTINUE
        credit balance routine
        GO TO 500
200 CONTINUE
        ok routine
        GO TO 500
300 CONTINUE
        payment due routine
        GO TO 500
400 CONTINUE
        payment overdue routine
        GO TO 500
500 CONTINUE
```

To encourage high-quality error-free coding, some FORTRAN users have established installation standards governing the use of FORTRAN language features in their particular programming environments. Some of these standards pertain to the use of comments and the formatting of source-program text, which we discussed at length in Chapter 7. Others deal often with the CONTINUE statement. In common practice, this executable statement is identified by a statement number; control is transferred to it by means of a GO TO statement, or it is the last statement in a DO loop headed by a DO statement in which the statement number appears. We recommended earlier in discussion of Figure 7-9 that each FORTRAN DO loop be terminated by a separate CONTINUE statement. This guideline is a natural fallout of other, more comprehensive standards that some FORTRAN users have adopted:

1. Do not use statement numbers on any executable statement other than CONTINUE.

2. Refer to each statement label in one and only one branching or control statement in a FORTRAN program.

We have followed the first of these standards in examples in this chapter. This standard helps to emphasize program structure, facilitates program debugging and maintenance, and helps to prevent errors related to the ends of DO loops. It also permits the programmer to insert comments that explain what a section of code is doing, after the CONTINUE statement preceding that code and yet before the statements that actually do the function. We have not followed the second, primarily because multiple references to the same CONTINUE are a more direct way of representing all potential transfers of control to the common collector node of a structured-programming control structure. The programmer may find this second standard advantageous, in cases where a program logic error is known to exist but cannot be isolated. It makes it possible for the programmer to determine with relative ease where a transfer of control came from. Particularly busy intersections of code are obvious, since several CONTINUEs occur at such points.

QUESTIONS

Q1. Support or refute the statement, "Structured programming is just a new name for techniques good programmers have been using for years."

Q2. Name as many characteristics of structured programs as you can.

Q3. Structured-programming techniques are interrelated with certain other improved programming technologies. Name them and describe the interrelationships. In doing so, be sure to show what the technologies have in common and how they differ.

Q4. (a) Why is the use of GO TO statements frowned upon by many computer professionals? (b) Describe specific situations (if any) where such use might be justified.

Q5. (a) What is pseudo code? (b) When, how, and why is it used?

Q6. Explain how structured-programming techniques can be employed in a high-level programming language of your choice.

EXERCISES

E1. (a) Using ANSI standard flowcharting symbols, sketch the three basic control structures of structured programming. (b) Next, label each structure. (c) Now, for each structure, use one or more English-language phrases to express the same logic.

E2. Distinguish between DOWHILE and DOUNTIL control structures.

E3. Construct a flowchart for a program to read individual records containing employee name and current position as input. Print the names of all employees who are auditors. For other employee records, no action is required. Program execution should terminate when a special 9s record is encountered. Be sure to plan a structured program.

E4. Repeat E3, but use pseudo code rather than a flowchart to specify the logic.

E5. Consider your work for E3 and E4. Which approach to program planning was more convenient for you? Why?

*E6. Have your flowchart (E3) or pseudo code (E4) verified by an instructor or a co-worker. Then use it as a guide to write a structured program.

E7. Construct a flowchart for a structured program to read N customer records, where N is a special data value read at the beginning of the program. Each customer record contains customer number, account action (DB for debit, or CR for credit), and amount. For each debit record, the program should print the customer number as output and add 1 to a count of debit records being accumulated for control purposes. For each credit record, it should print the customer number and amount as output, and add the amount to a total to be printed at the end of the list of amounts. When all customer records have been processed, the accumulated total should be printed. The constant DEBITS = and the count should be printed on the next line. Then program execution should terminate.

E8. Repeat E7, but use pseudo code rather than a flowchart to specify the logic.

*E9. Have your flowchart (E7) or pseudo code (E8) verified by an instructor or a co-worker. Then use it as a guide in writing a structured program.

E10. Not all programs that you encounter will be structured. Let us choose, as random examples, some of the programs planned in Chapter 5. Look first at Figure 5-4. (a) Use pseudo code to express the program logic described. (b) What control structures do you find? (c) Is this a design for a structured program?

E11. (a) Now look at Figure 5-6. Use pseudo code to express the program logic described. (b) In response to E11a, you should determine that the second decision-making step is set up appropriately, but the first does not lead to structured code. What alternative solution algorithm can you suggest? *Hint*: Try testing for a not end-of-data (that is, additional data to process) condition. (c) Redraw the flowchart in Figure 5-6 to plan a structured program that achieves the same output results. (d) Write pseudo code to express your revised plan. (e) What advantages do you detect in the structured form over the unstructured form?

E12-13. Use the approach of E11 for Figures 5-7 or 5-8 (their logic is very similar) and 5-9. You should find that you can express the logic of 5-7 (or 5-8) in pseudo code, but that 5-9 gives you trouble. *Hint*: To structure 5-9, try DO WHILE ($N \neq 0$) at the decision-making step.

*E14. Find a program that is not well-structured. Rewrite it in structured form.

REFERENCES

Aron, J. D. "The Superprogrammer Project." In J. N. Buxton and B. Randell eds., *Software Engineering Techniques*. NATO Scientific Affairs Division, Brussels 39, Belgium, April 1970, pp. 50-52.

Bohm, C., and G. Jacopini. "Flow Diagrams, Turing Machines and Languages with Only Two Formation Rules," *Communications of the ACM* 9, 5 (May 1966): 366-71.

Chapin, Ned, Roger House, Ned McDaniel, and Robert Wachtel. "Structured Programming Simplified," *Computer Decisions* 6, 6 (June 1974): 28-31.

Dijkstra, E. W. "GOTO Statement Considered Harmful," Letter to the Editor, *Communications of the ACM* 11, 3 (Mar 1968): 147-48.

_____. "The Structure of THE Multiprogramming System," *Communications of the ACM* 11, 5 (May 1968): 341-46 (a reprint of Dijkstra's ideas about top-down systems design as stated in a paper presented at the First ACM Symposium on Operating Systems Principles).

_____. "Structured Programming." In J. N. Buxton and B. Randell, eds., *Software Engineering Techniques*. NATO Scientific Affairs Division, Brussels 39, Belgium, April 1970, pp. 84-88.

Donaldson, James R. "Structured Programming," *Datamation* 19, 12 (Dec 1973): 52-54. This issue is devoted to *structured programming* with additional articles "Chief Programmer Teams," by F. Terry Baker and Harlan D. Mills; "Structured Programming: Top-down Approach," by Edward F. Miller, Jr., and George E. Lindamood; "A Linguistic Contribution to GO-TO-less Programming," by Lawrence R. Clark; and "Revolution in Programming: An Overview," by Daniel D. McCracken.

Hughes, Joan K., and Jay I. Michtom. *A Structured Approach to Programming*. Englewood Cliffs, N.J.: Prentice-Hall, 1977 (for anyone familiar with the basic concepts of programming).

IBM Structured Programming Flowcharting Template. IBM Corporation publication (SR20-7151). White Plains, N.Y., n.d.

IBM Structured Programming — Textbook. IBM Corporation, DPD Education Development, publication (SR20-7149). Poughkeepsie, N.Y., n.d. (an IBM Independent Study Program). See also *IBM Structured Programming — Workbook* (SR20-7150).

Kauffman, Richard L. "COBOL/Structured Programming — (Will the Marriage Survive?)" *Infosystems* 22, 2 (February 1975): 48ff.

McGowan, Clement L., and John R. Kelly. *Top-Down Structured Programming Techniques*. New York: Petrocelli/Charter, 1975.

Mize, Jan L. "Structured Programming in COBOL," *Datamation* 22, 6 (June 1976): 103-05.

Tenny, Ted. "Structured Programming in FORTRAN," *Datamation* 20, 7 (July 1974): 110-15.

Wirth, N. "On the Composition of Well-Structured Programs," *Computing Surveys* (ACM) 6, 4 (Dec 1974): 247-59. This issue is devoted to *programming* with additional articles on the subject, including "Structured Programming with Go To Statements," by D. E. Knuth, pp. 261-302.

Yourdon, Edward. "Making the Move to Structured Programming," *Datamation* 21, 6 (June 1975): 52-56.

_____. "Structured Programming," *Modern Data* (now *Mini-Micro Systems*) 7, 6 (June 1974): 30-35.

9

PROGRAM CHECKOUT - I

After a problem solution has been planned and a program coded accordingly, at least one major task remains: the programmer must make certain that the program performs as intended. This task is a part of the programmer's overall responsibility for complete, comprehensive program checkout.

As noted in Chapter 3, a major concern of programming has been the high frequency of errors, or bugs; the difficulty in isolating, identifying, and correcting those bugs; and the care required to avoid creating new bugs when correcting existing ones. Until recently, few persons, if any, thought to question a situation that appeared indisputable: programming was an error-prone activity. As programs, and interrelated sets of programs, became increasingly large and complex, more and more of the programmer's time was spent, not in program design and coding, but rather in debugging and testing.* If a program could be assumed to be correct, there would be no need for testing. If testing failed to reveal the presence of errors, there would be no need for debugging. Unfortunately, in common practice, neither was the case. And the situation has not changed much in many program-development environments.

Yet, today, there is evolving a thread of optimism. An increasing number of computer professionals are asking why programs should not be written correctly instead of debugged into successive "one less error than before"

---

*In this book, the term *debugging* is used to refer to the task of finding program errors (bugs) and correcting them so that a program runs correctly. *Testing* means exercising the program logic — actually, or in effect, operating on input data that simulates, or is a representative sample of, the problem-related data that will be processed by the program. For clarity, we shall consistently use these terms as defined here. However, the reader should expect that, in some references, testing is regarded as a subset of debugging; in others, debugging is regarded as a subset of testing; and in still others, the terms are treated as synonyms.

stages. It is much easier and less expensive in terms of both time and money to keep errors out of a program to start with than to isolate, identify, and correct them later, after trouble has appeared. Dr. Harlan Mills of IBM insists, for example, that programs can and should *ordinarily* execute properly the *very first time* they are run; that is, programming can be error-free.* This new level of precision programming is seen to be directly dependent on the improved programming technologies discussed in this book. It is expected to come about only when the technologies are accompanied by a new attitude toward programming expectations: a confidence on the part of the programmer that he can write programs correctly, coupled with a sustained, deliberate level of concentration on his part. The programmer must know that he can write error-free code. Then he must make an all-out effort to do so.

It may seem contradictory to discuss program checkout in a book that emphasizes the desirability — and even the real possibility — of error-free programming. But, even if we reject the idea that programming is doomed to be error-prone, we must admit that programmers as human beings are sometimes careless. External pressures such as budget and time constraints imposed upon programmers may prevent them from doing their best work. Even when maximum care and effort are exercised in programming, mistakes can occur. The programmer who has acquired debugging and testing skills is better equipped to find and eliminate errors than one who resorts to unplanned, hunt-and-peck methods of program checkout.

We shall not undertake to determine whether or not it is possible to prove program correctness — a topic often discussed lately. Instead, we shall direct our attention to what actions we can take to make reasonably sure that programs work as intended, without absorbing excessive amounts of both programmer and computer time in the program-checkout process. Those who are interested in proving program correctness are encouraged to pursue the topic independently in available computer literature.

TYPES OF ERRORS

In a very basic sense, an error is something that is not right — a mistake that we want to prevent or, if we fail at prevention, that we want to eliminate. Before we go error chasing, however, we need to understand the types of errors that may occur. Generally, they are either clerical or logical.

Most *clerical errors* occur during the coding and keypunching stages of program development; that is, when the programmer enters the statements of a program from a direct-input device (usually, a typewriter-like keyboard),

---

*Dr. Mills presents his ideas in *Mathematical Foundations for Structured Programming* and other writings. His views are also discussed in *IBM Structured Programming — Textbook*, which is listed in the references for Chapter 8.

or when he writes the statements on coding forms and later when those statements are punched into cards so that they can be read into the computer. For example, an assembler-language programmer may spell a mnemonic operation code incorrectly or use the label of a primary-storage location where a CPU register number is required. A high-level-language programmer may forget a closing right parenthesis or specify the wrong number or type of arguments in a call statement. A keypunch operator may press the wrong character on the keyboard or position entries in the wrong columns of a card.

Logical errors are errors in somebody's thinking. That "somebody" may be any one or more of a (usually) rather large number of persons involved in the program-development process. For example, the business management group for whom a computerized inventory-control system is being developed may assume that issues in response to customer orders are an accurate indication of decreases in inventory, only to discover that in-house transfers of stock play a significant role as well. A systems designer may account for all normal order-processing procedures, but fail to recognize that special action is needed when a short-on-storage condition exists for items ordered for a government-funded energy research project. The programmer may not thoroughly understand a phase of the problem to be solved, fail to account for certain situations that can (and do) arise during processing, misinterpret some steps in the solution algorithm, and so on. Not providing for the possibility of a negative charge (in effect, a credit) in accounts payable, or failing to initialize a primary-storage location used as an accumulator, are examples of logical errors in programming.

The possibility that as a programmer you may make either clerical or logical errors, or both, is very real indeed, as you have probably already discovered. What can you do to decrease the likelihood of errors? How can you determine whether or not you have made one (or more than one)? If you have made errors, how can you isolate, identify, and eliminate them? Only when a program has been designed, coded, *and* tested thoroughly can it be considered ready for production use. The care exercised in program checkout (or the lack of it) significantly affects the worth of the program.

VERIFYING THE PROBLEM DEFINITION

When our objective is to prevent errors, we must direct our attention to the start of the program-development process rather than the end of it. This means that a reasonable first step is to verify the completeness and accuracy of the problem definition. As we saw in Chapter 3, this definition is recorded in a problem statement, which often takes the form of not just one but several documents. For example, the highest level of problem definition may be a *user requirements document* containing the job description. Important reviewers of this document are representatives of the user groups for whom the program (problem solution) is being devised. Their participation is key at this point—not only to insure that the program or system being developed will meet their needs, but also to emphasize that the system is their system, not one imposed upon them by "computer bigots."

A lower, or more detailed, description of the job to be done appears in one or more *programming functional specifications*. Each specification gives a brief summary of the user requirements satisfied by the part of the design being documented therein. It describes the supported functions and their implications to the user. Hardware and software dependencies; reliability, availability, and serviceability (RAS) characteristics of the design; and performance considerations are other commonly included items. The specification should be reviewed by the chief programmer, team leader, or a coworker (say, a programmer who will help to implement the design).

Under one approach to verification of high-level (also called external or functional) design, the documentation of the design is distributed to selected reviewers. They are asked to study it and respond within an established time period. Each reviewer is directed to note, individually, any changes and additions required. This process is known as an *informal design review*.

Another approach that is gaining favor is the use of *structured walkthroughs*, which in this case are *formal design reviews*. Here, the design documentation is made available to from two to four people selected to serve as members of a review team. After a suitable length of time (allotted for preparation), these reviewers meet together with the designer and a moderator for an established time period, usually about two hours. Each reviewer is expected to have studied the design documentation (assume it is a programming functional specification) and is asked to comment on its completeness, accuracy, and general quality. Then the moderator "walks" the group through the specification in a step-by-step fashion, covering each point raised by a member of the review team.

During the walk-through, emphasis is placed on error detection rather than error correction. To maximize the effectiveness of the walk-through, a *minor error log* is usually distributed to each reviewer along with the specification. (See Figure 9-1.) The reviewer is encouraged to record minor problems such as typos and grammatical errors detected during preparation on this log sheet. These problems are not discussed at the walk-through. Reviewers are instructed to note more severe problems detected during preparation on a *problem log*, also distributed beforehand (Figure 9-1). These problems are discussed at the walk-through as the moderator leads the reviewers through the specification. Sometimes, a *review checklist* showing items to which reviewers should direct particular attention is also distributed. The purpose of this checklist is to help insure that errors of omission as well as of commission are detected. Examples of items that may appear on such a checklist are shown in Figure 9-2.

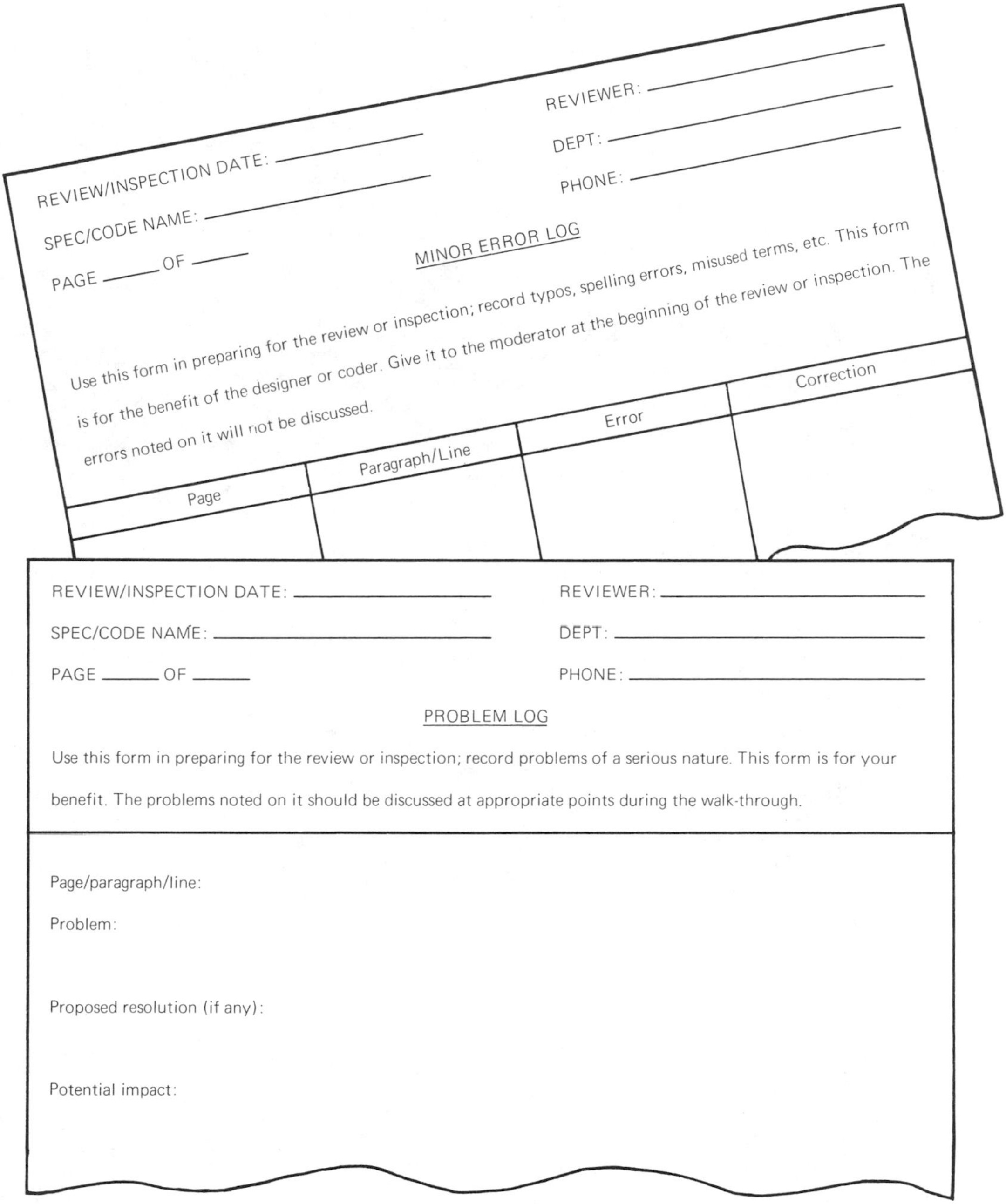

REVIEWER: _____

DEPT: _____

REVIEW/INSPECTION DATE: _____

PHONE: _____

SPEC/CODE NAME: _____

MINOR ERROR LOG

PAGE ___ OF ___

Use this form in preparing for the review or inspection; record typos, spelling errors, misused terms, etc. This form is for the benefit of the designer or coder. Give it to the moderator at the beginning of the review or inspection. The errors noted on it will not be discussed.

Page	Paragraph/Line	Error	Correction

REVIEW/INSPECTION DATE: _____   REVIEWER: _____

SPEC/CODE NAME: _____   DEPT: _____

PAGE ___ OF ___   PHONE: _____

PROBLEM LOG

Use this form in preparing for the review or inspection; record problems of a serious nature. This form is for your benefit. The problems noted on it should be discussed at appropriate points during the walk-through.

Page/paragraph/line:

Problem:

Proposed resolution (if any):

Potential impact:

Figure 9-1   Minor error log (top) and problem log (bottom) for structured walk-throughs

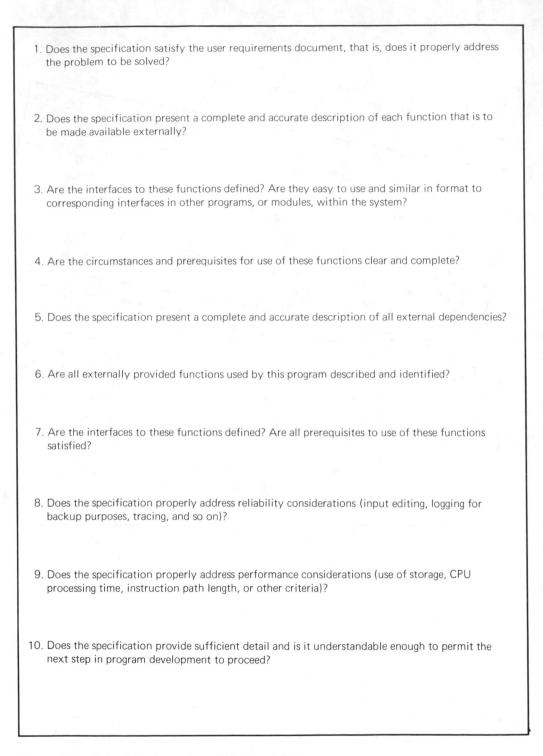

1. Does the specification satisfy the user requirements document, that is, does it properly address the problem to be solved?

2. Does the specification present a complete and accurate description of each function that is to be made available externally?

3. Are the interfaces to these functions defined? Are they easy to use and similar in format to corresponding interfaces in other programs, or modules, within the system?

4. Are the circumstances and prerequisites for use of these functions clear and complete?

5. Does the specification present a complete and accurate description of all external dependencies?

6. Are all externally provided functions used by this program described and identified?

7. Are the interfaces to these functions defined? Are all prerequisites to use of these functions satisfied?

8. Does the specification properly address reliability considerations (input editing, logging for backup purposes, tracing, and so on)?

9. Does the specification properly address performance considerations (use of storage, CPU processing time, instruction path length, or other criteria)?

10. Does the specification provide sufficient detail and is it understandable enough to permit the next step in program development to proceed?

Figure 9–2   A checklist for review of high-level design

If a problem is encountered during the walk-through, it is discussed to the extent necessary to understand it, but no attempt is made to devise a solution. Someone designated to act as a recording secretary notes any errors, discrepancies, exposures, and inconsistencies in the design. The notes are an action plan for the designer and a communication vehicle for the group.

If, at the end of the established time period, the review is not finished, another walk-through is scheduled. The group effort continues until all of the specification has been examined. Not until all points of concern on the action plan are resolved does the next program-development step begin.

When we advocated a top-down approach to program design (Chapter 4), we also advocated a top-down approach to writing the code and to program testing. This means that design reviews should be set up in a step-wise fashion. The design at each level must be accurate and complete, so that lower levels of the design can be developed independently without causing changes to have to be made to a previously verified specification. Because coding at a checked-out design level may proceed while the design is still in progress at one or more lower levels, explicit, correct documentation at each level is required.

REVIEWING THE DETAILED DESIGN

An equally important step in program checkout occurs after a lower-level (also called internal or logic) design of the program is complete. Generally, the basis for a review at this point is a *programming logic specification*, the detailed plan for all or a meaningful part of the solution algorithm. As we have seen, this plan may take any one or a combination of several forms — structure charts, HIPO diagrams, system and program flowcharts, decision tables, pseudo code, and so on.

As noted above for high-level design, either informal design reviews or structured walk-throughs may be carried out. In either case, the approach is basically the same, except that details at a lower level are dealt with. To participate effectively, reviewers must have significant technical knowledge of the subject area and must do their homework (that is, prepare for the review).

Where, or how, does one start when reviewing program logic set forth in a flowchart, decision table, or pseudo code? Some reviewers, individually or in groups, find that pretending to be the computer works well. Representative values for all types of input are selected: (1) data that is normally expected, (2) valid but slightly abnormal data (for example, maximum and minimum values allowable), and (3) invalid data. The individual or group follows the logic of the flowchart, decision table, or pseudo code step-by-step to process the input and determine what output will be produced. If the output matches predetermined correct results, the logic within the solution algorithm is upheld. Pretending to be the computer in this way is called *simulation*, *procedure execution*, or *desk checking*. Each reviewer must be careful not to make any assumptions as he traces the problem-solving steps, because the computer is a machine and can make no assumptions.

HELP FROM THE LANGUAGE-PROCESSOR PROGRAM

After a program, or module, has been designed and coded, it is submitted to the computer for translation to machine-language form. The language-processor program that performs the translation assists the programmer in checking out the program. In particular, it performs error detection by finding many types of clerical errors (misspellings, illegal names, missing commas, missing left or right parentheses, and so on) if they exist in the program. It may detect some types of logical errors (for example, illegally branching into a program loop, or failing to include a branch statement at a certain point and, therefore, providing no way to reach and execute a certain section of code). Some language processors are designed to be "forgiving"; they make assumptions in what appear to be minor error situations and proceed with the translation accordingly. For example, if the programmer appears to have omitted a required comma in an I/O list of variable names, the language processor may assume that a comma is present. Note, however, that the programmer who writes ONE TWO may mean either ONE,TWO or ONETWO; that is, the language processor's assumption may or may not be valid.

Having performed error detection, an assembler or compiler program also attempts to perform error isolation by indicating where each error occurs. It does so by printing a list of *diagnostics*, or error messages, at the end of the *assembly listing* or *source-program listing*, produced as one output of an assembly or compilation, respectively. In most instances, the language processor generates line numbers for all source-program statements. Each diagnostic calls attention to one programming error and contains the number of the line in which the error occurs.

An important guideline to be remembered here is: A bug at one point in a program may cause the language processor to interpret succeeding code incorrectly. That is, the language processor may be misled. For example, a misspelled label may be the basis for numerous UNDEFINED LABEL messages at other points in the program where the correctly spelled label is used.

Diagnostics may be any of three types, loosely termed fatal, non-fatal or warning, and advisory. The programmer must correct the source-program statements that cause fatal diagnostics, because, even if he resubmits the program for translation, no translation will be made so long as fatal diagnostics continue to occur. The programmer should check all diagnostics, even those that are not fatal, because they are often indicative of errors elsewhere. The programmer who verifies that a warning message points to a situation already known to him may choose to ignore the warning; for example, he may feel that an unreferenced label is needed for documentational purposes and, therefore, should not be removed. As another example, an advisory message may warn of possible overflow during an arithmetic operation or of over-lapping fields in a move; these situations may be symptoms of errors, or the programmer may have deliberately planned for either or both to occur during execution of the program.

One outgrowth of the increased awareness of the amount of program-mer time and effort spent in program debugging is the development of *checkout*, or *debugging, compilers.* Examples here are the WATFIV and PL/C compilers, which support student-oriented versions of FORTRAN and PL/I respectively. Another is IBM's PL/I checkout compiler. Such compilers do not analyze a program during translation in order to *optimize* the out-put they produce, that is, in order to set up the fastest-executing code possible. Instead, they often generate additional code not called for specifi-cally by the programmer, in order to help him find certain errors if they are present in the program. For example, such a compiler may include code to check whether or not variables used in a program are initialized before use. As another example, both FORTRAN and PL/I include capabilities for treat-ing individual data items as elements of a group of related data items, called an array; a debugging compiler can insert code to be executed whenever a subscripted array name is used to refer to a particular element, to insure that the value of a specified subscript does not exceed the bounds of the corresponding extent of the array.

A general rule well worth following is: If a debugging compiler is avail-able for the programming language in use, its capabilities should be taken advantage of during program development. After a program has been checked out, it can be submitted to a standard language-processor program for re-translation. The resultant object program can be stored in a system library for repetitive use.

INSPECTING THE PROGRAM

A "clean" (error-message-free) assembly or source-program listing is the basis for another type of review — the *code inspection.* This review is primarily one of careful scrutiny. There are several ways to proceed. The programmer himself may go over the program logic to verify that the program is complete, in effect stepping through the program manually (another form of desk checking), pretending to be the computer. Unfortunately, the programmer who is extremely familiar with a program may unconsciously read into it logic that is not there. For this reason, another programmer or a team of pro-grammers can sometimes play the role of the computer more effectively.

CODE DOCUMENTATION

1. Is a prolog included? Is it complete and accurate? If not, what discrepancies exist between the prolog and the code? Which is correct?

2. Are block comments included for each major function or section of code?

3. Are comments accurate, meaningful, and in sufficient detail? Do they provide additional information (rather than just parrot the code)?

4. Are meaningful names used for variables?

5. Are statement labels consistent with the functions of the code?

ADHERANCE TO STANDARDS

6. Does the code follow established intracompany standards? In particular:

   a. Does the code contain only symbolic names as addresses, with no references to absolute (machine) addresses, or use of relative addressing (e.g., HERE+4)?

   b. Is the total number of lines of code within established limits?

   c. Are THEN/ELSE and DO/END control structures aligned properly?

   d. Are nested IF and DO control structures indented properly?

NOTE: All standards established within the development organization, and not mentioned elsewhere on the review checklist, should be noted here.

VARIABLES

7. Is each variable defined?

8. Is each variable initialized before use?

9. Is each variable used as defined (no unanticipated conversions, truncations, or roundings)?

INTERFACE REQUIREMENTS

10. Are the correct numbers of arguments specified in all calls to other subroutines, modules, or macros?

11. Is each argument of the correct size and type (for example, binary or decimal, 16 bits or 32 bits in length)?

12. Are the arguments specified in the correct order (for example, does the called subroutine expect A,B, or should B,A have been specified)?

TESTS

13. Is the correct condition tested (If X = ON vs. If X = OFF)?

14. Are the correct variables, or constant and variable, used in the test?

15. Are values used in the test of acceptably comparable data types and lengths?

16. Are all possible conditions provided for (for example, equal to 0, as well as greater than 0 and less than 0)?

17. Are the branch paths correct (YES vs. NO)?

Figure 9-3   Examples of checklist items for use in code inspection

18. Is each branch target correct?

19. Are null THENs and ELSEs included where needed?

20. Is the most frequently exercised branch path the THEN clause?

LOOPS

21. Will any program loop be executed too many times? Too few?

22. Are there any loops that should sometimes be avoided altogether? If so, is this logic provided?

23. What assumptions are made about the values of loop variables at each loop exit? Are the assumptions valid?

24. Are all loop variables initialized, and reinitialized (or not reinitialized), as required?

INPUT/OUTPUT

25. Do field positions and descriptions specified in I/O statements match the layout specifications for the problem?

26. Will the first input be handled correctly? The last one?

27. Is an input value of 0 (or blanks) a valid input? What happens when 0 (or blanks) is received?

28. What happens when an invalid input is received?

29. What happens if no input is received?

ARITHMETIC

30. Will all arithmetic expressions be interpreted as the programmer intends (for example, is parenthesization correct; are rules of precedence within the language allowed for)?

REGISTER USAGE

31. Are register conventions adhered to (for example, in passing values to a common interface routine)?

32. Is each register initialized correctly?

33. Is the correct register specified for each usage?

34. Are registers saved appropriately on entrance to code?

35. Are registers stored on exit as required?

MODULE/MACRO LOGIC

36. Are built-in functions and/or subprograms available in the programming language used whenever such use is appropriate?

37. Do the entrance to, and exit from, the module/macro follow established conventions?

38. Are all possible error situations provided for?

39. Has all of the specified design been implemented?

40. Is all code within the specified design?

Figure 9-3   (Continued)

Going beyond individual effort, some programmers prefer to work in pairs, checking their own programs and the programs of another in informal code inspections. In some environments, structured walk-throughs, which in this case are formal code inspections, are used. Code listings are distributed to selected reviewers, along with minor error logs, problem logs, and review checklists, in much the same way as for other structured walk-throughs we have discussed. The moderator leads the reviewers through the code. It is not only checked for errors in what the programmer intended to do but also verified against the solution algorithm as expressed in the programming logic specification. Examples of items that may appear in the review checklist are shown in Figure 9–3.

As noted earlier for design reviews, the processing of normal data, valid but slightly abnormal data, and invalid data should be traced as part of the code-inspection process. Each flow of control through the program should be exercised. The overall objective is, of course, to detect and identify any clerical and logical errors still remaining. In the case of the formal code inspection, each problem found by the reviewers is recorded on a *problem report*, which is the mechanism used to track resolution of the problem. (See Figure 9–4.) As noted for formal design reviews, a maximum time period of about two hours should be established for one session of a formal code inspection. During that time period, reviewers can expect to cover from 200 to 400 lines of code. Subsequent review sessions should be scheduled as necessary until all of the code has been checked.

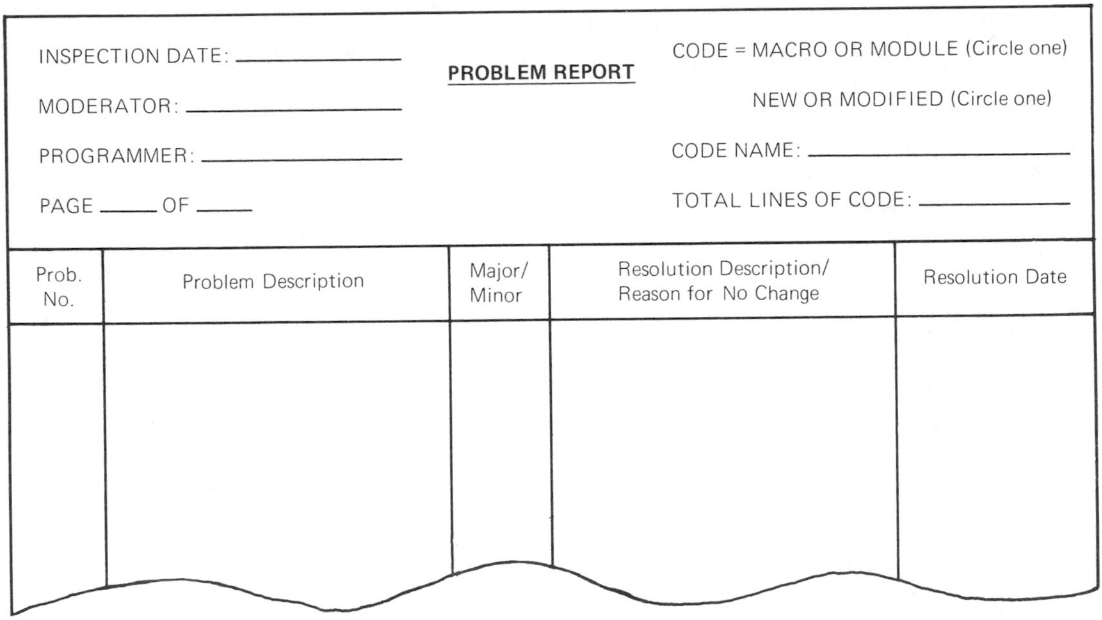
INSPECTION DATE: ______

PROBLEM REPORT

CODE = MACRO OR MODULE (Circle one)

MODERATOR: ______

NEW OR MODIFIED (Circle one)

PROGRAMMER: ______

CODE NAME: ______

PAGE ____ OF ____

TOTAL LINES OF CODE: ______

Prob. No.	Problem Description	Major/ Minor	Resolution Description/ Reason for No Change	Resolution Date

Figure 9–4 Code inspection problem report form

The criteria for successful completion of a code inspection should be established before the inspection begins. One criterion might be, for example, that the number of functional problems detected does not exceed an average of one per 20 lines of code. Another might be that no major problem — one requiring a significant design change to the specification for this code or any interfacing code — is encountered. If a re-inspection is necessary, the moderator and the programmer are responsible for setting a date for the re-inspection. That re-inspection should cover the entire program — not just a particular portion of it changed as a result of this inspection.

COMPUTER-ASSISTED TESTING

Every program must eventually be executed by the computer. In all but rare cases, to test a program thoroughly, the programmer requires computer help. If the programmer fails to test the program thoroughly, it will be tested anyway — in the actual problem-solving situation. But the costs of failure at that point are generally not worth the risk. What does a large manufacturing company do if a programming error prevents weekly payroll processing from being completed? How does a telephone company explain a computer processing error to hundreds of unhappy customers who have been billed incorrectly? It seems obvious that prevention is preferable to cure. So the programmer tests to detect, isolate, and remove errors, lest someone else discover them later.

Computer-assisted testing is an art. There is no sure-fire set of rules or formula that can be followed rigorously for all programs. The testing procedure for a program must be planned for that program. Experience is a good teacher. Hence, the programmer learns by working with others experienced in testing. He tries various approaches to testing, and he remembers and reuses those that work best for him, in similar situations. A major criterion for successful testing is the will to do it. Perseverence as well as creativity, time, and thought on the part of the programmer are required to try to find fault with code he has developed. A real desire to do a good job of testing goes a very long way toward building a high-quality program.

Functional Test

In the vast majority of cases, the first type of computer-assisted testing performed is *functional test.* The goal of this testing is to verify that the program does what it is supposed to do. Further, it must perform correctly, not just once, but consistently, in whatever situations may arise.

Normally, the person who has created a program does functional testing. Personpower permitting, another programmer or a tester should double-check the program independently. A person without prior knowledge of a program is more likely to create all types of test input; he may design a better testing procedure because he has no bias in favor of the program.

The execution of a program has three possible outcomes. First, the program may execute correctly and produce acceptable results. In this case, testing can proceed with another set of test data, or the program may be ready for execution with actual ("real," or "live") data. Second, the program may not execute to completion; that is, it may terminate abnormally because of an error condition that arises during processing. For example, an attempt to perform an arithmetic operation on a string of alphabetic characters, or to store such characters in locations reserved for decimal data, may cause abnormal termination. We say that the program "blows up." The third possibility is that the program may run to completion, but fail to produce acceptable results. Corrective action on the part of the programmer is required.

Making Test Runs

In a typical test environment, the testing procedure is broken into a series of *test runs*. The data for the first test run is usually low in volume and of the type normally expected. The purpose of this run is to check out the main processing functions of the program. A rule that applies here and to all subsequent test runs is: Always work out the results that should be produced *before* running the test. The programmer who fails to determine expected results beforehand is too apt to be prejudiced toward results actually produced. Stating this another way, if as a programmer you obtain computer-generated results and then try to verify them manually, the chances are very good that you will succeed — even if the computer-generated results are wrong.

If the results of the initial test run correspond to the expected results, a second test run is made. Valid but slightly abnormal data should be provided as input to the run. If the results of a test run are not correct, or if the program terminates abnormally, an error has occurred. The cause of the error must be identified and eliminated. Sometimes the cause is obvious; for example, the programmer may have coded a plus sign where a minus sign should have been coded. Sometimes the cause is not obvious. In this case the programmer may employ any of several debugging techniques to try to isolate it. (We discuss some of these techniques in the next chapter.) An important guideline here is: Do not let any program activity or any output that seems the least bit peculiar slip by without explanation. There is no such thing as a trivial bug during program testing; all too often that one bug is analogous to the tip of an iceberg. In a very real sense, either a program executes correctly or it fails to do so.

Test Planning and Tracking

Long or complex programs may require many test runs. To test all situations that could arise during processing may be next to impossible, but careful construction of a *test matrix* can help to increase the effectiveness of the testing process. Along the top of the matrix, the programmer lists all of the functions that the program can perform. Along one side of the matrix, he lists the *test cases* required. Each test case (the basis for a test run) should be limited to testing one or a very few functions (clearly identified on the test matrix by placing check marks or Xs in the columns for those functions, in the row describing the test case). Further, the test case should be fully documented as to purpose, prerequisites, dependencies, input, expected results, and so on. Figure 9–5 shows a sample test case form and explains in greater detail the individual test-case documentation required.

A *test library*, including a "regression bucket" of test cases used previously, can be established over time. It serves as an invaluable aid if existent but previously undetected errors are discovered later, or if changes in the problem to be solved necessitate changes to the solution algorithm in its computer-program form.

A *log* of test cases that (1) are to be run, (2) have been attempted, and (3) have been completed successfully should be established and kept up to date throughout computer-assisted testing. If significant changes are made to the program under test, it may be advisable to rerun certain test cases, even if they have been completed successfully before.

Ideally, every program should be tested in its entirety; that is, once a program executes successfully with some data, its functioning with all types of data must be checked out as thoroughly as possible. All paths, or possible combinations of branches, through the program should be exercised. A program flowchart or decision table created as part of the design documentation often proves to be a valuable aid at this time.

Generating Test Input

For other than very simple programs, generating a sufficient number of test inputs can be a major undertaking. Furthermore, considerations such as what combinations of input parameters are meaningful and which input sequences are appropriate must be taken into account. For typical business data-processing applications, this task is compounded by the requirement for master-file data as well as transaction inputs. Few if any programmers can be expected to relish the prospect of planning, keypunching, and verifying the data contents of 1000 or more records of an accounts-receivable master file.

TEST CASE

Numeric identifier
Descriptive title

DATE CREATED

mm/dd/yy

TEST PROGRAM(S)

If another program is created specifically for use in testing this program, or this and several other programs, it should be identified here.

TEST SCRIPT(S)

If the test case depends on one or more test scripts, they must be identified here. Such scripts may be either of two types: (1) a string of binary digits (bits) or characters that, when presented to the system, will cause a predefined result; or (2) a set of instructions to set up, control, or execute a test case or test cases.

PURPOSE

Indicates the function or very few functions that this test case is intended to check out; for example: "Verify the correct generation of terminal control table entries for 3270 terminal types."

TEST METHOD

Tells how the test case is run; for example: "This test case is run by a terminal operator using test script T411A to interact with the program under test and the operating-system command processor."

PREREQUISITES

Lists the JCL needed for execution, execution parameters, system generation requirements, primary storage requirements, and the like.

DEPENDENCIES

Identifies the operating-system environment in which the test case runs, the particular version(s) of operating-system programs and any other interfacing software, and the like.

INPUT

Shows the input data, or describes the input data contents and format, and indicates how test script(s) named above are related to it.

EXPECTED RESULTS

Describes the expected output of the test run, for example, the predetermined correct results of calculations, an instructional or error message, abnormal termination (abend) code, return code, or whatever.

VERIFICATION PROCEDURE

Tells how the test results are checked; for example: "The test program interacts with the terminal operator for required visual verification. Error situations are documented by dumps and logged messages. A positive message is logged if the test run completes with no apparent problems."

ERROR MESSAGES

Lists and explains error messages that may be generated during the test run, for example, if a terminal operator mistakenly enters an unacceptable value (note how this type of output generally differs from the expected results of the test run).

OTHER

Provides any additional meaningful information about this test case.

Figure 9-5 Sample of test case documentation

Fortunately, the programmer can call on the computer for additional help. One way to do this is to write a simple *test data generator program*, say, one that produces 20, 200, or even 2000 output values for each value submitted as input. Convenient formulas can be set up to do the generation, for example, $o = y + 2^m - y/m$, where y is submitted as input and m is increased by 1, each of 20, 200, or 2000 times that a loop within the test data generator program is executed. Some programming languages provide a random-number generator capability via a library routine or built-in function. This capability can be used advantageously in a program written especially to create test data. Another possible alternative is to engineer the purchase of a test data generator program from one of numerous software development firms offering such programs on a commercial basis. When using a program of this type, the programmer often specifies the formats and ranges of valid input, then causes the program to generate a very large volume of such input and select from it a reasonable subset, at random or at fixed intervals within the ranges. Invalid input can be generated in a similar manner.

When programs are developed in a top-down manner, the task of generating test data can be facilitated by planning the sequence of program development with this consideration in mind. As mentioned in Chapter 4, it may be desirable to write (and test) all segments related to input functions first so that other segments that process input data can operate on actual problem-related input, even in a test environment.

Verifying Test Output

A task closely related to generating test inputs is verifying the outputs of test runs. If the outputs are in machine-readable form, for example, the settings of bits in control blocks to be read as input by other modules, manual verification can be a tedious, time-consuming process. Here again, careful planning of the program-development sequence pays off. Sometimes, the process of verification can be done in a semiautomatic fashion. The programmer manually determines that for test input I1 the test output should be O1, and so on. Then he writes a simple verification program to compare the expected outputs with the actual computer-generated outputs of the test run and report any discrepancies.

With some types of problems, the technique of substituting the answer back into the original problem can be used for automatic verification of output. For example, a numerical case where this is possible is the solution of equations. The problem has the general form: "Find the xxx that satisfies the condition yyy." A check routine can be written to take the computed result xxx, substitute it back into the original problem, and have the computer itself determine whether or not the condition yyy is satisfied. To minimize the amount of special programming required, this routine can be included in the program under test. If the routine is short, requiring little time compared to that required to find the solution, it may be advisable to leave the routine in the version of the program released for production use.

Each time a test run yields incorrect results or fails, and the cause of the error is found and a correction made, the source program must be reassembled or recompiled before further testing can occur. As indicated in Chapter 7, a programmer who has access to an interactive terminal may be able to make numerous test runs in a relatively short time period. But waiting for job turnaround can be very frustrating to the programmer who works in a batch-processing environment.

Completion of Testing

How does one determine when enough testing has been done? Perhaps the simplest answer here is: when all test cases described in the previously agreed-upon test matrix have been completed successfully. This criterion appears straightforward, but in actual practice, a number of factors must often be taken into account.

For one, the test matrix itself should not be considered unmodifiable. If a particular section of code seems highly subject to error, it may be advisable to develop additional test cases to rigorously exercise that code. A tester may discover additional conditions or relationships that should be tested as he becomes increasingly familiar with the function under test. Here, too, additional test cases are apt to be required.

Typically, a major criterion governing test completion is the amount of time available for testing; a predetermined schedule and a promised program availability date may have to be maintained. The recipient of information to be produced by a program may be willing to forego some testing because the information is desperately needed. In other cases, not time, but rather cost, is a major consideration. What is meant by "enough testing" is determined by balancing the cost of additional testing against the penalties of acting on incorrect information.

Perhaps the major point here is that completion of testing is not a matter to be taken lightly. Generally, establishing measurable test goals beforehand and then working to meet those goals, while remaining alert to how the overall test is progressing, is the best practice to follow.

Other Types of Tests

Once the functional checkout of a program is complete, other types of tests may be called for, to verify other characteristics of the program. This is particularly true for both systems and applications software developed for widespread or extended use. Some types of tests that may be appropriate are:

- Performance Test—to determine how fast the program can accomplish its functions in one or more carefully selected EDP-system environments. For example, if the program is a part of systems software designed to provide rapid responses to users at terminals, tests can be made to determine the typical system response times when 10 users are active, when 40 users are active, and so on.

- Stress Test—to determine how the program performs under heavy usage. For example, if the system is designed to respond to customer inquiries about insurance, received at random from a variety of terminals at many branch locations, tests should be made to determine what happens if inquiries are entered from 80%, 90%, or all of the terminals at the same time.

- Usability Test—to determine how easy or difficult it is to use the program. This test must take into account many points of view: Will the computer operator at a user installation know what I/O media and devices are required for a run? Is the program designed to provide informational and/or instructional messages to the computer operator, user terminal operators, and/or others when necessary? Will the recipients of the normal program output be able to read and understand that output? Is it appropriate for their needs? Key items to be examined during this test, in addition to the messages provided by the program itself and its normal output, are the other types of documentation developed for it. These may include general information manuals, user's guides, instructional bulletins, and the like. Their technical accuracy, completeness, understandability, and ease of use should be evaluated. Any necessary changes should be made.

- Serviceability Test—to determine the ease (or difficulty) with which the program can be serviced. The question to be answered here is: What happens when an error occurs? Factors to be evaluated include the diagnostic information provided by the program (error messages, return codes, abend codes, or whatever); the general structure of the program code and the comments included within it to help those who must understand what is going on; whether or not it may be possible to insert a temporary fix or bypass so that the program, though known to be erroneous in one part, can perform other of its functions; and the documentation external to the program that has been developed to assist those who must service it.

Tests of the types described above are not necessarily easy to set up. They may be both time-consuming and expensive. Generally they are performed or directed by special test groups rather than by the development programmer. Special test tools are being developed for use in these tests. For example, test programs known as *simulators* can be run to make it appear to the program under test that input is being received from 200 different sources rather than from only one. Hardware devices known as *emulators* can be set up to imitate other hardware as well as software and user functions. Sometimes a program is distributed to selected field test sites for a predetermined period of time before it is made available for widespread use.

QUESTIONS

Q1. What do the terms *testing* and *debugging* mean to you?

Q2. What prerequisites do you see to error-free code?

Q3. (a) List and explain two general categories of programming errors. (b) Give examples of each (preferably some you have encountered).

Q4. (a) Distinguish between informal and formal design reviews. (b) Which approach do you believe is apt to be more effective and why?

Q5. (a) List four types of documents used in a formal design review. (b) Explain the purpose of each.

Q6. Explain one type of desk checking — what, why, when, how, and by whom is it used.

Q7. How does a language-processor program help the programmer?

Q8. (a) What is a forgiving compiler? (b) Argue for or against its use. (c) Give one or more specific examples to support your position of Q8b.

Q9. (a) What is a debugging compiler? (b) Argue for or against its use. (c) Give one or more specific examples to support your position of Q9b.

Q10. (a) During the testing stage, what are three possible outcomes of program execution? (b) What programmer action is appropriate in each case?

Q11. Why is it important to determine the expected results of a test run before making the run?

Q12. What are three general categories of input that should be submitted to a program during functional test?

Q13. (a) What is a regression bucket? (b) Describe a specific situation where such a tool would be especially useful. (Be sure to show how and why.)

Q14. List and explain five types of tests that a program may be expected to undergo.

EXERCISES

E1. Obtain an error-free source-program listing of a program being checked out, from your instructor or a colleague. Conduct an informal code inspection, or participate in a formal code inspection, of the program. (a) List all errors detected during the inspection. (b) Group the errors into categories such as shown in Figure 9-3. (c) What conclusions can you draw on the basis of this work?

*E2. Create a test matrix, documenting the testing required to check out a program you have written.

*E3. Using the test case documentation format shown in Figure 9-5, describe fully one of the test cases that you identified in E2 above.

E4. (a) Give an example of a program that could be tested more easily with a test data generator program. (b) Describe how you might expect to use the test data generator in this case.

E5. (a) Give an example of a program whose testing would be simplified by the use of an automated output checker. (b) Explain how you might expect to develop and use such a checker in this case.

E6. What factors would or do you consider in determining when a program you have written has been tested enough?

REFERENCES

Dijkstra, Edsger W. *A Discipline of Programming.* Englewood Cliffs, N.J.: Prentice-Hall, 1976 (a monograph stressing formal correctness proofs and the separation of mathematical concerns about correctness from engineering concerns about execution; not a book for the beginner).

Elspas, Bernard, Karl N. Levitt, Richard J. Waldinger, and Abraham Waksman. "An Assessment of Techniques for Proving Program Correctness," *Computing Surveys* (ACM) 4, 2 (June 1972): 97-147.

Fagan, M. E. "Design and Code Inspections to Reduce Errors in Program Development," *IBM Systems Journal* 15, 3 (Sept 1976): 182-211.

Helzel, W. C., ed. *Program Test Methods.* Englewood Cliffs, N.J.: Prentice-Hall, 1973.

Hoare, C.A.R. "Proof of a Program: FIND," *Communications of the ACM* 14, 1 (Jan 1971): 39-45.

King, J. "A Program Verifier." Ph.D. dissertation, Carnegie-Mellon University, Pittsburg, 1969.

Manna, Zohar, Stephen Ness, and Jean Vuillemin. "Inductive Methods for Proving Properties About Programs," *Proceedings of an ACM Conference on Proving Assertions About Programs; SIGPLAN Notices* (ACM) 7, 1 (Jan 1972): 27-50.

Mills, H. D. "Mathematical Foundations for Structured Programming." Report No. FSC 72-6012, IBM, Federal Systems Division, Gaithersburg, Md., Feb 1972.

Yelowitz, Lawrence. "A Symmetric, Top-Down Structured Approach to Computer Program/Proof Development." Ph.D. dissertation, The Johns Hopkins University, Baltimore, 1972.

10

PROGRAM CHECKOUT - II

Given the current state of the art, techniques for proving the correctness of a program depend heavily on assertions, axioms, and theorems. This work relates to the idea that, since a program is simply an algorithm by which symbols are manipulated, it should be possible to verify the correctness of the algorithm by a mathematical proof. Investigation has shown that the difficulty of proving the correctness of a program is closely related to its complexity and to the number of interactions between its component parts. One of Dijkstra's hopes in developing structured-programming concepts was that automated proofs might be easier to develop for programs expressed in structured form. Though some progress has been made toward automating the proof process, we still have no practical method for generating a rigorous proof. A great deal of work remains to be done.

Until techniques for proving program correctness are in widespread use, testing must be regarded as an integral part of programming. It is a necessary process for arriving at a belief that a program consists of high-quality code. Various techniques and approaches to program testing are discussed in Chapters 4 and 9 of this book. The reader who has not read these chapters should do so before reading this one. Why? Because we choose to emphasize the prevention of errors, or bugs, rather than the elimination of them, and to stress the very real value of removing any errors that do exist as early as possible in the program-development cycle.

We saw in Chapter 9 that the programmer can call for assistance in program checkout:

- Other members of the programming team can participate in informal reviews and inspections or structured walk-throughs.
- A language-processor program can detect, isolate, and identify certain types of errors during program translation.

- The computer itself is an exacting taskmaster, often revealing the presence of errors when code is actually run on the computer.

Our purpose here is to suggest techniques that can be used when errors are known to exist in a program, but are elusive. We go a step further by proposing that, in some situations, debugging facilities should be specified for a program at the design stage. Such facilities are apt to be needed, for example, if the programmer responsible for the code is not familiar with the programming language in use, or if complicated logic, with many control paths, is an integral part of the solution algorithm. Another point not to be overlooked is that many good programming practices are at the same time good debugging practices; we can deliberately put the program and, therefore, the computer to work, detecting errors for us.

SEGMENTING A PROGRAM

Once again, we recommend an approach to program development that involves looking first at the overall function to be accomplished by a program, then breaking that function into one or more lower levels, or subfunctions, each of which can be designed, coded, and tested with ease. The goal of this approach is simplicity. It is based on certain interrelated improved programming technologies: top-down development, modularization, and structured programming.

The programmer who follows the top-down approach to program development should not find himself confronted with long, complex sections of unverified code: (1) although there are no absolute size limitations, individual modules are kept small in size; (2) unnecessary complexity is avoided by separating identifiable functions in independent parts; and (3) these parts are checked out as they are completed, over time, until a fully integrated program or system of programs is produced. Why is this significant? As the length or complexity of code increases, so does the programmer time and effort expended during the program checkout process!

THE IMPORTANCE OF A
METHODICAL APPROACH

Debugging a large program as one unit should be avoided, whether or not the programmer has followed the top-down approach to program development. The functions performed within specific sections of code should be clearly established. Then debugging efforts should be directed to each of the specific sections, one at a time. As we will see, certain debugging techniques can be applied to confirm (or disprove) that "the program executed correctly at this point (or up to here)." The programmer should use each piece of information that he acquires in determining, very carefully, where to look next. Failure to adopt such an approach is akin to hunting for the proverbial needle in a haystack. Debugging degenerates quickly to the use of "bandaids." Pieces of code are patched to treat the error symptom of the moment without any real understanding of the basic cause of the problem.

Before chasing a bug at great length, the programmer should determine whether or not the bug is consistent and repeatable. If the programmer isolates a bug to what seems to be the responsible section of code, yet that code appears correct, then it may be worthwhile to rerun the program to make sure that the bug really exists. That is, an attempt to re-create the error may be advisable. If the problem reoccurs, so also may additional clues or sumptoms that the programmer can work with. If the problem does not reoccur, one possible action on the part of the programmer is simply to forget about it. An alternative action is to look beyond the program itself for potential causes of the problem:

1. A transient hardware error may have occurred. For example, a loose cable may cause a machine-language instruction to fail occasionally. If such a cause is suspected, one or more diagnostic routines usually can be run to investigate this possibility.

2. A systems software related error may have occurred. The most common examples here are timing problems. For example, in some EDP systems, two programs can attempt to update the same record on disk at the same time. In any situations of this type, the code being debugged may or may not have been involved in the problem.

3. The computer operator or a terminal user may have acted incorrectly. Jostling the I/O equipment, damaging the data-recording media, pressing keys that cause interrupts or other unanticipated actions, and failing to respond as requested to program directions or inquiries are human mistakes that can and do occur.

When pursuing any problem, the programmer should try to determine the general nature of the problem before looking for a specific cause. In an especially difficult situation, it may be possible to make some progress by eliminating certain factors because they are highly unlikely sources of the problem. Can the hardware be ruled out as a possible cause in a particular case? If the problem appears to be in the code itself, which parts of the code can be excluded? By narrowing the field to two or three likely causes, the programmer puts himself in a better position to determine how to proceed in his investigation.

ACTIVITY VARIABLES

A debugging technique that often works well when programs are designed in a modular fashion is the use of activity variables. Under this approach, a special variable is set up as an activity variable in each module of the program under test. The first action that occurs whenever a module is entered is to set its activity variable to a specific value, indicating that control has passed to the module during execution. (See Figure 10-1.)

```
      SUBROUTINE PRSUB (I,J,MAT)
C     THIS SUBROUTINE PRINTS TWO-DIMENSIONAL ARRAYS
C     NACT IS INCLUDED FOR USE AS AN ACTIVITY VARIABLE
      DIMENSION MAT (I,J), INTEG (10)
      NACT = 1
        .
        .
        .
      NACT = 0
      RETURN
      END
```

Figure 10-1   Use of an activity variable for debugging purposes

Some programmers include code to reset the activity variable of a module to an inactive state whenever control is passed from that module to another module (as in Figure 10-1). If an error occurs during execution, the programmer need only determine which activity variable was set at time of termination to determine what code was being executed when termination occurred.

Another approach that is sometimes used is to set each activity variable as described above, and to leave each variable that is set in its set state (that is, omit the NACT = 0 statement in Figure 10-1, for example). This approach helps the programmer to trace the flow of control through modules that have been active, until he arrives at the final one in which activity occurred. A structure chart or a visual table of contents for a set of HIPO diagrams created as part of the design documentation can be valuable here. (See Figure 10-2.) The programmer should be able to tell not only which module was active at termination but also which module transferred control to that module and for what purpose. Such information is particularly valuable when the cause of the error is not solely within the module active at termination, but rather depends also on processing carried out in one or more previously executed modules.

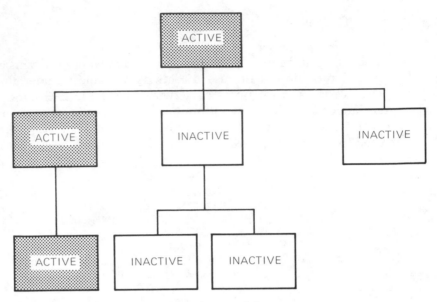

Figure 10-2   Checking activations in a modular program

STATISTICS GATHERING

A valuable complement to the use of activity variables is the technique of statistics gathering. Each module is designed and coded to keep track not just of the fact that it has been activated, but also of how many times activation has occurred. The most straightforward approach is to establish another variable within the module for use as a counter, set it to 0 initially, then add 1 to it whenever the module is activated. (See Figure 10-3.)

If an error proves to be particularly elusive, this technique can be expanded to monitor actions within specific modules. For example, if the code

```
      SUBROUTINE PRSUB (I,J,MAT)
C     THIS SUBROUTINE PRINTS TWO-DIMENSIONAL ARRAYS
C     NACT IS INCLUDED FOR USE AS AN ACTIVITY VARIABLE
C     CACT IS INCLUDED AS A COUNTER OF ACTIVATIONS
      DIMENSION MAT (I,J), INTEG (10)
      INTEGER NACT, CACT/0/
      NACT = 1
      CACT = CACT + 1
        .
        .
        .
      NACT = 0
      RETURN
      END
```

Figure 10-3   Use of a counter of activations for debugging purposes

within a loop is suspect, a special statement or routine can be inserted to count the number of times the loop is executed. If certain branch points or data items are key to the logic under examination, all references to those branch points or data items can be monitored in a similar manner.

DISPLAY TECHNIQUES

A simple, but powerful debugging aid available in most if not all programming languages is the statement ordinarily used in the language to provide printed output. This statement can be used not only to print final results, say, a sales report or a table for use in mortgage loan calculations, but also to display other information that can be very useful to the programmer.

Through judicious use of output statements, the programmer can provide a *built-in trace* of the execution of a program, showing both where it has been and the values of important variables when it was there. Strategic locations for the statements will generally suggest themselves during initial stages of program coding. Some likely points are: (1) just before or after calls to other modules, subroutines, or functions available in the language; (2) as the first statement inside a program loop; and (3) just before a branch point in the program. Each statement should print a unique constant and the current values of selected variables, as do the WRITE statements in the sample FORTRAN coding in Figure 10–4.

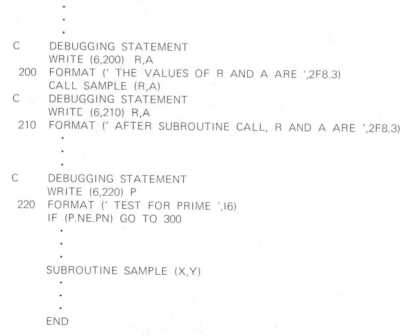

```
        .
        .
        .
   C      DEBUGGING STATEMENT
          WRITE (6,200) R,A
   200    FORMAT (' THE VALUES OF R AND A ARE ',2F8.3)
          CALL SAMPLE (R,A)
   C      DEBUGGING STATEMENT
          WRITE (6,210) R,A
   210    FORMAT (' AFTER SUBROUTINE CALL, R AND A ARE ',2F8.3)
          .
          .
          .

   C      DEBUGGING STATEMENT
          WRITE (6,220) P
   220    FORMAT (' TEST FOR PRIME ',I6)
          IF (P.NE.PN) GO TO 300
          .
          .
          .

          SUBROUTINE SAMPLE (X,Y)
          .
          .
          .
          END
```

Figure 10–4   Setting up a built-in trace in a FORTRAN program

If a long or involved sequence of calculations must be performed, the programmer should insert output statements at points along the way so that intermediate results can be checked. There is little to be gained by writing one very long arithmetic expression rather than two or three shorter ones, even if the rules of the programming language permit it. If errors exist, they are likely to be camouflaged. Any required modifications are apt to lead to new errors. A better approach is to compute intermediate results and print them out. For debugging purposes, periodic output during execution of a program is far more valuable than a ton of output printed at the end of the run.

The use of invalid or incorrect data is a common cause of programming problems. Programmers tend to be overly optimistic about the quality of use and, especially, the quality of data their programs will be subjected to. A highly advisable technique is to have the computer do some error-checking of input. Most if not all input data values can be tested for validity or reasonableness; they should be, whether read from an I/O device or received as parameters from another program module. It is especially important for the programmer to know exactly what data values are being dealt with during the testing and debugging stages of program development. Hence, the rule here is: Print out (*echo*) all input and check it carefully. The computer should be put to work as a meticulous, untiring surveillant; otherwise, the checking must be done manually.

DEBUGGING STATEMENTS

As mentioned in Chapter 9, special checkout, or debugging, compilers have been developed for some programming languages and should be used, if available, during the program-development cycle. In addition, special language features have been included in some languages, primarily or solely for error-checking and debugging purposes. These, too, should be taken advantage of by the programmer.

As an example, assume an unwary COBOL programmer sets up a sequence of operations as shown in Figure 10-5a. Further assume the MULTIPLY statement causes calculation of a result that is too large to fit in NET-PAY, the receiving field specified for it. The computer continues to execute the program even though the value in NET-PAY is wrong. The programmer may search fruitlessly for an error occurring inconsistently in program output, not realizing that bad data generated when this instruction is executed is the cause.

To prevent such an error (called an *overflow exception*) from going unnoticed if it does occur, the COBOL programmer can include an ON SIZE ERROR clause in an arithmetic statement. Thus, our same problem situation, redone, is shown in Figure 10-5b. If an overflow occurs when the result of the multiply operation is stored in NET-PAY, control is transferred to

```
          .
          .
ADD SHIFT-PRE TO HOURLY-RATE.
MULTIPLY HOURS-WORKED BY HOURLY-RATE GIVING NET-PAY.
MOVE NET-PAY TO DL-NET-PAY.
ADD NET-PAY TO GROSS-PAY.
          .
          .
          .
```

(a) Allowing overflow to go undetected

```
          .
          .
          .
ADD SHIFT-PRE TO HOURLY-RATE.
MULTIPLY HOURS-WORKED BY HOURLY-RATE GIVING NET-PAY
    ON SIZE ERROR PERFORM ERROR-ROUTINE.
MOVE NET-PAY TO DL-NET-PAY.
ADD NET-PAY TO GROSS-PAY.
          .
          .
          .
ERROR-ROUTINE.
    MOVE EMP-NO TO EL-EMP-NO.
    WRITE EL-LINE AFTER ADVANCING 3 LINES.
          .
          .
          .
```

(b) Directing the computer to check for overflow

Figure 10-5   Use of ON SIZE ERROR in COBOL programming

ERROR-ROUTINE where appropriate remedial action is taken under stored-program control.

An additional word of caution is in order for the programmer who uses ON SIZE ERROR: this clause applies only to the final result calculated under control of the statement in which it appears. To fully understand this point, look at Figure 10-6a. An overflow will occur if A * B is too large to be stored in RESULT, even if A * B / C is not too large. The COBOL programmer must make the receiving field of an arithmetic statement large enough for any intermediate result, irrespective of whether or not ON SIZE ERROR is specified. A desirable alternative may be to specify operations by means of slightly different coding, as shown for our same problem situation in Figure 10-6b.

The capability to check for overflow is also provided in the PL/I programming language. Many other error or exceptional situations, known as *conditions*, can be checked for as well. Among these are attempts to divide by zero, to read past the end of an input file, to write past the end of an output page, to perform illegal conversions on string data items, to place data in primary-storage locations outside the area established for the pro-

```
             .
             .
             .
    COMPUTE RESULT = A * B / C
        ON SIZE ERROR PERFORM ERROR-ROUTINE.
             .
             .
             .

    ERROR-ROUTINE.
             .
             .
             .
```

(a) Permitting overflow to go undetected in intermediate results

```
             .
             .
             .
    COMPUTE RESULT = A * B
        ON SIZE ERROR PERFORM ERROR-ROUTINE.
    COMPUTE RESULT = RESULT / C.
             .
             .
             .

    ERROR-ROUTINE.
             .
             .
             .
```

(b) Setting up a sequence of computations as distinct operations

Figure 10-6 Eliminating the possibility of undetected overflow in calculation and storage of intermediate results

gram, or to use a subscript value that is outside the bounds declared for the corresponding array extent.

To invoke such checking, the PL/I programmer need only include code to cause a particular condition to be tested for, and additional code to be executed (or a default system action will be taken) if the condition occurs. For example, the ON statement on-unit in Figure 10–7 says that if an illegal conversion on string data is attempted at any time after the ON statement has been executed, the data item RESULT is to be set to a character string consisting of zeros. The message ILLEGAL CONVERSION ATTEMPTED is to be printed as output. We can assume that whenever conversion is attempted and RESULT contains a value that cannot be converted successfully, the CONVERSION condition will be raised. Zeros will be placed in RESULT. The conversion message will be printed to alert the programmer to what has occurred. Then control will be transferred back to the statement where conversion was called for, to reattempt the conversion. Since RESULT will now contain a character string of zeros, the conversion will be made successfully (and no program termination need occur at this time).

Much more could be said about PL/I's debugging features — enabling and disabling conditions by means of condition prefixes, the scopes of prefixes, the CHECK condition capability to tell whenever a specified statement or data item is referenced, the SIGNAL condition capability to simulate various conditions that may arise during processing in order to verify that the program handles them correctly, and so on. PL/C, the student-oriented version of PL/I, provides even more. However, our goal at this time is not to teach the PL/I or PL/C programming language. The major point to be made here is: Both PL/I and PL/C provide a wide variety of powerful debugging features; the programmer is well advised to take advantage of them in checking out programs.

```
PROCA:      PROCEDURE OPTIONS (MAIN);
              .
              .
              .
            ON CONVERSION BEGIN;
                            RESULT = (4) '0';
                            PUT LIST ('ILLEGAL CONVERSION ATTEMPTED');
                            END;
              .
              .
            RESULT = ...
              .
              .
            VAR1 = RESULT;
              .
              .
            END;
```

Figure 10-7 Use of an ON statement for the CONVERSION condition in a PL/I program

The sole debugging aid in standard FORTRAN is the WRITE statement, which we saw in the built-in trace of Figure 10-4. Many implementations of FORTRAN have added facilities for use in debugging. With some, DUMP and PDUMP statements give the programmer the capability of printing selected areas of storage in integer, floating-point, octal, or alphanumeric format. Some permit the programmer to include *debug packets*, groups of statements specifying debugging actions to be taken at selected points in a program. (See Figure 10-8.) The DEBUG statement in Figure 10-8 establishes debugging options that apply to all debug packets in the program unit; the AT statement indicates that the debugging operations specified in the first debug packet are to be performed just prior to execution of statement 100; the TRACE ON statement initiates tracing of program flow by statement number; and DISPLAY causes the current values of the variables BAL and N100 to be printed out. Note the standard FORTRAN assignment statement N100 = N100 + 1 in the debug packet; both standard FORTRAN and special debugging statements can be included in a debug packet if the programmer chooses. Note also that it is generally unwise to include implementation-dependent language features as part of the production version of a program, but it is foolish not to take advantage of them during program checkout.

```
          REAL QOH, ORD, BAL
          INTEGER N100/0/
            .
            .
            .
100 CONTINUE
          BAL = 4.5 * FUNCIN(P,R,T)
            .
            .
            .
          DEBUG TRACE
          AT 100
          TRACE ON
          N100 = N100 + 1
          DISPLAY BAL, N100
          AT 300
            .
            .
            .
          END
```

Figure 10-8   Use of debug packets in a FORTRAN program

AFTER DEBUGGING

A wise programming practice is to use comments to flag any use of variables and/or statements for debugging purposes. Another technique that can be employed within the constraints of the programming language in use is to group debugging routines, say, near the beginning or end of the module, or program, being checked out. By doing so, the programmer makes it easy to find the statements when he wants to remove them, after the program has been checked out. In some cases, he may decide not to remove them, knowing that they will be very useful if additional, unknown errors are detected during subsequent use of the program. Another technique that can be used after checkout is complete is to insert branch statements around code inserted for debugging purposes. This approach is particularly advantageous if the debugging code is relatively long or complex, or if modifications to the program are apt to be required at a later time.

SYSTEM DEBUGGING AIDS

At most installations, system debugging aids are available for the programmer's use. The oldest and most common are *trace programs* and *dump programs*.

They offer a wide range of facilities for tracking down the impossible-to-find errors in a program. Our purpose here is to suggest the kinds of situations where these tools can be used with maximum effectiveness. Details of how to use a particular debugging package should be obtained from vendor-supplied information developed in support of the package.

Trace Programs

In some program-development environments, a trace program can be activated by the programmer to monitor the execution of every instruction in a program. It reflects in great detail the sequence of program execution. For example, it may print out copies of the before and after contents of primary-storage locations, whenever those contents are changed. Some trace programs print out the actual machine-language code of every executed instruction. While such information is valuable in that it shows the flow of processing, step-by-step, there are certain drawbacks to this approach: (1) the printer is a relatively slow-speed I/O device, so printing of all the information takes a very long time and program execution is slowed accordingly, and (2) the programmer may be so overwhelmed with output that he does not know how to isolate the cause of a problem, or even where to look first.

To overcome these drawbacks, the designers of most trace programs incorporate *snapshot* facilities in their programs. As we might expect, a "snapshot" is a picture — taken only under a particular processing situation and/or showing only selected parts of a program being debugged. For example, the trace and resultant printing may be specified to occur only when a branch instruction is executed, or only the contents of selected primary-storage locations may be printed out. The total output of the trace program is a series of snapshots that together give an accurate indication of what happened during execution of the program.

There are obvious similarities between a trace program and the trace capability that a programmer can build into a program by means of output statements inserted for debugging purposes. A programmer may employ the latter approach because no trace program is available to him. Some programmers prefer to use their own built-in traces because they are confident they can set up exactly the tracing they need. Others may not want to take the time to learn how to use a trace program. The output statements of the programming language in use are apt to be already familiar to them because these statements are ordinarily used in problem solving.

Dump Programs

A dump program may be invoked automatically by systems software or manually by the programmer to display the contents of primary storage (or selected portions of it) as output. This output is known as a *storage printout*

```
GR 0-7    000030C8   000030C0   00000019   0000000B   00000043   0001E240
GR 8-F    585F3031   00000063   00003010   00003010   4A003002   00004E90
003000    05C05820   C0525830   C0561A23   5840C05A   1B245020   C0625A20
003030    C07EC070   D213C093   C08292D2   C0A79869   C0AA4110   C0BE4100
003060    00000021   FFFFFFF8   00000019   F1F2F3F4   F5F60123   456F0006
003090    405C6B4B   5BC1C2C3   C9D1D2D8   D9E2E3E8   E9405C6B   4B5BC1C2
             .          .          .          .          .          .
             .          .          .          .          .          .
             .          .          .          .          .          .
```

or *memory dump*. In common practice, a dump program is loaded into primary storage and executed to capture an accurate representation of storage contents at a particular time — say, just after the program being debugged has been loaded into storage, or upon abnormal termination of the program.

Figure 10-9 shows a portion of a storage printout provided by one type of dump program. The contents of CPU general registers 0 through F and of primary-storage locations, beginning with location 003000, are represented in hexadecimal notation. Each 8-digit hexadecimal numeral shows the contents of 32 binary-digit (bit) positions. The programmer who studies this printout must have a good working knowledge of hexadecimal notation, and of the machine language of the computer in use, in order to find the machine-language instructions of the program and the data used by it. So equipped, he can determine whether or not the correct instructions and data are stored in the locations they should be stored in. If this is not the case, he can examine related parts of the source program to discover why errors have occurred.

Today most programmers do not concern themselves with what is going on inside the computer at the level of machine detail shown in a memory dump. They do not know how their programs are translated, organized, and loaded into storage by systems software. Such programmers should attempt to use memory dumps only as a last resort, after all other attempts at debugging have failed. Experienced programmers who are familiar with the internal operations of both the hardware and the software of the computer should be called upon for assistance.

Programmers who are using machine-oriented languages (usually, to develop systems software) often find dump programs to be invaluable. What address is contained in CPU register 8, or whether the contents of primary-storage location 004000 are positive or negative, can be very meaningful. Hours of programmer time may be saved if the programmer is given an accurate representation that helps him to determine exactly what is going on inside the computer.

```
0000000C  00000FFF
000001D8  0000008B
C05E5020  C066F235  C070C96A  F275C076  C05A4F50  C076FA33
COC60A02  4110C0CE  0A020000  00000030  0000000B  00000043
00000000  0123456F  0123466C  C1C2C3C9  D1D2D8D9  E2E3E8E9
C3D20000  0000000C  00000FFF  585F3031  00000063  00003010
     ·          ·          ·          ·          ·          ·
     ·          ·          ·          ·          ·          ·
     ·          ·          ·          ·          ·          ·
```

Figure 10-9   A storage printout

Some dump programs are being enhanced, and new ones are being developed, to print out the contents of storage as we have described, but to identify more clearly what is being printed (instead of leaving it to the programmer to figure out). For example, if tables created and used by operating-system programs are displayed, they are identified as such. Or if data referred to by a high-level-language program is displayed, the names of the data items as well as their values at the time the dump was taken are printed as output.

PARALLEL OPERATIONS

Some programs are developed to do new things — to accomplish tasks never before completed, or even attempted, or to solve heretofore unsolved problems. Other programs are developed as replacements to existing systems — say, an application previously run on an older computer system or on a punched-card data-processing system, or one performed with the use of a bookkeeping or adding machine, or a totally manual procedure. When a program is a replacement, parallel operation of the new program and of that which it replaces is usually advisable. The new program operates on the same data as the old system and on the same time schedule, over an agreed-upon period of time. The outputs of both are compared, and the reasons for any discrepancies are identified. For example, if a company is preparing to shift from a manual accounting operation to a computerized application that performs the same function, both systems may be used for a 3-month or 6-month period to verify that the new system is capable of replacing the old one. If there are errors in the new system, they can be corrected, without the strain of a panic mode caused by the knowledge that work must get done but will not until all required corrections have been made.

There are several good reasons why parallel operations should not be carried out any longer than necessary. To achieve duplicate results by different means when only one set of results is really needed is, from many points of view, a luxury that a company can ill afford for long. Remnants of an existing system may be hard to get rid of unless they are cut off promptly. Personnel who have to be involved in both methods of processing may be placed under considerable strain for the period of parallel operation. To gain the confidence and respect of its users, the new program must stand on its own without an assumed backstop.

DOCUMENTATION

Computers generate a lot of paper in a hurry. This means that programmers often accumulate a lot of listings, console logs, outputs of test runs, and so on. The obvious temptation is to get rid of much of this recorded evidence of activity quickly — to submit the paper for recycling as soon as possible. But a guideline well worth following here is: Keep it, at least until the project is finished. Being able to refer to a preceding version of the program, which worked, can save hours of programmer time during testing and debugging. In a chief programmer team environment, where the programming librarian submits all jobs and picks up all results, not only test matrices and test plans but also the inputs and outputs of all test runs are filed as public records of the project.

Documentation must be developed so that a computer operator can run the program without the programmer having to be present. Many of the operator actions required should be established already as standard operating procedures for the installation. The standard operating procedures, together with any special operating instructions for the program, should be stated in a *console run book*, or *operator's manual*, that can be kept on or near the computer console. The operator action required in the event of a program failure or a failure of I/O equipment — say, an unrecoverable read error on magnetic tape — should be covered by the standard operating procedures. Messages that may be printed on the console printer-keyboard or display screen and their meanings; automatic halts that may occur (if any; not a generally approved-of practice in some EDP-system environments); and special setup and takedown instructions for I/O devices and media (say, the type of printer paper to be used and its alignment) are examples of program-specific operating instructions that may be required.

A wise programming practice is to develop and test the operating instructions for a program at the same time that the program itself is being tested. As noted in discussion of top-down development in Chapter 4, the JCL statements needed to run the program may be the first item checked out.

If a program is being developed for widespread use, the *run manual* for the program may serve as a basis for one or more types of *user's manuals.* Such manuals need not include the running historical record of program development. They should restate the program objectives and explain, to some extent, the solution algorithm employed, EDP-system resource requirements such as primary storage needed and disk or tape usage, running-time estimates, and the meanings of messages that may be issued by the program. The user should be told how to prepare input and how to use output, as necessary. In short, he must be able to determine what the program does, how it does it, and how it can best be used. In some program-development environments, where programs and documentation of them are developed and sold to other EDP-system users, technical writers are employed to assist programmers in meeting documentation requirements.

PROGRAM MAINTENANCE

A vital consideration of program development is one that actually comes to pass after the program has been released for production use. In some rare instances, a program may be run, unchanged, throughout its lifetime, until it is either obsoleted or replaced. More commonly, a program undergoes periodic if not continual revision. It is corrected, improved, updated, or expanded, either to bring it closer to the original intentions for it, or to reflect changed or new conditions in the problem it is supposed to solve. The task of revising an existing program is known as *program maintenance.* The term *maintenance documentation* may have either of two meanings. To some, it is a detailed record of all the changes made to a program after it is released as an operational program. Alternatively, it may be used to refer to the information needed when making changes to a program.

Business data-processing applications are especially subject to revisions, due to changes in company policies, business operations, governmental regulations, and so on. For example, assume a firm uses an hourly payroll program to calculate the wages of its employees. Further assume that income tax rates, basic wage rates, and standard medical and insurance deductions are coded as constants in the program. Program maintenance is required whenever any of the constants must be changed. If the program has been coded in a structured manner, and is documented properly, either by comments or by hard-copy (printed) reference materials, the statement (or statements) containing the constant should be easy to find. Once it is found, the task of replacing the constant with a current one should be relatively straightforward. On the other hand, if a program is not well-structured, or if it is not documented properly, the programmer may spend considerable time searching through the program for the constant. He may find some uses of it, but be totally unaware of others (until newly introduced errors turn up later).

A fact too often overlooked is that program maintenance is not just coding. When done correctly, it involves definition, design, coding, verification, and documentation of changes, just as does the original development of a program. The programmer called upon to do program maintenance may have a difficult task, especially if he must work with a program that is totally unfamiliar to him. Straightforwardness and naturalness in the program coding are much appreciated. If the computer-program representation of an algorithm has a simple correspondence to a real-world algorithm that might be used to solve the problem, the programmer has a base from which to start.

To facilitate the task of program maintenance, the wise programmer consistently follows a basic rule: Keep all programs simple; avoid clever, or tricky, coding. As a programmer, you should not make the mistake of assuming that any program you write will be used once or twice and then thrown away. There are a few cases where this happens, but they are extremely rare and should be recognized as exceptions. In general, any program that is worth anything at all will be around for a long time. Therefore, it is essential to plan, design, code, test, and document with this in mind.

QUESTIONS

Q1. Discuss the state of the art, as far as proving program correctness is concerned.

Q2. Give at least three reasons why debugging is likely to be easier if a program is developed in a top-down fashion.

Q3. (a) Why does it make sense to check to see if a bug is repeatable and consistent? (b) Give some examples of situations where a bug may not be repeatable.

Q4. Why is it wise to check the simplest clues first when looking for a bug in a program?

Q5. What is a built-in trace?

Q6. How can the programmer tell what data values are processed by a program?

Q7. Give at least two reasons why commenting any use of variables and statements for debugging purposes is advisable.

Q8. Why might it be wise to leave debugging statements in a checked-out program?

Q9. What are the primary differences between a trace and a dump?

Q10. Why are dumps sometimes printed in hexadecimal notation?

Q11. Explain when, why, and how parallel operations are employed.

Q12. Give a brief definition of program maintenance.

EXERCISES

E1. (a) What are activity variables? (b) Describe how they might be used in checking out a modularly designed airlines reservation system.

E2. (a) Describe a specific situation in an information retrieval application where the technique of statistics gathering may be helpful in debugging. (b) Explain how you would apply it.

E3. Give an example of a situation where failure to check the validity of input data could cause abnormal termination of a program.

E4. Give examples of checks that can be built into a program to be sure that the console operator or a user terminal operator has responded as required.

*E5. (a) Describe a bug that proved to be particularly elusive in a program that you wrote. (b) How did you finally determine its cause? (c) How might the bug have been avoided?

*E6. Experiment with the use of a built-in trace in a program you have written but not tested fully. (a) Discuss how you have implemented the trace with your instructor or a colleague. See whether they have any suggestions that may increase its effectiveness. (b) What errors, if any, did the trace help you to find?

E7. Describe the special debugging features included in a programming language of your choice.

E8. (a) What does it mean to say that a trace program has snapshot capabilities? (b) Suggest some rules that might govern the taking of snapshots in a customer-billing program.

E9. Give three examples of situations where program maintenance is required.

REFERENCES

Gilb, Tom. "Parallel Programming," *Datamation* 20, 10 (Oct 1974): 160–61.

Grabowsky, Norman. "What Kind of a Programmer Are You?" *Datamation* 23, 3 (Mar 1977): 134

Green, Sandra L., and Robert J. Greene. "Overtime Pay for DP Employees," *Datamation* 23, 5 (May 1977): 215–16.

Mercer, Robert J. "Simplicity in Programming," *Datamation* 20, 6 (June 1974): 96–97.

Mills, Harlan D. "Top-Down Programming in Large Systems." In R. Rustin, ed., *Debugging Techniques in Large Systems*. Englewood Cliffs, N.J.: Prentice-Hall, 1971, pp. 41–55.

Van Tassel, Dennis. *Program Style, Design, Efficiency, Debugging, Testing*. Englewood Cliffs, N. J.: Prentice-Hall, 1974 (covers the subjects indicated for programmers wanting to increase their proficiency).

Yourdon, Edward. *Techniques of Program Structure and Design*. Englewood Cliffs, N.J.: Prentice-Hall, 1975 (more than 100 pages of this programming tutorial are devoted to debugging and testing).

APPENDIX

RESPONSES TO SELECTED EXERCISES

CHAPTER 1

Q1. Data processing is the collecting, processing, and distributing of facts and figures to achieve a desired result.

Q3. (a) The three basic elements involved in any data-processing operation are input, processing, and output.

Q5. One person uses as input (data) to a data-processing operation that which another has produced as output (information). For example, a requirements document produced as information by a planning committee serves as data for upper management decision-making.

Q7. (a) A data-processing system is a device-oriented view of operations, whereas an information system is organization and application oriented.

CHAPTER 2

Q1. Hardware is the equipment that performs operations. Software is the instructions that direct those operations. Firmware is the microcode and instructions that tailor the operations of the computer to meet particular data-processing needs.

Q3. (a) The CPU consists of a control section, an arithmetic/logic unit, and an internal storage unit.

Q5. (a) An EDP system may have primary (main), secondary (auxiliary), and virtual storage.

Q7. (a) A symbolic-language programmer uses mnemonics for operation codes and labels for data and instructions. Unlike the machine-language programmer, he does not have to code using binary digits, and he does not have to know the exact storage locations of data and instructions.

CHAPTER 3

Q1. (1) Defining the problem to be solved, its inputs, and its desired outputs in a readily understandable manner. (2) Developing a solution algorithm that can be used to solve the problem. (3) Expressing the solution algorithm in a computer-program form. (4) Checking out the program to insure that it performs as intended. (5) Completing all required documentation throughout the program-development cycle.

Q3. Historically, programmers worked individually and developed programs as independent components. Then small groups or teams were formed, as recognized needs and relationships made such organization convenient. In recent years, team organization structures have been formalized. The chief programmer team is perhaps the most formal method of structuring activities within the program-development environment.

Q5. (a) A chief programmer team consists of a chief programmer, backup programmer, programming librarian, and additional team programmers, analysts, and technicians as needed for the project.

Q7. There are internal records such as job-control statements, the program code, and test data on disk storage, and external records such as filed listings, current copies of code, and current directories for all internal data sets.

CHAPTER 4

Q1. An algorithm is a set of instructions that specify a finite number of operations from a given set required to solve a problem.

Q3. (a) Top-down development comprises top-down design, programming, and testing. A program or set of programs is developed in successively lower levels of function, or detail. All segments along any given top-down path must be developed in sequence, but, for example, coding at one level may begin before the design of all segments at that level has been completed. Similarly, testing at one level may begin before other segments at that level are coded or even designed.

Q5. A HIPO diagram contains a visual table of contents that acts as a hierarchical guide to the package contents; overview, or high-level, diagrams that describe the inputs, processes, and outputs of major functions in general terms; and detail, or low-level, diagrams that tell the inputs, processes, and outputs of specific functions at the lowest level needed to understand those functions.

Q7. (a) Under one approach to top-down coding, all design is completed before coding begins. Code for the top level is written, then the second, and so on. Under another approach, both design and coding at any given level are completed, before any design or coding at the next lower level are carried out.

CHAPTER 5

Q1. (a) The two types of flowcharts are system flowcharts and program flowcharts.

Q3. Flowcharting worksheets provide an arrangement of 50 blocks with alphabetic co-ordinates that the programmer can use in positioning symbols, squaring up flowlines, and referencing from one part of a flowchart to another. Flowcharting templates are plastic or metallic cards containing the flowcharting symbols as cutout forms that can be traced on flowcharts.

Q5. (a) The loop index is initialized. The processing steps in the loop are executed. The value of the loop index is modified. The loop index is tested for a terminating value.

CHAPTER 6

Q1. (a) Flowcharts work well when there are few different types of input or output and correspondingly few decision-making steps. When there are many different types or conditions of input and output, with many control paths, decision tables work well.

Q3. Limited-entry decision tables permit only Y, N, and dash or blank as condition entries. An extended-entry decision table permits the conditions listed in the condition-stub portion of the table to be extended into the condition-entry portion. The condition-entry portion defines values for elements in absolute (for example, 100, 200) or relative (for example, > 100, $\leqslant 200$) terms. A mixed-entry decision table has some rows of each type.

Q5. (a) Decision tables require that conditions and actions be separated and that every possible useful combination of conditions be covered in a separate, mutually exclusive rule. Keeping decision tables to manageable size leads to program segments of manageable size. Both of these factors lead to program modularity.

CHAPTER 7

Q1. (a) A coder converts a solution algorithm into computer-program form. A programmer has much broader responsibilities, covering not only coding but also defining the problem, planning the solution algorithm, checking out the program, and documentation.

Q3. Language availability involves (1) whether or not an appropriate language-processor program is available or can be obtained, (2) whether or not the assigned programmer knows the language, and (3) whether or not a change in EDP-system hardware is expected, and, if so, whether or not the program will be usable on the new hardware.

Q5. A cataloged procedure is a prewritten sequence of job-control statements that have been placed on a system library, from where they can be retrieved by only a single job-control statement to control execution of a job.

Q7. Good code is well-planned, straightforward, and easy to follow. Carefully chosen names for variables are used, and the names are declared before use. Attention is given to program format—use of blank lines, indentions, etc. In effect, since the code becomes self-documenting to a significant extent, it is generally true that fewer comments are required.

CHAPTER 8

Q1. Structured programming involves a definite commitment to use of only three basic patterns and to certain programming techniques and concepts (which should be named in your response to Q2). While these ideas may not be new, little emphasis has been placed on them heretofore. Good programmers may indeed have employed some or all of them at times, but it is doubtful whether many did so with the consistency, discipline, and deliberate awareness that is being advocated by structured-programming enthusiasts.

Q3. Structured programming is the implementation of the concepts of top-down design and program modularity at the program-coding level. A program can be developed from the top-down, and may even be modular, yet not be coded using only the basic patterns of structured programming. A structured program is modular, but it may not have been developed from the top down. A chief programmer team organization is generally effective in implementing programs in a structured manner, though members of such a team may, of course, write unstructured code if they choose to do so.

Q5. (a) Pseudo code is an informal, easy-to-read language that can be used during the program-design stage to express the logic of a structured program.

CHAPTER 9

Q1. As used in this book, testing means exercising the program logic — submitting input to the program, processing that input, and producing output that can be verified against predetermined correct results. Debugging is necessary when the actual output does not match the predetermined correct results; it is the task of finding the errors in a program and correcting them so that correct output is provided.

Q3. (a) Programming errors may be either clerical or logical. The former deal primarily with whether or not each statement is written or keypunched correctly, according to the rules of the programming language. The latter are concerned with the program logic, whether or not the computer program is an accurate representation of the solution algorithm, and whether or not that algorithm solves the problem it is intended to solve.

Q5. (a) The four types of documents used in a formal design review include: (1) the design documentation itself, such as a user requirements document or a programming functional specification, (2) minor error log, (3) problem log, and (4) review checklist.

Q7. A language-processor program translates the programmer's coding into a machine-language form. In doing so, it checks for certain types of errors and detects errors of those types if they exist in the program. It isolates the errors by associating them with specific statements. Then it notifies the programmer of its findings by means of error messages produced as part of the output of the translation process.

CHAPTER 10

Q1. Techniques for proving program correctness have been developed. They are mathematical in nature, depending heavily on assertions, axioms, and theorems, as do other mathematical proofs. Some progress has been made in automating these techniques, but there is no practical, easily applied approach to proving program correctness at this time. Much work is being done and remains to be done in this area.

Q3. (a) There are certain factors, external to a program, that may cause what appear to be errors in the program. If a bug is repeatable and consistent, the code itself is probably erroneous. But if the bug is not repeatable and consistent, the programmer may unknowingly spend much time looking in the code for an error that does not exist or that is caused by factors external to the code.

Q5. A built-in trace is a record of program execution produced via output statements inserted at strategic points throughout the program for debugging purposes. The trace output usually shows the flow of program control (through the strategic points) during execution and the values of selected variables at each strategic point, each time the point is encountered.

Q7. Commenting the use of variables and statements for debugging purposes helps another reader of the code to understand what is being done and why. It also makes it easier for the programmer himself to find the code inserted for debugging purposes if he wants to remove it later, after the program has been checked out.

INDEX

To assist the reader in understanding and doing program documentation, all index entries directly related to documentation are italicized in this index. "See" and "see also" references to documentation entries are also italicized.

WITHDRAWN